OUTPEDALING "THE BIG C"

**bancroft
press**

Pulitzer Prize Winner
ELIZABETH MCGOWAN

Cover Design and Photography, Interior Design, and Photo Insert Design by Dani Williams
Author Photo by David Watkins
Many Insert Photos taken by Marny A. Malin

978-1-61088-514-0 (HC)
978-1-61088-515-7 (PB)
978-1-61088-516-4 (e-book)
978-1-61088-517-1 (PDF)

Published by Bancroft Press: "Books that Enlighten"
410-358-0658
P.O. Box 65360, Baltimore, MD 21209
www.bancroftpress.com

Printed in the United States of America

OUTPEDALING "THE BIG C"

MY HEALING CYCLE ACROSS AMERICA

TABLE OF CONTENTS

To Don,
whose unwavering faith in me sometimes feels undeserved.
And to my father,
who I wish could read these words now that I know him so much better.

INTRODUCTION

Absorbing a cancer diagnosis from a doctor feels the same as tumbling to the ground from a bicycle, smacking the unforgiving asphalt. It's scary and hurts like hell. You can choose to lie there in a dejected heap, waiting until an eighteen-wheeler squashes you into roadkill. Or, you can pick yourself up and get on with living. I chose to climb back on the bike.

I n the spring of 2000, I was thirty-nine and had reached a major milestone: five consecutive years of cancer-free living. My oncologist in Wisconsin had just given me a clean bill of health after an exhausting eleven-year escapade with an insidious type of cancer called melanoma. Most people know melanoma as a skin cancer that can be tamed if caught early enough. What they don't know is how deadly it can be once it penetrates the skin. It will kill 7,230 men and women nationwide in 2019, according to the latest estimate from the American Cancer Society. More than 96,480 new melanomas will have been diagnosed that same year.

For years, I had been toying with the idea of cycling solo from the Pacific Ocean to the Atlantic Ocean. Now, I had a legitimate excuse. But I wanted my transcontinental journey to be more meaningful than simply checking off an item on a bucket list. I envisioned my undertaking as a fundraiser for cancer research in southeastern Wisconsin, where medical specialists at Waukesha Memorial Hospital had labored so diligently to keep me alive.

My ride was also about resilience. I wanted people to see that it is possible to survive the frightening plunge into the black hole of cancer and emerge with renewed physical and mental vigor. That meant being forthright and adept enough to talk about cancer in small-town diners, corner stores, health clinics, campgrounds, and people's houses as I explored new territory. For a few shining moments, I wanted to galvanize folks across a horizontal sliver of this glorious, sublime, complicated, and often frustrating country that we all call home.

Why would an ordinary recreational cyclist bother to devote an extraordinary effort to engaging in daily conversations about this disease?

As corny as it might sound, I believe that most people want to be part of the greater good. Sometimes you have to be the one who holds the door ajar. Deep down, we all know that nobody gets out of here alive. But I think most of us have the urge to make our stay, however brief, somewhat memorable.

Another reason I was inspired to pedal coast-to-coast was to pay tribute to the spirit of my father, Ronald McGowan. I wanted that time on the bike to give me the courage to delve into the pain of his death twenty-four years earlier. Melanoma, the same type of cancer that had wrapped its voracious tentacles around my skin, lymph system, lungs, liver, and abdomen, had dogged my father for decades. It devoured him whole in October 1976, a month after he turned forty-four. I was just fifteen. When I received my first melanoma diagnosis as a new college graduate, was it any wonder I figured his fate was mine too?

My route included several places where my father and I had spent time together. I wanted my journey to be cathartic so I could understand the complex person I believed he was. My childhood memories seemed too one-dimensional and superficial. I remembered his charm, quick temper, dedication to teaching, and how he minimized being consumed by a disease with no cure. I wanted to expose the connective tissue that bound those disparate pieces. This pursuit would allow me to seek my own truths about my father because I realized that I could never know who I was if I didn't know him. What surprised me is how my journey also let me dig deeply into my grief over his death, deep sorrow I was hardly aware I had been lugging around since high school.

I named my cross-country endeavor "Heals on Wheels" because the rhyme was catchy and the title was succinct. As my plan took shape, everything seemed perfectly aligned. I had my health, the luxury of time, and the proverbial—and mandatory—fire in my belly. Every cell in my body was itching to go. Before I could settle into the next stage of my life—whatever that might be—I absolutely had to ride that bike. I outfitted my bike, fleshed out a fundraising proposal, and settled on a sensible west-to-east route.

Then, I started pedaling.

CHAPTER 1
THE WAY WEST: WHAT HAVE I BITTEN OFF?

For what was probably the 150th time on an oppressively searing afternoon in early August 2000, I peered into the rearview mirror of our maroon Nissan Sentra to sneak another peek at my traveling companion—a bicycle. The pockmarked road caused her to rock ever so slightly, even with bungee cords securing her sleek, forest-green form to the rack on the trunk.

I was driving westward across the thickest section of rural Idaho's distinctive "stick," the part of the state that juts northward like an index finger between Oregon and Montana. Don, my steadfast and dedicated partner of eight years, sat in the passenger seat. We were in the midst of a twenty-two-hundred-mile road trip from southern Wisconsin to Astoria, Oregon, the launch point for Heals on Wheels. Driving not only saved me the hassle of schlepping a disassembled, boxed bike via plane or train, it also allowed me to preview geography I would eventually be pedaling across.

On two-lane Highway 95 near Riggins, Idaho, I veered into the climbing lane as the car's four-cylinder engine groaned up yet another mountain. Crampons seemed more appropriate than tires. Soon, it was abundantly clear we had left behind the lush, green conifer forests of western Montana and eastern Idaho. We were navigating a vertical desert with peaks topping four thousand feet.

Minutes later, we dropped down, down, down more than two thousand feet through a canyon colored in dozens of shades of brown. Each distinctive layer resembled the edge of a gargantuan stack of pancakes cooked on an ancient geological griddle. The Hells Canyon name fit this bone-dry high desert, where temperatures hovered near a hundred degrees. I half-expected to hear sparse clumps of sagebrush, rabbitbrush, bunchgrass, and other native vegetation pleading for water. The only obvious moisture appeared at the very bottom of the descent, where an earthen embankment—Brownlee Dam—restrained the Snake River to form a mild, fifty-eight-mile-long reservoir on the Idaho-Oregon border.

Phew, I thought, watching wavy lines of heat ripple from the baking asphalt. *Did the Idaho Department of Transportation actually vet this road, or have we been mistakenly catapulted aboard a sick sort of amusement park ride for adults who have committed heinous sins?* A dribble of macadam that stretched beyond the white stripe at the road's edge served as a shoulder where bicyclists could sequester themselves. Coasting down that canyon had been intimidating enough in a car, but I would be going in the opposite direction on my bike. Could I even manage such an ascent? My stomach flip-flopped.

My racked bike remained composed. How liberating to be free of awareness, emotions, and hormonal fluctuations. I guess there were advantages to being thirty-six pounds and twenty-one gears of elegantly engineered plastic and aluminum pieced together for an affordable $279. As I peeled my sweat-drenched back from the car seat, I realized I was feeling a bit jealous of this inanimate object.

"Why are you suddenly so quiet?" Don inquired, interrupting my silent reverie.

He could read me well. Nine years earlier, we had met on the Appalachian Trail. It's impossible to hide your true self on such a long-distance hike. Shortcomings and strengths are quickly exposed in a place awash with challenges and short on everyday comforts. The only doors in the woods are attached to intermittent privies.

"This terrain intimidates me," I replied, feeling puny and vulnerable. "I know it's a stereotype, but potatoes, not peaks, come to mind when I think of Idaho." My nerves jangled. "Am I even strong enough to pedal while carrying gear? It will take forever to push a fully loaded bicycle uphill here. I don't have forever."

I knew not to expect an immediate answer because Don rarely gave a rapid-fire response.

"Remember," he eventually offered, as we crept out of Idaho and through tiny Oxbow, Oregon, "you only have to climb these hills once. I know you. You have good tools and instincts. Trust yourself and you'll be fine."

I hung on his every word because I wanted them to be true. Still, the hamster of doubt spun even faster on my inner anxiety wheel.

"What the hell was I thinking?" I continued, tugging at the blue bill of my Boston Red Sox baseball cap in a futile attempt to block the sun's laser-like rays. "What an impulsive fool I am. What an absurd idea this is."

Why hadn't I just promised the hospital team that I would pedal the perimeter of relatively flat Wisconsin clockwise, then counterclockwise? Certainly circling the Badger State twice would be enough for anybody else. But evidently not for me, the queen of grandiose ideas. I had to concoct an elaborate 4,250-mile scheme.

Had I been too cavalier in assuming that a reasonably fit thirty-nine-year-old woman could start slowly in Oregon and count on gaining stamina and confidence along the way? I figured riding cross-country was about enduring, not sprinting. I was no "Lancette" Armstrong—my wardrobe didn't include a yellow jersey—but I wasn't a cycling novice either.

Bicycles were a staple of my childhood in Philadelphia and rural western Massachusetts. I'd been riding a two-wheeler since my father had pushed me, wobbling, down a city sidewalk on an adult-size, dark-blue one-speed Schwinn with balloon tires and coaster brakes. I dismounted by falling sideways onto a neighbor's grassy embankment. At age ten, I graduated to a green secondhand, three-speed boy's Raleigh that I joyfully found under the Christmas tree. A metallic-blue ten-speed Motobecane I bought at age fifteen with my earnings from cleaning houses, mowing lawns, and babysitting became my main mode of transportation throughout high school and college.

Decadent as it seemed, at least to me, I became a two-bike household shortly after moving to Wisconsin in the late 1980s, acquiring a mountain bike to complement the trusty Motobecane. Mountain biking on forest trails left me wracked with guilt, convinced I was irreparably damaging the soil, plants, and creatures that, like so much of the natural world, were already under siege from human behavior. Instead, I stuck to the lengthy network of defunct railroad beds the state had converted to paved bike trails.

In my pre-Don days, I logged hundreds, then thousands, of miles pedaling paved trails and rural roads. My most cherished adventures included three separate weeklong trips organized by bicycling enthusiasts. On the most difficult one, Ride Around Wyoming, we traversed peaks as high as ninety-six-hundred-plus feet in the Big Horn Mountains. I wrote articles about that escapade for the Wisconsin daily newspaper where I was a reporter at the time. The other two rides were Wisconsin-centered. On vacations in the 1990s, Don and I had ridden trails in Maine, West Virginia, Pennsylvania, and New York.

Never before, however, had I bicycled with panniers, or saddlebags. Organized tours hauled riders' gear to campsites in trucks. Those same vehicles served as "sag wagons." In bicyclist lingo, that meant they cased the route periodically, sweeping up riders with malfunctioning bikes, as well as those who had run out of daylight or were too drained to finish. I had always vowed that barring a broken bone or a complete bicycle meltdown, I would pedal every inch of every day. I didn't want the words "sag wagon" in my vocabulary. Or so I thought.

Driving along the Idaho-Oregon border made me rethink that bravado. This time, it would be just the bike—equipped with two loaded panniers on the rear rack—and me. Sagging wasn't an option. Nor was letting down those who backed my enterprise during six months of planning and fundraising. It would be more difficult to fail my supporters than myself.

Early that spring, a handful of hospital fundraisers, marketers, and public relations specialists had agreed to design a Heals on Wheels logo for the white cotton T-shirts I would be wearing. My key outreach tool would be a simple trifold brochure they created that explained the how and why of my journey. I also had stacks of sunscreen coupons to hand out.

The hospital's webmaster designed a digital map of my route so followers could "travel" with me by tracking a small blue dot that moved eastward as I did. This was long before the wholesale conversion to digital photography, so I would be mailing rolls of film to the hospital. Plus, whenever I tracked down a computer with internet access at a library or school, or at the home of a generous person, I would record my observations on geography, natural history, culture, and human encounters. Today that electronic journal would be called a blog, a term that was not yet a household word.

I had transformed my living room into a temporary post office/clearinghouse/print shop as my fundraising project switched gears from the light-bulb-over-my-head stage to rubber-hitting-the-road reality. I snail-mailed and emailed letters to friends and acquaintances explaining that I would cover all expenses—gear, food, and overnight accommodations—so that every penny of every donation would go to a cancer research fund at the hospital. My hospital support team arranged interviews with their in-house publications as well as local newspapers, and radio and television stations.

I was overwhelmed by the response to my tiny, grassroots effort. Pledges of single, double, and even triple digits started to roll in from friends, co-workers, relatives, and cancer patients I had never met. Reporters wrote and broadcast stories. A pair of popular disc jockeys at a Milwaukee radio station interviewed me on-air and scheduled ten from-the-road updates.

A local woman named Joanne, whom I had never met, called to invite me to dinner at her house, along with her best friend, Elaine. Both of them lived just a few miles from my house. In 1985, they had bicycled the same route to celebrate Joanne's fiftieth birthday. The bike ride wasn't the only thing that Joanne and I had in common. She was a breast cancer survivor and had recently finished treatments at the same hospital I was supporting with Heals on Wheels. Joanne's call was just one in an avalanche of correspondence that descended as my departure date neared.

After those initial highs, the car ride west had me questioning the limits of my intestinal fortitude.

"Don't forget about *River-Horse*," Don piped up, reminding me of William Least Heat-Moon's 502-page epic that had inspired me to act boldly. The Missourian's wanderlust had first appealed to me decades before with his classic *Blue Highways*, about exploring the nooks and crannies of back roads in a van. He traded the van for a boat in *River-Horse*. It recounts his coast-to-coast voyage from the Hudson River in New York to the Columbia River in Oregon. The destination for his C-Dory, christened *Nikawa*, was the same as my starting point, Astoria.

Not far from Brownlee Dam, the winding roads were making Don feel sick in the passenger seat. When we stopped to switch seats, I reread the wisdom from Least Heat-Moon's book that I had jotted in my journal: "Proceed as the way opens." The phrase had served as a reminder for the author to rein in his temper, follow his instincts, and endure those grueling miles. It would do the same, I hoped, for me.

Before my departure, my friend and former co-worker Anna had interviewed me for an article for the daily newspaper in Janesville, Wisconsin. "It takes will," I had told her. "Preparing myself for this and executing it involve more than mental and physical gymnastics. I have to keep reminding myself when I'm out there that every uphill leads to a downhill. It's exhilarating to fly down those hills and pretend that you're ten years old again." I wanted to highlight the upside of the undertaking. "This isn't a chore I'm taking on. It's supposed to be a celebration of being alive."

Yes, as I had told other reporters, you need physical stamina to pedal from coast to coast. However, it's mostly about persistence, vigilance, and keeping your eye on the prize. I might be hauling twenty-five to thirty-five pounds of gear, but more importantly, I would be carrying along the love, energy, encouragement, and hope of hundreds of supporters. None of those intangibles weighs an ounce, but they made all the difference to me.

I thought back to a phone call I had fielded a few weeks earlier from a brokenhearted father who lived near Madison, Wisconsin. He had read about my planned adventure in the hospital newsletter. The father was still grieving for his son, who had died recently of melanoma at age nineteen. In his son's memory, he had created a website dedicated to melanoma survivors. He asked about including a link to my journal entries on the hospital website.

"Of course," I replied. Then, silence. I thought our connection had been lost. Then I heard a deep breath, and a shaky voice continued: "Elizabeth, we all cheered on Lance Armstrong when he won the Tour de France because he wasn't only a world-class bicyclist. He was also a brave cancer survivor. But now we have a new hero, and it's you."

"We can skip the hero part," I told him. "But I'm honored to ride in your son's memory."

Recalling that Wisconsin conversation perked me up as Oregon unfolded before me. *You can do this thing, Elizabeth*, I thought, realizing that a dose of fear was an asset. Without it, I could become too cocky or confident and lose my humility. Maybe I couldn't ride 4,250 miles in one day. But breaking it down into doable pieces would eventually add up to something significant.

CHAPTER 2
OREGON: DIPPING INTO THE PACIFIC

MILES RIDDEN: 0
MILES TO GO: 4,250

Wander any farther north or west from Astoria, and you would fall into the Columbia River, Oregon's border with Washington. Don and I arrived there late on the morning of August 16. It was a glorious Class A day. Humidity was low and cotton candy clouds accented a Maxfield Parrish blue sky.

I had intentionally bucked the traditional June-August timetable for a west-to-east ride to train in Wisconsin's relatively mild spring and summer. That later start was appealing because I figured I could avoid one-hundred-plus temperatures in Kansas and the nation's summertime parade of gargantuan recreational vehicles equipped with bicyclist-maiming side-view mirrors. I just had to be speedy enough to haul myself over the Rocky Mountains before fall snowstorms so I could eventually bask in the beauty of Appalachia's autumn.

From the severely limited wardrobe I had squeezed into my two rear panniers, I had selected the white T-shirt emblazoned with the Heals on Wheels logo and a pair of loose, padded black cycling shorts. I shunned reveal-everything Spandex shorts because of the cringe factor. Perhaps they make cyclists more aerodynamic, but they didn't seem appropriate for my tour of small-town America.

My bike had been captive on the rack since Wisconsin, so I wheeled it to Hauer's Cyclery for a quick checkup. The shop was adjacent to the trailhead. "Where are you headed, and why?" the congenial owner asked while pumping up my tires. I figured he had posed that same question hundreds of times. But he dropped the air hose upon hearing my response. "Melanoma!" he exclaimed, explaining that a large, black mole on his wife's arm had been diagnosed as malignant melanoma in 1980. She had endured surgery and chemotherapy, and had not had a recurrence. Already, I had connected with a melanoma survivor—and I wasn't even pedaling yet. I considered that a positive omen and handed him a brochure. He hugged me and urged me to send him a note from the Atlantic.

Astoria, the oldest permanent white settlement west of the Mississippi

River, is named for entrepreneur John Jacob Astor. (No doubt native people had a more melodious name for these shores.) In the early 1800s, he sent two fully outfitted expeditions to the mouth of the Columbia River to establish a fur trading post. Scandinavians drawn to the coastal climate started a thriving fishing industry. That more recent history is depicted in a mural that spirals around the 125-foot concrete-and-rock Astoria Column, a landmark for bicyclists. The elegant column, rising like a monadnock from nearby Coxcomb Hill, is modeled after a structure the Roman emperor Marcus Trajanus erected two millennia ago.

The column was too tall to serve as a suitable backdrop for obligatory start-of-ride photographs, so Don and I instead settled on an immense anchor in front of the city's Maritime Museum, and a pier jutting into the mighty Columbia's mouth. Don would hand-deliver the film to the hospital so the pictures could accompany my first journal entry.

"OK, enough procrastinating," I said. "It's time to pedal." And away I went.

Don was ahead of me in our car. He had offered to "escort" me twenty or so miles out of Astoria before heading to the interstate for his solo return to Wisconsin.

Even though my last training ride had been ten days prior, my legs felt strong and I didn't wobble because my loaded panniers felt well balanced. Trickier, however, was flicking my eyes between the road and my map, which was tucked into a plastic sheath atop my handlebar bag. The mileage and routing information was in tiny print—and there was a lot of it. Rather than try to read and ride, I stopped periodically to memorize turns and landmarks.

Just as I gained a rhythm navigating the twists through Astoria's hilly neighborhoods, an approaching van slowed, and a fit-looking woman leaned her blond head out the window: "You look like a serious bicyclist," she called out, introducing herself as a member of the local cycling club. "I'm out doing some scouting. We're always looking for new routes for our rides. Where are you headed?"

"Actually, I'm on my way to the Atlantic Ocean," I told her, laughing. "But I got a late start so I guess I'll have to settle for the Pacific today."

"What route are you taking?" she asked.

"The TransAmerica, the granddaddy of all cross-country trails," I replied, holding my waterproof map aloft. I explained that I was counting on a set of twelve maps for guidance across Oregon, Idaho, Montana, Wyoming, Colorado, Kansas, Missouri, Illinois, Kentucky, and Virginia. "I'm sure you could order just the map for western Oregon."

I wheeled closer so I could hand her a brochure and give her the number for Adventure Cycling, the map supplier in Missoula, Montana. "Wow, you're brave," she said. "Good luck, and thanks for the advice."

On Astoria's outskirts, I passed the Fort Clatsop National Memorial, a replica of the stockade Meriwether Lewis and William Clark built to overwinter their Corps of Discovery in 1805–1806. Expedition members had relied on leg muscle, horses, and man-powered boats as they bravely slogged west from St. Louis to follow President Thomas Jefferson's edict to find the shortest passage to the Pacific. What's now a three-day car trip in the age of asphalt, speed, and the infernal internal combustion engine took those long-ago explorers eighteen months.

Minutes later, I slowed my pace while approaching the bane of any cyclist—road construction. Cautiously, I pedaled my way across ankle-deep gravel, my sturdy tires carving temporary channels in the grit. Then, an unexpected sound. A grinning construction worker with big, beefy hands set his rake aside and started clapping.

"This is from the whole state of Oregon," he said. "We want you to make it to Virginia." Ahead, a truck driver hauling a giant water tank doused the gravel to minimize dust clouds. I flashed a thumbs-up, thankful I was not relying on the ridiculously skinny tires of a racing bicycle, which surely would have caused an embarrassing wipeout.

That warm reception clicked when I caught up with Don. He had given the construction crew a heads-up. Coincidentally, the applauding worker was a Wisconsin native.

After meandering through resplendent pine forests lining the roadways, I rolled into the resort community of Seaside, where Don photographed me baptizing my tires in the salty waves of the Pacific. Then, at a nondescript place called Cannon Beach Junction, twenty-five coastal miles south of Astoria, Don pulled onto the shoulder. This was where he needed to head east. It was time to say goodbye. I don't think I had ever hugged him that hard. "You can do this, Elizabeth," he said, while cupping my cheeks and looking me in the eye, not letting go until I nodded. Then, I watched him blend into traffic—thinking how naked the trunk end looked without a bicycle rack. I was beginning the ride of my life, and elation and fear jousted in my gut.

I didn't cry often, but the white line along Highway 101 blurred as I rode it alone. The tears weren't a pity party. They were my unscripted reaction to being separated from an exceptional partner who had quietly taught me to be kinder to myself by not expecting perfection. He never met my father but he understood what I was trying to accomplish with this ride, and he knew the tenacity it would take. Don had always offered support in his unobtrusive and steady manner, refusing to see me as a cancer victim or damaged goods. As a mountain climber and long-distance hiker, he grasped how formidable such sojourns could be. In 1991, the two of us were among the hundreds of hikers who flock to Georgia's Springer Mountain each spring with the wild idea of following the Appalachian Trail's iconic white blazes more than twenty-one hundred miles before snow closed the northern terminus in Maine. Don and I didn't know each other that April, but we ended up climbing Maine's Mount Katahdin together on the same blustery day in October.

Not long after parting with Don, I began scouting for a campsite. All I needed was a small strip of out-of-the-way green space. Our hundred-mile drive from Portland to Astoria that morning had cut into my pedaling time. It made sense to channel William Least Heat-Moon and proceed as the way opened. Arch Cape, a tiny seaside community 35.5 miles from Astoria on Highway 101, felt right. I declared it my temporary home by pitching my tent next to St. Peter the Fisherman Catholic Church. And though I felt as if I were violating a covenant of small-town America, I locked my bike to a tree. After all, my mission would be hopeless without it.

To save weight and open up space in my panniers, I had opted to leave my camp stove at home. I would eat when food was available. In Arch Cape, my dinner source was a small grocery store. I tried to ignore the imposing homes that clogged the beachfront as I ambled along the sand exploring caves carved into cottage-size rocks by the relentless pounding of salt water. From a beachside seat on a hefty driftwood log, I gobbled my sandwich while watching bucket-billed pelicans in pursuit of a fish supper acrobatically dive-bomb the waves.

Finally, I was scratching my bicycle-journey itch. Years ago, I doubted I would be allotted this time. Watching my father die in such an excruciating manner when I was in high school, and then grappling with my own cancer for most of my adult years, had forced me to pursue an accelerated schedule and take a less orthodox route. I never felt invincible. With so much to fit in, I felt I lived in speed-it-up, speed-it-up, speed-it-up rhythm. Planning for the long term had always seemed ludicrous, if not impossible. People encouraged me to be patient, but I never felt as if I had the luxury of waiting years to tackle the proverbial to-do list stuck under a refrigerator magnet. "It can't wait," I would tell them, trying to convey my sense of urgency. "I have to do it now."

On that beach, I allowed myself to believe that I might linger on the planet longer than I had ever expected, perhaps even outlive my father's forty-four years. How liberating to accept that cancer wasn't necessarily a death sentence and to know that surviving didn't mean shriveling. When I had stood in the shadow of my dying father during that summer of 1976,

13

I was unaware that hundreds of bicyclists—part of Bikecentennial—were streaming east and west across the continent to inaugurate the spanking-new 76 Trail. A small group of cycling enthusiasts had invited goodwill ambassadors—"spokes"-people, if you will—from around the globe to join the cause. I had no inkling that twenty-four years later I would be following that same Bikecentennial route, which morphed into what is now the TransAmerica Trail.

Soon, vacationers were scurrying to the shore like parishioners to pews. They seemed to need to savor the remains of the waning summer, knowing their lives would shortly resume a more frenetic pace. I was doing the opposite. My "vacation" season had just begun.

I watched fingers of seawater massage the pebbles on the sand. Suddenly, a cheer erupted from a throng of teenage boys who had hoisted themselves upon a fifteen-foot-high shiprock as the darkening Pacific swallowed the blood-red ball of sun. Their spontaneous celebration of a daily astronomical occurrence as old as our world resounded like an amen. "My sentiments exactly," I wrote in my journal.

CHAPTER 3
THE INTERGENERATIONAL BEAST

When I first spotted the black, raggedy-edged mole about the size of an M&M on the left side of my heavily freckled upper back, I nearly teetered off the rickety wooden chair I had shoehorned into my tiny bathroom. The year was 1985, and I had just turned twenty-four. I was two years out of college and living by myself in a second-story apartment in a Victorian house adjacent to the University of Vermont campus in Burlington. It was a beautiful city on the eastern edge of Lake Champlain.

Melanoma awareness was quite limited, but a Missouri doctor I had visited in college had recommended that I see a dermatologist regularly and closely monitor the multiple moles and freckles dotting my skin. The mirror above the bathroom sink was the only way to examine my backside. What I eyed that day was similar in size and shape to a mole that had appeared on my father's arm fourteen years earlier. While alarming, it would have to wait because I had to go to work.

I had recently left my editing job at the daily newspaper to take a different position editing academic journals. I didn't mention the suspicious spot to anybody; my gut feeling was to keep quiet until I knew more. Maybe it was nothing. About a week later, I worked up the nerve to call the hospital affiliated with Dartmouth College in Hanover, New Hampshire. That's where my father was treated after our family moved to western Massachusetts in 1973, for what turned out to be the last three years of his life. Hanover was a two-hour trip from Burlington, but instinct told me I needed to seek help in a familiar place. At my initial visit, the dermatologist opted to skip a biopsy and remove the entire invader. He promised to call with test results.

Within a week, he confirmed what I suspected: a malignant melanoma. Fortunately, no immediate follow-up treatment was necessary because the growth was evidently not thick enough to have penetrated my epidermis. Early action seemed to have nipped the stinker in the proverbial bud. The three-inch-long incision on my back healed.

Instead of asking "Why me?" I asked "Why *not* me?" Watching my father die had made me hyperaware that the bad things many people assume will happen to others could strike anybody. With a system as complex as the human body, why should I be shocked that a wrong switch, so to speak, had activated long-dormant cancer cells, ones my vigilant defense system must have beaten back with relative ease up until then?

I remained mum. After all, I had followed medical protocol and gotten the damn thing removed. Why did I need to worry my three sisters and my mother? It hadn't even been ten years since that nasty disease had killed my father, and the gaping wound it had inflicted on our family was still too raw.

I rationalized my silence by telling myself I was protecting people I cared about. But I wasn't able to stay quiet for long. Shortly after moving to Burlington, I had joined the women's rugby team so I could continue with a sport I had played in college and exercise my desk-bound body. In the autumn of 1986, I ran a hand over my surgical scar during a break at practice and traced a new bump. Uh oh. Even as my internal alarm buzzed, my anti-drama side prevailed. It could be a bug bite, a knot where job tension had gathered or swelling from an especially hard tackle. After all, our only protective gear was a plastic mouth guard. But that harping inner voice, the one that spoke truths I was reluctant to hear, knew it was none of those. The cancer was back.

Once again, I trekked to Hanover. This time I had an appointment with a young, cheerful dermatologist whose pleasant, confident, and professional demeanor relaxed me. She had played goalie on her college field hockey team. After listening thoughtfully to my concerns, she smiled and said, "Well, there's one way to find out. Let's take a look." An hour later, she was sewing the last stitch into an anesthetized section of my left upper back. I focused on my breathing to try to block out the jarring sound of the piercing needle and thread being tugged through numbed skin so close to my ear.

The telephone call I anticipated but still dreaded came a few days later. Pathologists confirmed that the extricated lymph node was swollen with malignant melanoma. Damn.

Lymph nodes are tiny, bean-shaped organs tasked with fending off infections. Simply put, they are part of the body's janitorial system. Lymphatic vessels are positioned just below the epidermis—within the inner layer of skin known simply as the dermis—tucked among blood vessels, hair follicles, and glands. Their valiant challenge is to detect, capture, and dispose of bacteria, cancer cells, or other lurking detritus. At least my immune system had sensed something was awry and hoisted a red flag by causing my lymph node to swell. Unfortunately, once melanoma enters the lymphatic system, it's possible for cells to break off and hitch a ride via the bloodstream to the brain, liver, lungs, bones, or beyond.

This time I couldn't just let the wound heal and return to work. The Dartmouth doctors were worried that the string of connected lymph nodes near the malignant one might also be cancerous. They helped me scout out a Burlington oncologist so I wouldn't have to drive so far for follow-up care. I spent hours being poked, prodded, and questioned.

Specialists recommended I undergo a neck dissection to rid my body of any stray melanoma cells not captured by that one lymph node. But first, doctors had to trace which direction those cells might have traveled. That required a technician to stab my scar with what he called a dye-loaded needle, which I was convinced was the size of Blackbeard's sword. Oh, how that hurt.

Scans of my dyed innards indicated that any cancer cells would likely follow a circular route on my left side. This time, the doctors said, it would not be outpatient surgery. That's when I knew I had to gather the courage to tell my mother.

Coincidentally, my mother had scheduled a weekend visit that autumn. On the day she drove up from western Massachusetts, I took her to dinner at a restaurant overlooking Lake Champlain. I had asked a female co-worker who had become a good friend to join us. During that first hour, we covered every topic but my health. I couldn't find the words. Fearing the unintended pain I would cause, I almost chickened out.

My cut-to-the-chase friend, however, wouldn't let me off the hook, which is probably why I invited her. "Don't you have something to tell your mother, Elizabeth?" she blurted out. Now I couldn't avoid the truth. My top lip began to quiver as I slowly recited in a shaky monotone the details of the two small surgeries, the melanoma diagnosis, and the looming neck surgery.

I could barely maintain eye contact with my mother. Just looking at the shock and sadness enveloping her face made me feel as if I were pummeling her with my fists instead of speaking the difficult truth. Nobody was to blame, but I felt that this terrible news was my fault and I was a failure as a daughter. I was ashamed.

"Oh Elizabeth," my mother whispered, her eyes tearing up. "Don't worry. We'll work something out."

She didn't ask about my feelings, and I didn't divulge them. I suppose our mutual chop-wood, carry-water approach to obstacles meant we responded to cancer with logic rather than emotion. We devised a plan. She would be with me in Vermont during my surgery and hospital stay. Then, while I recovered in my apartment, she would visit again, accompanied by a longtime family friend.

Immediately after the operation, I spent several days recovering in a shared hospital room divided by a curtain. For reasons I could not fathom, my roommate was permitted to smoke. "Great," I remember thinking, my black humor still intact, "I can get lung cancer while I try to beat back melanoma." Hospital authorities finally put the kibosh on her smoking after my mother and I complained repeatedly.

Downtime in the hospital left the two of us vulnerable. I was finally emotionally comfortable enough to ask my mother about my father's early melanoma. What little I did know was hazy.

It was downright eerie how my cancer mirrored my father's. Both of our initial brushes with the beast came in our early twenties. The melanoma had planted its evil seed in the same manner—first on our skin and then in our lymph system. I knew it had eventually gorged on his internal organs. But I didn't yet know what it had in store for me.

My father's first encounter with melanoma happened in March 1955 when he was just twenty-two. He and my mother, Susan, had married in their Ohio hometown in June 1954 and rented a second-story walk-up apartment near Philadelphia that December. My father was finishing up his four-year commitment to the US Navy by serving his final year as a captain's yeoman at the Philadelphia Navy Yard. In the spring of 1955, my mother was on the verge of graduating from college with a teaching degree. She had left her college in Ohio after her junior year to get married, then completed her university studies via correspondence courses.

My father had enlisted in the navy in 1951, shortly after he and my mother graduated from the same high school in Mount Vernon, Ohio. He completed two tours of duty in the Korean War, one eleven months and the other fourteen months, aboard a navy ship.

He and my mother had met through a mutual friend in the summer of 1949, between their sophomore and junior years, as she and a girlfriend were walking to a community dance on the tennis courts at a local park. My parents both sang in the high school choir and acted in plays together but didn't begin dating until my father invited my mother to a high school basketball game their senior year. On Valentine's Day, my father sent half a dozen roses to my mother's house.

"It wasn't just his white buck shoes, his white pressed shirts, his height, and his red hair that attracted me to him," she told me. "He also had manners, modesty, and a certain sophistication that other boys lacked. Instead of talking about himself incessantly, he usually asked questions about others, and that made him popular and pleasingly different."

In March of 1955, my father went to a navy clinic in Philadelphia because the collar of his uniform had rubbed raw a blackish-blue mole on the front of his neck. A biopsy proved it was melanoma, and follow-

19

up examinations revealed that it had most likely spread to the lymph nodes on the right side of his neck. He matter-of-factly announced to his twenty-one-year-old wife that surgeons wanted to eradicate any lingering melanoma cells by performing a radical neck dissection. Rather than delicately extracting the lymph nodes, they would have to carve through wide swaths of tissue and muscle.

In late March, my mother visited him in the communal ward of the navy hospital where he was recovering along with at least twenty other patients. Doctors had cut out thirty-eight lymph nodes from his right side. Several were malignant. The bandages around his neck were so thick that he appeared to be wearing an enormous collar. It was pierced with an array of tubes designed to drain fluids. "I remember his lips were so dry that the nurses constantly applied glycerin to keep them from cracking," my mother said. He stayed in the ward through April and most of May.

When he was finally released, my mother found him waiting on a bench outside the hospital. He was beaming, a neatly wrapped package resting on his lap. That morning, he had picked out a set of kitchen utensils for her at the hospital gift shop. "I didn't really need or want those utensils," my mother revealed, "but your father seemed so thrilled to be giving me a present that I told him they were just what I needed."

Once he folded his frail body into the car's passenger seat, he told my mother, "I wanted to come home earlier, but the doctors thought it was too risky. I kept telling them that I needed to be out in time to march in the Memorial Day parade." Parades weren't really his thing, but he wanted to prove to himself and anybody watching that he wasn't an invalid. And he followed through, marching that entire, miles-long route through Philadelphia.

Though he joked that the neck surgery made him look like Andy Gump, the chinless comic strip character popular in newspapers for several decades, my father was initially self-conscious about his prominent Z-shaped scar. Until it fully healed, he covered it with a kerchief or an ascot.

I understood his urge to hide that scar. Fortunately, post-surgery, none of the twenty-six lymph nodes doctors removed from my neck showed any traces of melanoma. But I still had to heal. Doctors had sealed the ten-inch wound that encircled close to half of my neck with metal staples and massive amounts of surgical tape. The skin on the left side was so taut that I had to practically rest my head on my left shoulder. It would take months for the skin to stretch. But that didn't deter me from returning to my editing job within a week. My co-workers jokingly called me Frankenstein's monster. I was so happy to be mending and focused on something beyond hospital walls I just laughed.

Surgical techniques had improved significantly in the three decades since my father's operation. Whereas I merely had to wait for skin and nerve endings to knit back together, surgeons had removed so much muscle mass from my father's right side that he always had to exert extra effort just to lift his arm. He willed himself to perform somersaults off a diving board, but if you paid careful attention, you noticed that he favored his weaker right side.

While I healed from my own neck dissection, one tricky challenge was learning how to position pillows under my neck so I wouldn't be so sore. The harder challenge, however, was trying not to be overwhelmed by the fact that my father had lived just two decades after undergoing almost exactly the same surgical procedure.

It wasn't until much later, in fact years after my neck surgery, that I gathered enough courage to ask my mother what it felt like to see her twenty-four-year-old daughter undergoing the same operation her husband had had at about the same age. If I thought about asking those questions about our parallel cancers in the 1980s, I certainly didn't vocalize them. And my mother didn't volunteer her thoughts until I questioned her all those years later.

"I just remember thinking that this melanoma was never going to end," she said, explaining that she would "cry and drive and cry and drive" on that 3.5-hour trip from western Massachusetts to Burlington, Vermont. "I thought I was never going to get there. I had that terrible feeling where your gut just sinks to the floor."

She said she always figured she would be able to handle anything that came her way after her husband died because she assumed his dying was the very worst thing that could happen.

Seeing me in that hospital bed, however, made her even more aware of the intensity of a parent-child bond. Not only was she heartsick about me, but for the first time she could empathize with the depths of pain my father's mother had experienced.

"It was much worse with you because you are my own," she explained. "It's horrible to lose your husband, but losing your child is like an amputation, like a piece of you is being taken away."

CHAPTER 4
OREGON: RESOUNDING SHOTS

MILES RIDDEN: 35.5
MILES TO GO: 4,214.5

I swear I heard my energetic friend Joanne laughing all the way from Wisconsin as I pedaled along the Oregon coast on August 17, my second day out. We had met just a month before when she invited me to her house for dinner before my departure. Joanne, who lived in the next town over, tracked me down after reading about my upcoming ride in the newspaper. We bonded instantly because in 1985, she and her best friend, Elaine, had bicycled cross-country—on the same route I had selected—to celebrate Joanne's fiftieth birthday.

Elaine's husband, Chuck, had served as their support crew. Not only did he carry the bulk of their gear in his vehicle, he also toted his golf clubs in the trunk. Chuck spent his days racking up birdies and eagles at golf courses along the route while Joanne and Elaine pedaled together. Each afternoon, they met at a pre-arranged campsite or hotel.

During that Wisconsin dinner, Joanne and Elaine regaled me with the highlights and lowlights of their adventure fifteen years earlier. Hands down, Joanne insisted, their most strenuous day in all ten states was the twenty-two-mile stretch along the Oregon's Three Capes Scenic Loop, around Meares, Lookout, and Kiwanda. "Just wait and see," she told a skeptical me. "You'll think of me then." She was so emphatic that I jotted notes on my map.

Nearing that section on my bicycle, I still wondered if maybe Joanne was exaggerating. After all, the Oregon coast wasn't exactly the Rockies. My Wyoming and Colorado maps had a special profile section outlining severe altitude changes. This one didn't show any ups and downs. Evidently, the editors thought the geography was flat enough not to merit such detail. How hard could it be?

Shortly after passing through Tillamook, I discovered there was nothing wrong with Joanne's memory. Reluctantly, I had to suck up my pride and crank down into "granny gear"—the lowest and easiest one of my twenty-one options—to hoist myself over those beastly bumps north of Cape Meares State Park. Yikes!

A very fit male cyclist, who looked like a set of robust lungs with legs, was on a lightweight, skinny-tire bike just ahead of me. He asked me to snap his photograph when we pulled over to admire the brilliant blue water and white-capped waves smashing against a steep coastline. Although he was not burdened with panniers, he sheepishly admitted that those mini-hills were much rougher than he anticipated. *Phew*, I thought. *Now I don't feel so weenie-like.*

"My quadriceps have voted," I scribbled on my map. "Joanne was dead-on!"

That deceiving topography is at the western edge of the Oregon Coast Range. Summits along these bands of ridges, which start south of the Columbia River and merge with the Klamath Mountains of southwest Oregon, average two thousand feet above sea level, with many peaks measuring four thousand feet. The cycling route isn't anywhere near that high because it hugs the Pacific Ocean, tracing the edges of Tillamook Bay and Netarts Bay. Still, climbing mere hundreds of feet can feel like thousands when you're carrying thirty-five pounds of gear. The sight of tree-covered foothills jutting almost straight out of the salt water is a surprise for those of us accustomed to the broad beaches of the Atlantic.

Early that afternoon, I stopped in Netarts to scout around for delicacies I had been craving—chocolate milk and a banana. I devoured both at a picnic table. My goal was to minimize my trash footprint by keeping meals simple. The banana peel was easy to compost in a nearby grove of trees. The milk carton was more challenging because there was no trash can in sight. I knocked on the door of a real estate office. The jovial agent who invited me in joked that I could use her garbage can "only if you buy a house."

"Well, I guess it'll have to be a vacation house, because I'm a long way from home," I told the woman, who introduced herself as Pam.

After I handed her a brochure, she shocked me by writing out a fifty-dollar check to the hospital foundation before I'd even completed my thirty-second elevator speech. I was comfortable doing charitable outreach with strangers, but I never expected them to hand over money on the spot. "My sixty-year-old husband is still struggling to recover three years after surgery for brain cancer," Pam said, explaining her spontaneous donation. "His trauma has altered every aspect of our lives."

It didn't matter that the money would go toward cancer research in Wisconsin, she told me. "Anything anybody can do to stamp out cancer is worth the investment." Who knew a simple request for a trash can could yield such generosity?

I continued about thirteen miles toward the remote farming community of Sandlake. Fittingly, one towering sand dune after another formed the scenic backdrop for this town of twenty-five. Such grandeur made me feel like a midget. Some dunes were scarred with the telltale tracks of off-road vehicles, but I was heartened by a roadside sign explaining the state's attempts to limit that type of recreation to a designated area.

When I pulled into the parking lot next to the little Sandlake grocery store, I was the sole two-wheeler in what appeared to be Pickup Truck Central. Inside, I foraged for more "health food" before joining a handful of locals seated at picnic tables on the attached deck. I perused the Major League Baseball standings in a stray section of a Portland newspaper while refueling on a hot dog and cookies. An older man seated nearby had watched me roll in earlier. Gradually, I realized his nonstop chatter was directed at me.

He peppered me with questions, ostensibly to strike up a conversation, but his tone had an edge. I answered him politely, choosing to do more listening than speaking. My mere existence seemed to annoy him. "I bet you were surprised to see all the trees out here," he said snidely, his bluish lips exposing an array of crooked teeth. "One lady from out east didn't know she would see all these trees. She thought we'd cut them all down." A hee-haw of a laugh followed. Resolving not to become riled, I retreated to a Zen-like state that practiced reporters on the receiving end of rants are adept at achieving. But I did chew faster, eager to be on my way.

He rambled on. "Logging old-growth forests in the state has nothing to do with a drop in the population of endangered spotted owls," he said, clearly hoping I would counter his statement. An uptick in the coyote population is to blame, he explained, adding that the coyotes horn in on the owls' food supply of mice and other critters. I still wouldn't take his bait.

Instead, I focused on how the sun highlighted a golden expanse of freshly cut hay across the road. Then, a slight movement caught my eye. As if on cue, a coyote pup appeared, cavorting through the stubble, his blondish-gray coat blending almost seamlessly with the brush he ambled through. I was thrilled. My first instinct was to point out the little guy to my neighbors. But, remembering where I was, I squelched that urge.

I diverted my eyes, sneaking only occasional glances at the critter, hoping the chatterbox would leave. I tried to conjure up mammalian telepathy to urge the innocent creature to beat a hasty retreat to tree cover. But my will wasn't enough. The babbler, his eyes now locked on the pup, yelled, "Look! Coyote!" His alert prompted a little girl eating candy nearby to dash inside the store and scream, "Quick, call my father and tell him there's a coyote!"

"Oh no," I mouthed, my chest tightening, sensing the episode would turn grotesque. I felt helpless. Why was everybody so wound up by the sight of a harmless baby likely tracking mice feeding on the scattered grass seeds? The pup wasn't hurting anything or anybody.

Within three minutes, a man driving a pickup truck screeched to a halt in front of the meadow where the oblivious pup romped. I spied the candy-eating girl in the passenger seat. Seconds later, her father poked a rifle out his open window and fired a single blast. Stunned, I watched the animal twist sickeningly before landing, limp. The man on the deck who had lectured me about the spotted owl whooped loudly. I glared at him in disgust.

As I rode away, sickened by what I had witnessed, a familiar verse played in my head. *Oh, Elizabeth, you're being too sensitive. Just let it go.* But a stronger and louder refrain—the one reminding me that I don't need to apologize for feeling empathy—quickly drowned it out.

My stomach knotted as I pedaled past the pickup, watching two small blond girls—the candy eater and her sister—gleefully helping their gun-toting father drag the dead animal across the field as if it were a sack of potatoes instead of a recently sentient being.

What a peculiar irony. My bicycle journey was about the preciousness of being alive after coming so close to dying. Before riding off, I heard chatter about the dead coyote at the Sandlake store. The goal was to make a souvenir of the tail, not to eat the meat or use the coat. Watching a father acting so casually about life in front of two young daughters seemed a cruel juxtaposition. In good faith, I had left one of my brochures with the storekeepers when I purchased what had passed as my dinner. I figured by now it had gone in the rubbish—unread.

A few miles down the road, I was relieved to discover how devoted Oregon is to protecting avocets, great blue herons, and other shorebirds at a sanctuary called Whalen Island County Park. It would be my nest, too, for the evening. I walked off my lingering anger over the coyote slaughter by thinking about the bald eagle I'd been lucky enough to see soaring over the Nehalem River earlier that day. I also pondered how the natural world persists when humans—who are part of it, not a separate entity—seem so intent on beating it down out of fear, ignorance, and thoughtlessness. We think nothing of destroying animal habitats, then become indignant when opportunistic creatures such as coyotes adapt to our changes. Will we not be content until every square inch of the planet is under our control?

I was the only cyclist in the campground that night, but I wasn't alone. Fellow campers Bill and Becky, retirees from Washington State, graciously served as my sounding board as I relayed the story of the coyote's untimely death.

"I'm not naïve enough to think this doesn't happen regularly," I told them. "It's just that killing for sport—for a trophy—shocks me."

"I'm afraid our evolution as an ethical species has been mighty slow," Bill said. "Looking back, future generations will be alarmed by what we find acceptable."

They both told me how much they enjoyed catching the fish they eat. "Last night we fed three really hungry young guys cycling across Oregon," Becky said. "I wish we had leftovers for you."

I described how my relationship with the land was changing since I had begun spending weekends with a crew of volunteers on nature preserves in Wisconsin trying to rid abused patches of land of buckthorn, honeysuckle, garlic mustard, and other invasive plants. We restored those plucky pieces of Earth so native plants could thrive and support the turkeys, deer, beavers, opossums, and other wildlife that evolved in those distinct regions since the ice sheets had retreated ten thousand years ago. Hunters lucky enough to access those lands with their guns and bows and arrows for a short window of time each year wasted no part of any deer they killed.

"Put that away," Becky told me when I opened a county-provided envelope to make the honor-system payment for an overnight stay. "Bill and I already covered your fee. It's the least we could do for your venture."

We talked around their campfire until hordes of voracious mosquitoes descended. Before Bill and Becky headed to their trailer, we cursed the wretched insects for the misery they inflicted. In the next breath, of course, we laughed and thanked them for being at the bottom of the songbird food chain.

"But the birds in this sanctuary might be living on borrowed time if they don't pick up their mosquito-eating pace," I joked before slipping into my tent. I was grateful I had zipped my tent door closed hours earlier to keep the mosquitoes out. Otherwise, I would have been a captive—and undoubtedly sleep-deprived—blood donor.

CHAPTER 5
TESTING, TESTING: THAT GUINEA PIG FEELING

I f annihilating cancer were as simple, quick, and effective as firing the shot that dispatched that Oregon coyote pup, doctors would be standing in long lines for such medicinal ammunition. But eradicating such a complex disease is beyond difficult. At least 150 types of cancer exist, and silver bullets to destroy them don't. As Dan Fagin wrote in his epic 2013 book, *Toms River: A Story of Science and Salvation*, "Their only common characteristic is supercharged cell division, growth run amok."

Basal cell, squamous cell, and melanoma are the three types of skin cancer. Melanoma is the deadliest. It accounts for less than 5 percent of all skin cancer cases but a majority of the deaths. That lethal trait comes from its expert ability to mutate. Melanoma, the fifth most common cancer among men and the seventh most common among women, begins its sordid life growing in cells known as melanocytes that are stored in the inner part of the epidermis. The epidermis is the outermost layer of skin. Skin, our largest organ, is forced to tolerate all manner of hazards. It is the melanocytes' job to crank out melanin, a pigment that gives skin its color. The more sunlight a body absorbs, the more melanin it makes.

Until recently, numbers from the National Cancer Institute revealed that deaths from melanoma had always increased, though sometimes only very slightly, every year since 1950, when cases were first recorded. Today, however, the outlook is far less grim as those trends are beginning to reverse.

In the last several years, melanoma has had the largest mortality-rate decrease of all cancer types, according to the American Cancer Society report released in January 2020. For instance, the one-year survival rate for patients with advanced melanoma rose from 42 percent in the 2008–2010 period to 55 percent between 2013 and 2015, according to "Cancer Statistics 2020." That dramatic improvement is mostly due to cutting-edge immunotherapies and genetically targeted treatments developed over the last decade. Melanoma authorities also attribute success with survival rates to the wider use of sunscreen and awareness campaigns focused on early detection.

Even so, melanoma kills a relatively tiny percentage of people. For instance, in 1955, the year my father was first diagnosed, close to 165 million people lived in this country and 1,805 of them—967 males and

838 females—died of the disease. By 1976, the year my father died, the US population had grown beyond 217 million, and melanoma killed 4,181 Americans. In 1985, the year of my first diagnosis, melanoma killed 5,529. The country's population stood near 238 million that year.

Early on, researchers were aware that people with blue eyes, blond or red hair, numerous freckles, and fair complexions who had suffered multiple severe and blistering sunburns in childhood were prone to developing melanoma. My father and I fit the bill in all of those categories. Over the years, scientists have also learned that ultraviolet B radiation, which causes sunburns but can't penetrate glass such as car windows, can increase the risk of melanoma. They are still unsure about the possible threat of ultraviolet A radiation, the type that causes aging and wrinkling and can penetrate glass.

In 1986, as I was recovering range of motion in my neck after major surgery, I had another decision to make. It involved an experimental follow-up treatment with injections of something called interferon. Doctors spelled out two potential benefits. The interferon could boost my immune system by tamping down melanoma cells' propensity for rapid division. Also, it could serve as a liquid sponge, scrubbing away any renegade melanoma cells that might be lingering in my body after my operation. The doctors seemed quite certain they had removed any melanoma near my neck, but they couldn't be sure that cells hadn't traveled elsewhere. The yearlong regimen with interferon seemed to be my only post-surgery option. Or I could choose to forgo further treatment altogether.

Interferon treatment is called immunotherapy, or biological therapy, as opposed to chemical therapy, or chemotherapy. Interferon occurs naturally in our bodies. It is categorized as a signaling protein, one of the "good guys" that not only stimulates T-cell activity but also signals the body to produce more T-cells, a cancer patient's ally. These lymphocytes, a type of white blood cell, regulate and activate the body's response to diseases and foreign agents.

Remarkably, interferon is capable of a three-pronged attack on melanoma. First, it can eliminate cancer cells by interfering with growth and multiplication. Second, it can encourage killer T-cells and other white blood cells to destroy the melanoma. Third, interferon can stimulate cancer cells to release certain chemicals, which in turn attract the immune system cells to them so they can dispatch the melanoma quickly.

Of course, each body is different. For me, it was possible the interferon injections would do all of those things or none of them. The doctors couldn't give me any guarantees. If I opted in, I would become one of dozens of cancer patients signing up for a clinical trial with interferon. My regimen would entail taking the interferon intravenously at the hospital three times a week for a month, then injecting it myself for the eleven remaining months using a supply of syringes stored in my home freezer.

My squeamish side wanted to vote no on the interferon because just mentioning the word *needle* made my already-shy veins seek cover. But my idealistic side won out. Volunteering to be a data point for the potential advancement of medical science wouldn't ensure me protection from cancer, but maybe this study would eventually uncover some of the secrets to containing melanoma. Perhaps it would save lives on a large scale. Plus, I reasoned, my father probably would have exercised this option too because contributing to the greater good was important to him. After all, wasn't I living for both of us now?

I started treatment in late 1986. I was twenty-five but felt much older. I figured more than half of my life was already over at that point, and I sure didn't have much to show for it yet. The picture of cancer I carried in my head was of a rope tightening around my neck until it finally choked the life out of me. In my family, cancer meant death. Yes, I was scared. But I didn't tell that to the cheerful oncology nurse who was hanging the bag of clear liquid, the interferon, from a hook on a metal pole as I settled into my reclining chair outfitted with a mustard-colored plastic cushion and adjustable armrest. Telling her I was frightened would have meant talking about my feelings, and I wasn't prepared for that. I needed logic to navigate this mess.

"I figure we'll use your left arm because you're right-handed," the nurse said, tying a rubbery tourniquet around my upper arm.

"Please, use this one," I pleaded, pointing to the semi-visible vein in the crook of my right arm. "I know the ones on my hands and wrists look promising, but they'll retreat like spooked prairie dogs when they sense a probing needle."

She gracefully inserted the needle on her first try.

I might have felt mature, but the nurse holding my left hand while the interferon started coursing through me saw a baby-faced young woman with unlined skin, abundant freckles, big blue eyes, and shorn blond hair. Through tears, she told me I shouldn't have to be going through cancer treatments at my age. Watching her cry made my eyes fill for the first time ever in a doctor's office. I felt embarrassed and silly being the center of attention, so I attempted to lighten the mood by talking.

"As much as I hate doctors' offices and needles, I figure being a guinea pig is a wiser choice than just hoping the melanoma doesn't return," I told her. "I'm an individual after all, not some lousy statistic. Who says I can't beat the odds?"

What I didn't tell her was how much I hoped that saying these words out loud would make me believe them.

Right after the interferon treatments, I felt like I had a low-grade flu. I endured daily bouts of chills, fatigue, muscle aches, and nausea. The intensity of these symptoms tapered off somewhat when I was weaned from the larger intravenous doses. Still, I was adamant about keeping a full-time work schedule, playing on a competitive women's soccer team in a recreational league, and tending a vegetable garden. I was determined not to sit at home playing the victim.

To get the hang of injecting myself with a hypodermic needle, I practiced on an orange. After experimenting on my upper thighs and stomach, I found that poking my belly was the least painful option, especially when I iced my pinched flesh first. Fortunately, this wasn't a solo venture. My stalwart friend and co-worker, the one who accompanied me to that dinner with my mother, volunteered to help. She would have made an exceptional nurse because she wielded a syringe needle with much more authority than I ever did. She agreed to jab me on the days I couldn't stomach the procedure.

When I revealed to my invaluable friend how much cancer cells in my body scared me, she tried to help me form a less frightening image of the disease. She suggested I concentrate on living each day instead of worrying about the weeks, months, and years ahead. She was a recovering alcoholic who had started going to Alcoholics Anonymous meetings five years earlier. Alcoholism, she explained, was a disease she had learned to cope with daily. She was convinced it could kill her just like cancer if she didn't stick with her twelve-step recovery program. *Perhaps she's right*, I thought, as I mulled over her insights. But I realized I wasn't nearly as convinced of the comparison as she seemed to be. In my mind, if you don't drink, then it's clear alcohol won't kill you. But what surefire preventive measures could I take that would keep cancer from infiltrating my body? After all, I couldn't alter my genetic makeup or erase my childhood sunburns.

That interferon routine lasted until 1987 was almost over. By then, I was ready for a change. A big one.

CHAPTER 6
OREGON: BANGED UP IN MONMOUTH—AGAIN

MILES RIDDEN: 100
MILES TO GO: 4,150

Ominous clouds that had drooped from an ash-colored sky the evening I camped with Bill and Becky still lingered early on August 18 as I rolled up my damp tent. They were a reminder of why western Oregon is so green.

A drizzle morphed into chilling torrents fifteen miles later in Neskowin. Sensing that the deluge wouldn't let up soon, I took refuge in a bustling café where I was the least-dry diner. My map's description of the state's coastal economy served as my companion as I savored pancakes, yogurt, and hot chocolate. Herds of cows I had passed that morning confirmed that dairy was still king in the Tillamook Valley. It is home to the world-famous Tillamook Cheese Factory, an imposing—and pungent—behemoth.

The steady slap of raindrops hadn't halted while I lingered over breakfast. I would have to move on, even if they didn't. Northbound Appalachian Trail hikers have a motivational rhyme: "No rain, no Maine." What they mean is that if you intend to traverse twenty-one hundred miles from Georgia to Maine in one continuous hike, you won't reach your coveted destination if you wait out nasty weather under cover. My outdoors experience had proved that neither low-tech garbage bags nor high-tech Gore-Tex can keep long-distance hikers or cyclists dry for long. Wetness was part of the adventure.

But on a bike, visibility is crucial. I feared that drivers distracted by beating windshield wipers might miss my bold yellow safety vest. As I stood under the restaurant overhang, a passerby seemed to sense that I was on the verge of psyching myself out. We examined my map together. He reassured me that traffic would slow to a trickle shortly, once I turned onto Slab Creek Road and joined Old Scenic Highway 101.

Back on the bike, I quickly discovered how well that Good Samaritan knew his neighborhood. The only "traffic" I encountered climbing the scenic highway was a waterlogged, gear-laden male cyclist sloshing toward Neskowin. We exchanged nods and "yes-we-are-really-doing-this-and-it's-a-heck-of-a-lot-better-than-sitting-in-an-office" grins. Lush roadside ferns glistened in the rain. I felt like I was pedaling through an emerald forest.

About fourteen miles beyond Neskowin, I arrived in Rose Lodge, a booming metropolis of twenty-five where eastbound riders take a sweeping left turn, away from the Pacific Coast, into Oregon's heartland. There, the owner of a thriving garden center assured me dry territory lay ahead. I doubted him as I slopped through Boyer, Grand Ronde, Valley Junction, and Fort Hill along Highway 18. Then, near the junction with Highway 22, Mother Nature turned off the spigot, just as the gardener had promised. I figured I could dry out on the twenty-three-mile ride to Monmouth.

I picked Monmouth for an overnight stay because it would be a homecoming of sorts. Back in 1971, our family of six had squeezed ourselves into a two-bedroom apartment in this college town of almost seven thousand for a couple of summer months while my father, a teacher, studied race relations at Western Oregon University courtesy of a National Science Foundation grant. We had spent every glorious weekend camping and exploring the Pacific Northwest.

When I coasted into Monmouth twenty-nine years later, it was much too early to pitch my tent. My quest for more exotic cuisine landed me at a Japanese restaurant, where I feasted on tempura and teriyaki. As usual, I had carried in a short stack of brochures and the sunscreen coupons. I didn't want to come across as some kind of Jehovah's Witness, but my goal was to lighten my load by distributing them early and often. My waitress, who had immigrated to the United States from Taiwan in 1989 to attend college in Portland, was full of questions. As we conversed, our voices evidently carried. The man in the adjacent booth was soon sitting next to me, pushing his hair aside to reveal a large but neat scar near his right ear where surgeons had removed a melanoma tumor the year before, when he was twenty-four.

Melanoma was rare enough that most people were unfamiliar with the word. Still, I was only three days into my journey and I had already heard about two cases. The disease was also in the headlines that August because US Senator John McCain, the Arizona Republican and Vietnam War veteran who would later run for president, had undergone surgery for malignant melanoma on his face.

When I tried to pay my bill, my waitress, Mei-Chin-Yeh, wouldn't take my money. "This is something I can do for you, Elizabeth," she said sweetly, hugging me. "You're already doing enough. Please let me help." A few minutes later, when I was outside switching from boots to cycling shoes, she rushed toward me with a handful of green tea bags. "Good luck," she said. "Use these on your journey. They have good energy. Maybe they'll help make your travels a little easier."

Within twelve hours, I would be convinced she had a prescient streak.

After dinner, I scouted out a campsite behind a Baptist church. I wandered around the university campus searching for landmarks I had last seen when I was ten—the apartments our family shared with a group of nuns and families from Nebraska and Washington; the shop where we rented bicycles; the block where I'd wiped out on one of those bicycles; the storefront where my mother, older sister, and I took macramé lessons; and the campus auditorium where we watched movie classics such as *True Grit* and *King Kong* on blissfully long summer evenings. I found the auditorium, but the other places were either long gone or unrecognizable to my adult eyes. That night, I zonked out and enjoyed my deepest sleep since leaving Wisconsin. I attributed that to riding seventy-eight miles and gaining confidence I might go the distance.

Early on August 19, I merrily set off for Coburg, about fifty-seven miles away. While coasting through a quiet residential Monmouth neighborhood that connected me to State Highway 99 West, I committed a major bicycling no-no: I diverted my eyes from the road to my map for just an instant. Suddenly, an unforgiving cement curb loomed inches ahead. I was in trouble. *BAM!* Miraculously, my sturdy front tire bounded over it. I hung in midair like a clueless cowgirl on a bucking bronco. Desperately, I twisted both feet, trying to disengage the cleats on my cycling shoes from my pedals. At the same time, I made a last-ditch effort to brace the airborne bike, hoping to stay upright. Instead, I crashed to the asphalt. With my feet still attached to the pedals, my left elbow smacked the ground with a revolting crack.

I've barely started this ride and it could end right here, I thought, stifling the urge to throw up. Slowly, I unclipped one shoe, then the other. As I inched my body and bicycle to the safety of the sidewalk, I glanced around to see if anybody had witnessed my embarrassing spill. It was a relief not to have an audience, although part of me didn't want to be alone.

Seated on the sidewalk, I did a quick once-over and found three wounded entities—my aching left elbow, my bleeding left knee, and my pride. The latter two would heal, but I wasn't so sure about the first one. *Damn it, Elizabeth*, I scolded, my anger and fear flaring. *Can't you get out of Monmouth without falling off your bicycle?*

I cursed the salesman at the Wisconsin bike shop who had convinced me to trade in my easy in-and-out toe clips for fancy shoes and special pedals. He assured me that state-of-the-art gear would provide maximum leg-pumping power while climbing hills or pushing through long straightaways.

I walked around for a few minutes just to clear my head. *You've put too much effort into surviving cancer and organizing this ride*, I thought. *I guess now is a good time to find out what you're made of. A ridiculous spill isn't going to stop you.*

After my venting session and pep talk, I remounted, balanced my tender left forearm on the handlebars, and pedaled off, hoping my body would prove to be as resilient as my still-intact bicycle. Somehow, my front tire had not deflated in the crash.

Oddly enough, that summer of 1971 was the only other time that I had injured myself falling off a bike. I was racing along a Monmouth side street on a rented bicycle trying to keep pace with my older sister. When I lost my balance and tumbled to the road, blood spurted from a wound when a bent piece of metal near the bike chain pierced my left leg. My sister was too far ahead to hear me yell. A kind woman who had witnessed the crash tended to the wound and propped me up in her comfy recliner before my mother arrived and rushed me to the hospital emergency room for stitches.

This time around, there was no kind woman or recliner, but not much blood either. Putting pressure on my left arm hurt immensely, but I was determined to take a wait-and-see approach. I rode slowly, eyes focused on the road, trying to assess the arm injury. It felt more like a minor dislocation than a broken bone, but that didn't explain the horrible cracking sound. Had that been my body or the bike?

In the mid-1980s, I had severely dislocated my right elbow while playing on a competitive soccer team, the same one that helped to keep me sane during interferon treatments in Vermont. That injury happened just a few weeks before my older sister's August wedding. As the maid of honor, I pulled the long sleeve of my blue-green silk dress over the top of the cast and strategically covered the rest with a flower arrangement. Nobody knew I was wearing a sling.

However, negotiating this latest elbow injury was more problematic. After experimenting with various positions, I found that bracing my left arm on the handlebar grip at close to a forty-five-degree angle didn't make me wince too badly. Switching gears was challenging. I had to either stop completely or make a quick maneuver to the gear shifter on the left side of the bike with my right hand. It wasn't pretty, but it would work for the time being. I dulled the ache with over-the-counter painkillers from my tiny first-aid kit.

Fortunately, the Coast Range of Oregon, which required constant gear-shifting because of severe ups and downs, was behind me. I spent most of the day rolling through the moderate terrain of the Willamette Valley. On either side of Corvallis—Latin for "heart of the valley"—the soothing scent of commercially farmed peppermint wafted through my nostrils. For centuries, sediments that washed in via periodic flooding of the Willamette River have enriched that soil. Even though dams have limited that natural cycle, the beautiful dirt also grows crops of apples, hops, celery, cherries, grapes, and filbert nuts.

The most amusing "crops" I saw in this fertile agricultural valley were the distinctive blue and white ADT Security signs planted in front of dozens of well-tended farmhouses surrounded by gigantic swards of green. Encroaching subdivisions suggested that perhaps the thieves these farmers were trying to stave off were none other than real estate developers. Nothing inside those homes could possibly have been more valuable than that alluring acreage.

Late that afternoon, I was relieved to spot the lone store in Coburg because I anticipated burying my wounded elbow in a bag of ice. But my attempt to bond with my fellow cyclists delayed such relief. My hello to two older—and evidently lonely—male cyclists near the store prompted them both to drone on—and on—about their long-past bicycling exploits and challenges with the weather. When the gloom-and-doom twins warned me that I would be snowbound if I did not cross the Rocky Mountains by the end of August, I knew that was my cue to leave them behind. With a sore arm, I wasn't sure I could even make it to the Oregon-Idaho border.

So much for encouragement from fellow cyclists, I thought, finally able to enter the air-conditioned store. I bought a chicken dinner. A clerk let me fill a plastic bag with ice to soothe my swollen, tender elbow, which by now resembled a freckled sausage. After walking to a nearby park featuring a prominent "No Camping" sign, I shared my meal with a persistent cat that reminded me of Wilbur, my comical Maine coon cat back in Wisconsin. When my iced arm was numb, I scoped out a vacant space between two dilapidated houses where my tent fit perfectly. Before drifting off, I propped my injured arm on a packed pannier so I would be less likely to jar it.

My faith in bicyclists was restored the next morning, August 20, as I pedaled to the Lucky Logger Restaurant beyond Coburg for breakfast. I spied an ancient three-speed bicycle leaning by the side of Camp Creek Road. "Hello!" said an elderly gentleman emerging from the roadside thicket. I watched in awe as he deftly attached a dented metal bucket full of blackberries to his handlebars with a leather strap. I wished I had met such a pleasant cyclist in Coburg.

My goal for that Sunday was the blink-and-you'll-miss-it community of McKenzie Bridge, Oregon. I needed to be near a telephone for the first of my scheduled on-the-road interviews with a Milwaukee radio station early the next morning. After that, I would be climbing intimidating McKenzie

Pass. I wanted to be fresh for that elevation gain of 4,000 feet.

McKenzie Bridge had my chief necessity, a pay phone, and a bonus, ice cream. Shade provided by stout-trunked pines near the plain but elegant McKenzie Bridge Christian Church beckoned me on that toasty afternoon. I imagined how luxurious a pine needle mattress would feel. As it was Sunday, I figured somebody would be around so I could ask permission to pitch my tent. I knocked on the door of a house on the church grounds. And that's how I met Roseanne.

She did not appear flustered when my knock interrupted her piano practice. "We'll just go ask the pastor," she cheerfully replied to my camping question. It turned out she was married to the pastor, Gary. Though I was somewhat ripe after five days of shower-free cycling, they extended me every courtesy. They insisted that I set up camp in the carpeted church nursery, use the telephone in the second-floor office, and boil my tea water on the church stove. Roseanne even gave me a bag of ice so I could nurse my elbow. All she and Gary asked in return was that I tell my story at their evening service. That sounded fair enough.

I wasn't drawn to camping at churches out of any religious fervor. It was more a practical decision. Churches had open space and always seemed receptive to low-key, solo cyclists making a quick overnight stop, especially in towns that barred bicyclists from parks. For the most part, I had not been linked to any organized religion since last attending Quaker meetings as a child in the early 1970s. Although the intricacies of world religions fascinate me, my urge to participate teeters between minuscule and nonexistent. Not even my bouts with cancer had caused me to budge on that front. Chalk that up to my reporter instincts. That is, observing and asking questions is kosher, but joining isn't part of the package.

If there is indeed some sort of higher power—be it sacred animal, volcanic mountain, god, goddess, or great spirit—I am convinced that he, she, or it has a devilishly rich sense of humor. Otherwise, how could I possibly have found myself relaxing with a cup of green tea, courtesy of the Monmouth waitress, in the embrace of a church nursery rocking chair? I was counting on the good energy she told me it had to heal my arm quickly. As I leaned back in the only adult-size piece of furniture in the room, surveying my diminutive surroundings, I felt like Gulliver in a land of Lilliputian accoutrements. My sleeping bag was unfurled on the blue carpet opposite a baby crib full of plush critters. Nearby, pint-size chairs were tucked under a matching table. In one corner, a series of videos featuring bible stories were stacked under a small-screen television. My bicycle leaned against a bookcase overflowing with art supplies and colorful volumes featuring Jesus in the title.

The coursing McKenzie River served as background music as I reviewed my progress thus far. It was thunderous enough to drown out traffic noise on Highway 126. Pedaling 56.5 miles from Coburg that day meant that I had reached the end of map number one in my series of twelve. It was the first item I would mail home—lightening my load by about two ounces. Even with 289.5 miles down, the salt water of the Atlantic was still at least 3,960.5 miles away, I told Don when I called him that evening. I didn't mention my sore arm because I didn't want to worry him. "One map at a time is my approach," I joked about creating my own twelve-step plan for crossing the country.

To prepare for my evening talk at the church, I took a notebook and pen to the Log Cabin Inn, tucked along the river near a grove of statuesque Douglas fir trees. It housed the only restaurant in town. The inn, built as a stagecoach stop in the 1860s and rebuilt after a 1906 fire, boasted the signatures of Herbert Hoover, Clark Gable, and the Duke of Windsor in its registers. As if the church's hospitality weren't enough, Diane, my server, refused to let me pay for my fish dinner. She was a cervical cancer survivor, and my meal was her donation to my cause.

An hour or so later, I stood in front of the rustic church sanctuary wearing what amounted to my Sunday best—patched blue nylon rain pants, a pair of worn lightweight hiking boots, and my soiled-at-the-neck Heals on Wheels T-shirt. My only props were a map, a pannier full of gear, and brochures. I didn't have a fancy slide show to present, but the attentive parishioners in the pews were there to listen, not to judge. Not only did they ask intelligent questions, they also vowed to monitor my electronic journal. And for one magical evening, they felt like my adoptive family.

CHAPTER 7
CAPTURING THAT SMILE

D uring my interferon treatments, my older sister gave me several black-and-white family photos in antique frames as a birthday present. My favorite one captured my young father standing with his only sibling, William "Bill," eighteen months older, in the tiny central Ohio town of Gambier.

Their mother, Mary Higgins, had married their father, William Herron, in Cleveland in 1928. By 1933, William had died of an infected pericardium, a thin double-layered sac that encloses the heart. He was just twenty-seven.

In November 1934, Mary married her second husband, Stuart Rice McGowan, who adopted both Bill and Ron, my father. Shortly after the wedding, she and the children joined Stuart in Gambier, where he taught political science and was the registrar at Kenyon College.

In that photo, taken in the yard of their house on the college campus, the brothers are wearing knickers. Bill, looking studious and composed, tenuously holds a football. My smiling father, half a head shorter, is squinting. He looks to be seven or eight years old. Even in black and white, it's easy to tell he had red hair and freckles. The family story is that he is grinning lopsidedly because he had to go to the bathroom badly when Stuart snapped the picture.

My father grew taller—six foot one—and his red hair turned black, but that mischievous smile remained. And throughout my childhood, I monitored his face carefully so I would know which version of my father I could expect.

The cheerful one emerged one summer day in the late 1960s in Philadelphia. I remember being elated as my older sister and I, then about ten and eight, walked with our father to the neighbors' built-in swimming pool, which we had permission to use anytime. That was the day he taught us how to dive, first off the side of the pool and then off the diving board. We didn't care that shade from mature oak trees kept water in the deep end bracingly cold. We were just thrilled he didn't lose his patience when we belly-flopped or momentarily lost our nerve.

He gently guided us as we practiced over and over. Eventually—and most surprisingly—we graduated to experimenting with what he called a sailor's dive, launching ourselves headfirst and missile-like, arms straight at our sides. I was amazed my safety-conscious father would even allow it, but I kept quiet because I didn't want to break what felt like a spell. "Just don't tell your mother I taught you that dive," he warned us, and then winked, as we reluctantly prepared for the walk home. It was our secret.

My father's smile was also predominant during our summer camping vacations in the early 1970s. By 1970, for the first time, both of my parents had their summers off from work. My mother tutored students, and my father no longer had to make extra money teaching summer school because he had finally paid back the colleague who had loaned us the down payment for our Philadelphia house. In June, we borrowed a tent, lantern, propane-fueled stove, and other camping gear from neighbors and explored the coasts and mountains of Maine.

Maine was merely a rehearsal for a more intensive summer the following year in the Pacific Northwest. We rented out our house for three months and learned to be minimalists. Each of us girls was issued one blue duffel bag about the size of a large sleeping bag for clothes and necessities. In early June, we crammed everything into the back of our creaky Ford Fairlane, the station wagon my father nicknamed the Fix or Repair Daily model. Only three of us could fit on the bench back seat, so he cleared a tiny square of space in the rear cargo area for one sister.

We spent about a week tracing a northerly route to Oregon, stopping to explore the natural wonders and small towns. Every night, we pitched our pair of tents—one for my parents and one for my sisters and me—in a different setting. One evening we were serenaded by a herd of boisterous cows along the Mississippi River in La Crosse, Wisconsin. In the Black Hills of South Dakota, we stopped at Mount Rushmore. We spent much longer than desired in that state when our secondhand car lived up to my father's low expectations, and our entire exhaust system failed in Rapid City.

Farther along, we were awed by the wide-open expanses of Wyoming. At nightfall, lights from indistinguishable ranch houses miles from the highway pricked the darkness, one by one. We savored the sight of elk grazing in the Bighorn Mountains and relished the geysers and rivers of Yellowstone National Park. We marveled at the endless wheat fields of Washington and were entranced when fourteen thousand and four hundred-foot Mount Rainier seemed close enough to touch with our grubby little fingers, though it was a hundred-plus miles away.

On our return trip from Oregon, along a more southerly route, we admired the incomparable blueness of Crater Lake. We stopped to gawk at California's magnificent redwood trees and then San Francisco, Monterey, and Big Sur on our route to Los Angeles to see my father's brother, Bill, and his family. Near Albuquerque, we were fascinated when a husband and wife pulled into a campsite on a motorcycle towing a small boat. It was a trailer for their gear.

In the summer of 1972, after our western trip, we headed north to Canada to camp across the provinces of Quebec, Nova Scotia, and Prince Edward Island. On all of these long trips, my father controlled the pace of our travel by driving every mile. My mother was the navigator. For him, order mattered and time couldn't be wasted, even—especially—when traveling. And sleeping in wasn't an option. Our predawn alarm clock was the distinctive ZZZZZZZZ of my father enthusiastically unzipping our tent. We all had camp takedown chores, and if you didn't finish before sunrise, you ate breakfast in the car after brushing your teeth. Knowing how icky it was to chase toothpaste with instant orange juice, we all hurried to eat breakfast first.

Though my father's attempts to cook at home were usually unmitigated disasters, he delighted in preparing his so-called campfire Supreme Dinners. Usually the menu was steak, potatoes wrapped in tin foil, and corn on the cob. He would get so excited about fixing them that you felt obligated to enjoy every bite, even if the potatoes had shriveled in the coals. My sisters and I never quite grasped how this amiable version of my usually tense father emerged, but we always welcomed him to the picnic table.

On the road, my father would let a red beard and mustache grow over his normally clean-shaven chin and cheeks, prompting him to christen himself Captain Spiffy. Those whiskers scratched our cheeks when he kissed us goodnight.

My mind has protected that image of him, probably because that is who I wanted him to be all of the time. No photos I had of him hinted at his explosiveness. My father's ire went far beyond the impatience he displayed when he thought it took us too long to get ready for school. His raw, volcanic temper was unpredictable and downright scary. When my older sister was a toddler, she developed her own barometer to gauge the severity of our father's anger. "It's OK, Mommy's smiling," she would say, checking my mother's face to decide how frightened we should be. We knew spilling a glass of milk or leaving a bicycle outside overnight were akin to criminal offenses in his mind. So we tried to be perfect. But that was impossible, and futile, in a house where the ground rules were always changing and an ordinary evening could devolve into a calamity.

When our family played rounds of Old Maid on New Year's Eve, my father could be as comedic as the affable Dick Van Dyke. He made that tradition memorable by sticking one of the cards in his dealt hand way up high. It was so tempting to trust him, but you never knew if he was taunting you with a card you needed to make a pair or the stinker card you didn't want to be saddled with at game's end. Those were the times it felt safe to laugh without suffering consequences.

Other times, however, something—who knows what—would light his incredibly short fuse and put an abrupt end to any hilarity. I knew to brace myself when his upper lip would curl into a foreboding sneer, a precursor to his yelling and cussing. That dark, frightening version of my father left me speechless. I would hold my breath and freeze, hoping stillness could deter a tirade. Often the torrent of fury would travel from his mouth to his hands, and he would hurl a plate of spaghetti across the table at dinnertime, tear a shower curtain from its rod, or throw a heavy rotary telephone across the room hard enough to scar the wall plaster. He could turn on his own family in a malicious and terrifying manner, but would never unleash such fury on his students, fellow teachers, or friends. No amount of avoiding contact, remaining silent, tiptoeing around the house, or praying that it would stop kept that internal beastliness from awakening. It was always lurking.

My mother often bore the brunt of his venom. Sometimes, when our windows were open on summer evenings, my father's angry rants would reach the yard and front stoop where my sisters and I were playing with friends. "Maybe our television is just on too loud," I would tell playmates who asked about "all of that noise." What I didn't tell them was that I was terrified for my mother, reasoning that she was OK as long as I could still hear her voice. Occasionally, he spanked my sisters and me, but he wasn't physically abusive. Even so, on those summer evenings, I half-expected to find my mother broken into a hundred pieces in the living room. I was always relieved to find that only her eyes were red, from all of the crying.

An especially petrifying day came in the late 1960s when he ordered my three sisters and me to sit on the wooden steps near the second-story landing of our three-story house in Philadelphia.

"Which one of you did this?" he barked, the most prominent vein in his neck bulging.

Sitting ramrod straight, we turned our eyes to the long, crooked crack on the wall he was pointing at. Chunks of old plaster from a long-ago repair job were missing.

"You're not going anywhere until somebody confesses to picking at this wall," he shouted, behaving as if one of us had murdered the family pet.

Nobody piped up, which only fueled his anger. He wanted a whipping girl. I concentrated on not smirking or making eye contact with my sisters. After an hour of ranting, he must have worn himself out because we were all sent to separate bedrooms for the afternoon.

Years later, the "guilty" sister apologized to the rest of us, saying she was too frightened to admit her transgression during the staircase interrogation. We all understood and forgave her.

Despite my father's sometimes despicable behavior, my eagerness to please shaped my loyalty to him. For instance, I knew instinctively that on school days I had to be standing at his coat-and-tie-clad side by the time he gulped down his last swallow of orange juice—all the breakfast he ever ate—to avoid a glare or reprimand. He would kiss my mother goodbye, then I would follow him through the red front door with the brass knocker and across the glassed-in porch of our semi-detached Tudor-style house. We would march down our front walkway to the big, slightly wobbly, smooth stone step where my older sister and I often played Jacks and where our exotic neighbor—the boy who was allowed to keep pet snakes in his house— taught us how to wield a ball-peen hammer to get the biggest bang from a paper roll of gunpowder caps.

Then we would turn left and head up West Penn Street for half a block before turning left once again. Our destination was the same: William Penn Charter School, a K–12 private Quaker-founded school with the motto "Good Instruction Is Better Than Riches." My father taught history, geography, political science, and urban planning in the Upper School. I was one of six sorely outnumbered girls in Mrs. Yocum's first-grade class. Daughters of faculty and staff members were allowed to attend this boys-only school through second grade tuition-free.

Our morning walk usually lasted about fifteen minutes. The most adventurous part came early on when we dashed across four-lane Midvale Boulevard at an intersection without a stoplight or a crosswalk. That crossing made me jumpy because of an incident that happened there a year earlier on the trek to school with my father and sister, a second-grader. As a kindergartner, I had been mortified to watch the clasp give way on my older sister's square metal lunchbox, the one decorated with a yellow-haired princess. Out tumbled her matching Thermos, a sandwich, an apple, and a handful of potato chips sealed in a plastic bag. Predictably, my father, who knew we didn't have a minute to spare, blew up. My sister and I cringed. Even an accident had to be somebody's fault.

From then on, I was convinced that I couldn't trust the shiny latch on my own metal lunchbox, a more utilitarian red plaid model. Every day, I pressed my right index finger over the latch, even in winter when I had to slip the finger from my mitten. Protecting my lunch that way became a ritual. I didn't care how red, chapped, or cold that finger was, I didn't want to trigger another outburst from my father.

When he was holed up in his study, my sisters and I wouldn't dare interrupt him as long as we could hear him pounding out lesson plans on his Royal manual typewriter, with the carriage bell chiming its familiar ding at the end of each line. He had once told me that he depended on that typewriter—which had been my mother's in high school—because his handwriting was so difficult to decipher. He attributed his poor penmanship to the schoolroom rigidity of the 1930s, which forced naturally left-handed people such as my father to write right-handed.

At home, my sisters and I ached for my father to adopt his vacation persona of Captain Spiffy. Sometimes, that happened on Sunday evenings. If he finished preparing for school early enough, we would hear a different sound emanating from his study—chords from the acoustic guitar he was teaching himself to play. That sweet sound was a cue. His furious strumming was an invitation for four small, pajama-clad girls to bound into his cramped study and dance. We called it dancing, but it was really feverish head-bobbing and leaping—as high as we could without banging our skulls on the ceiling's sloped eaves. We probably looked like those stick-necked cartoon kids from the 1960s Charlie Brown Christmas television show. It was such genuine fun. My father would smile his engaging smile, and we would bask in his genuine pleasure. We would flail around and laugh for a half hour or so before trundling off to bed in a sweaty heap. I like to believe my father was capable of fully loving us during those moments.

CHAPTER 8
OREGON: THE ULTIMATE YOGI

MILES RIDDEN: 289.5
MILES TO GO: 3,960.5

M *ind believes, body achieves.* I rotated my pedals to the chant of those seven syllables—a mantra from my rugby-playing days in Madison—while grinding my way up an intimidating maze of switchbacks on the McKenzie River Highway on the morning of August 21. I was in pursuit of McKenzie Pass, a 5,324-foot jewel on the green necklace of Oregon's Cascade Range. This mountainous spine, stretching from southern British Columbia to northern California, roughly divides the wet of western Oregon from the dry eastern section.

I felt dog-like, panting my way up the mountain. It's little wonder that some white westbound settlers on the Oregon Trail in the 1800s viewed those peaks as such an impediment to their quest for the Willamette Valley that they resorted to rafting the Columbia River. The few cars that passed me on the winding ascent did so gingerly. Businesses from nearby Eugene funded initial construction of this road, and the first car chugged to the summit in 1910. I doubt I could have beaten even that jalopy to the top, but at least I didn't have to pay a toll to use the road. That practice had been abandoned in 1891.

Partway up the twenty-two-mile climb, a sign pointing to Proxy Falls Trail beckoned. My instinct was to ignore it, so as not to interrupt my rhythmic, albeit glacial, pace to the summit. But my inner voice interceded. *Elizabeth*, it admonished, *one of the reasons for this journey is to explore. You're setting your own schedule. It's OK to take a break.* Stepping from the asphalt into the woods, I entered soul-soothing silence. Then, minutes later, I heard the whisper of water.

Silvery tongues of liquid tumbled at least two hundred feet, lapping at shelves of moss-covered columns of basalt on their long slide to a pool. Sun-kissed droplets sprayed the thirsty ferns in this isolated cathedral of pines and rhododendrons. I took a ringside seat on a piece of forest furniture, a log with the girth of a tractor tire. I felt fortunate to have access. Authorities often closed the road due to lingering snow or bad potholes. Most long-distance bicyclists, including my Wisconsin friends Joanne and Elaine, were forced to take a less strenuous and scenic detour.

Up the road, I joined a clot of cyclists at a narrow, well-worn spot for a few sips of lukewarm water from my bottle. "I'm Andrew," one lean man said warmly, extending his hand. "Hey, are you the one doing that ride for cancer? We stayed at the Log Cabin Inn last night, and the bartender told us all about you. Where did you stay, anyway?"

I told him about my welcome stay at the church in McKenzie Bridge. Andrew, an anesthesiologist from Philadelphia, explained that he was out with about fifteen other riders from across the country for a weeklong tour of the Pacific Northwest. They were unencumbered by gear because everything, including a kitchen sink, was crammed in the Olympia-based Bicycle Adventures van tailing them. They invited me to lunch, telling me to stop when I spotted the large white van with bike racks. I had planned on eating the peanut butter, honey, crackers, and raisins I'd stowed in the pantry part of my pannier. I figured their invite meant I'd be supplementing my rations with a sandwich or maybe a piece of fruit.

Some two miles shy of the summit, however, I thought I was hallucinating from dehydration when I saw what looked like a blue-and-white circus tent billowing in the brisk wind. But no. Soon, I realized it was a tarpaulin staked over tables. Then, a white van came into focus. The motionless herd of riderless bicycles stashed near the roadside confirmed that, yum, I could be in for the ultimate Yogi. The term is part of any long-distance traveler's vocabulary. It has nothing to do with somebody in the lotus position and everything to do with that rascally cartoon bear Yogi and his sidekick Boo-Boo, who roamed Jellystone Park to score whatever was in visitors' "pic-a-nic" baskets. But I didn't have to fool anybody into sharing. I'd been invited.

I joined the buffet line, eagerly piling my plate with tortellini, fruit salad, beans, cookies, green salad sprinkled with pine nuts, and bread smeared with brie. (The curious always ask what long-distance bicyclists eat. The succinct answer is: "Pretty much anything they want.") They even had china plates and metal utensils. Oh, how splendid and restorative it was to sit elbow-to-elbow in a circle of folding chairs with a gaggle of more than a dozen other sweaty cyclists immersed in the same physical ups and downs. They all led interesting lives and had clearly developed an easy rapport in their few days together. Most of them were seasoned riders, but a few rookies admitted to having tender hind ends on their second day out.

"Your body always barks the loudest on day two of any long ride because it figures day one was an error that you wouldn't dare repeat," Andrew said, laughing.

"Don't worry," I chimed in. "Each part toughens up and adapts. Your lungs gain capacity, your legs and back stretch, and your butt develops a callous right where you need it."

Back on my own, I thought about how timing is everything. Early that morning, I had been annoyed when last-minute changes for a Heals on Wheels interview with the Milwaukee radio station had delayed my departure from McKenzie Bridge. Poor reception and roaming charges made traveling with cell phones dicey and prohibitively expensive back then, so the trick was finding a pay phone at the right time.

I had prepared my radio script at the church so it could be taped early that morning. But the harried technician in Milwaukee told me he wouldn't be able to field my call for another hour. I fumed because if I dillydallied in the morning, I wouldn't be able to maximize daylight for the four-thousand-foot climb from the river to the summit. I was a hostage to the phone at the church, so I waited around and called at the newly appointed time. If not for the morning wait, I realized, I would have been lunching alone at the summit. *Proceed as the way opens,* I reminded myself.

I reached the top of McKenzie Pass with a full stomach. The summit bisects an ebony-colored, rocky armada that long ago spewed lava from an ancient volcano eight miles long and a half-mile wide. I felt as if I were riding on the moon. Giant chunks of basaltic lava, which geologists say flowed from the Yapoah Crater twenty-seven hundred years ago, created otherworldly formations such as pressure ridges, lava gutters, and cooling cracks. Pieces of this basaltic aa (pronounced "ah ah") lava have rough, jagged surfaces. Lava blocks, broken and jumbled like ice being burped out of a thawing river in springtime, formed as air rapidly cooled the surface flow. The insulated molten flow below, however, continued moving. As the lava cooled and hardened, it formed still-visible lava gutters, which look like rocky riverbanks, and pressure ridges, which are a series of distinctive mounds.

Around me, about half a dozen types of resolute conifers, distended and gnarled by the harshness of this sub-alpine environment, clung to life at this seemingly barren altitude. Dead and dying trees jutted upward like sickly stick ghosts. Remarkably, white pioneers had carved a wagon trail out of this unforgiving landscape in the late 1860s and early 1870s.

The Dee Wright Observatory at the tippy-top of the pass was, well, a delight. Wright, a Civilian Conservation Corps foreman who devoted twenty-four years of his life to the US Forest Service, began constructing the building in 1933, and it was dedicated as a memorial when he died the next year. The lava-block structure looms like a small but impenetrable summit fortress. Peepholes notched in the circular walls allow visitors to walk 360 degrees and stop for bullseye views of mountains at the heart of the Cascade Range: snow-covered Middle Sister, North Sister, Mount Hood (on a clear day), Mount Jefferson, and Mount Washington, and also the bare but equally beautiful Black Crater, Black Butte, Little Belknap Crater, Belknap Crater, Scott Mountain, and Horsepasture Mountain.

Diminishing daylight tugged me away from that alluring panorama because I needed to travel another fifteen miles before sunset. And what a reward that was. Wheeee! My odometer reached thirtysomething miles per hour as I descended out of lava fields into forests of robust ponderosa pines. I had to stop for a close-up sniff because the vanilla scent wafting from ponderosas is one of nature's most exquisite fragrances. I like to think that the carload of Washingtonians that passed me at that moment still talks about that weird woman in biking shorts they saw along Highway 242 embracing a ponderosa pine, her nose deeply embedded in its ridged bark.

That heaping helping of downhill meant I made double time to the community of Sisters. From its name, I figured it was some sort of feminist enclave or, from the way certain Oregonians talked, a remote mountain outpost. It was neither. Instead, it was a sanitized tourist trap overflowing with scented candles, outlet clothes, food from nowhere in particular, and every kitschy doodad imaginable. Among all of that nonsense, however, I found a young mind that would bend. The amiable teen tending the deli at the small grocery store agreed to sell me two pieces of bread because I didn't need a whole loaf.

At the community park where I pitched my tent, I met a husband and wife who had started cycling on New York's Long Island and would be finished when they reached the Oregon coast within a week. They lived in Connecticut and Florida. Severe wildfires in Montana had forced them off secondary roads and onto busy Interstate 90. I was surprised how nervous the woman was about climbing McKenzie Pass the next day. "What could possibly scare you now?" I asked, puzzled. "You've struggled over the Appalachians, battled the winds of the Midwest, and put the Rockies behind you. This will just be a blip to you. By now you could probably pedal with one leg and do just fine."

"I'm the one who should be fretting," I continued, "People keep warning me that my late start means snow will keep me from crossing the Rockies."

She didn't offer any encouragement.

CHAPTER 9
THE GIFT OF THE COUNTRY

Late or not, I was not going to call off a two-day hiatus scheduled to begin the next day. It would be my first break after six days of riding, and I bet even Lewis and Clark would have traded the hard ground for a mattress. I would be staying with Mary Ellen and Larry, anthropologist friends from Wisconsin who had opportunely transplanted themselves to Madras, Oregon, about thirty miles off my route. It would be a chance to wash myself and my pungent shirts on what I jokingly called a "lowgiene" tour.

I spent my restorative day and a half off visiting a Native American museum, tumbling with my friends' rambunctious kittens, and overindulging in huckleberry pie and Mary Ellen's incomparable meals. Larry didn't flinch when I asked him to drop me off at the exact spot where he had picked me up on the trail in Redmond so I could keep my don't-miss-an-inch purist credentials. The rest meant my elbow was still stiff but less sore. Bracing it precariously on the handlebars allowed me to resume shifting gears the normal way, which was a much safer option than the cross-handed system I'd developed when leaving Monmouth.

One of the two roads from Redmond to Mitchell was the O'Neil Highway, which roughly parallels the Crooked River. A headwind was the most momentous challenge to climbing about eighteen hundred feet to Ochoco Pass at 4,720 feet. The highway was a delightful stretch of junipers and blooming sagebrush tucked among stunning canyon walls lined with endless columns of prismatic basalt. I kept expecting—and hoping—to spot a bobcat, though I spied only vultures and magpies.

Arriving in minuscule Mitchell, Oregon, the afternoon of August 24 with my bicycle odometer reading 422.5 felt significant. I was one-tenth of the way to the Atlantic. Granted, I wasn't out of Oregon yet, but the arithmetic gave me a boost. The neatly stacked firewood, operating water faucet, pavilion, picnic tables, and flat tent site at the quaint Lions Club Park seemed like luxurious amenities after pedaling seventy-one miles in temperatures hovering in the low nineties.

On Mitchell's deserted main street, somebody had painstakingly handwritten a somewhat convoluted town history on posterboard taped to the windows of a defunct business. The faded words revealed that hellacious floods and fires had devastated the community not once, but four times between 1884 and 1904. Somehow, the old mining hotbed still clung to a skeletal existence with a population of two hundred.

Origins for the town's name vary. The ho-hum version claimed that blacksmith William Johnson established a post office and requested that the settlement be named for Senator John Hipple Mitchell, a Pennsylvanian who migrated west. The more exotic version unfolded like this: A traveler was driving his Racine, Wisconsin-made Mitchell wagon full of whiskey from The Dalles, a rough section of the Columbia River that stretched from east of Portland to Canyon City, Oregon. When the wagon broke down, the disgusted driver sampled his load and became, er, loaded while commiserating with passengers, who also imbibed. That breakdown site evidently birthed the Palace Saloon, the first establishment in Tiger Town, the rowdy commercial district of Mitchell. Early settlers built their homes and churches in uptown, also known as Piety Hill.

I was partial to the more colorful creation story, probably because it highlighted my adopted home state of Wisconsin, and Racine, the city where I had worked as a newspaper reporter and met the friends I had stayed with in Madras. Still, that entertaining tale didn't prepare me for the John Irving moment that jolted me before entering the only extant business, Little Pine Café. Something large, dark, and furry was a few hundred feet from the doorway. And it caught my eye because it moved. I figured it was an off-leash dog or my sunbaked brain playing tricks, until I walked closer and confirmed it was neither dog nor delusion. I was staring at a black bear pacing in an open-air pen.

Hugh, who greeted me with a dinner menu in the welcome coolness of the café, turned out to be the answer man for my bear questions. He was a bear of a man himself. The fabric of his white T-shirt was stressed not only by his Popeye-like arms but also his prodigious stomach, which nearly obliterated the shiny Colt revolver belt buckle looped through his jeans. His baseball cap couldn't contain his unruly blond hair. He reminded me of a gruffer rendition of the Skipper, the boat captain of *Gilligan's Island* fame.

A boys club from a nearby Oregon town had purchased the declawed bear from an Iowa outfit that supposedly trains animals to "act" in movies. Sadly, the bear became homeless when the club left town, burdening a local sheriff's deputy with the nasty chore of shooting the innocent animal. The sympathetic deputy told Hugh about his dilemma. Hugh, a mechanic, construction worker, and jack-of-all trades, added savior to his resumé by converting his truck garage into a house for the eighteen-month-old bear he named Henry.

"I've been training Henry because he has a future in Hollywood," the

51

garrulous Hugh told me as I shoveled in forkfuls of vegetable omelet. "I have connections at Universal and with them Japanese. This bear could be my meal ticket." *It must be true what Wallace Stegner said about the West being the native home of hope*, I thought, *because clearly this stretch of soil is deeply embedded with optimism and initiative.*

Outside the café, Hugh and I watched Henry, his lustrous black coat tinged with auburn, devour a heaping portion of dog food from an enormous bowl fashioned from a rough-edged semi-trailer tire. Hugh fed him two gallons of apples daily and rewarded him with treats for following one-syllable commands. To motivate Henry to perform, he dangled cookies, the same edible lures he deployed to coax his hunting dogs. "I'm his toy," Hugh said about his pet project. "He's lonely when I'm not in the pen with him. And he sure does like them cookies. I think that other owner taunted the bear and played too rough. So I have to watch that. You know, I would shoot him if he ever got too ornery."

Afterward, while I sat at the park's picnic table, the sun dropped into glowing clouds smudged with exotic streaks of pink and orange caused by drifting ash from a not-too-far-away wildfire. A cricket provided reassuring harmony to the wind's melody. Then, a splash. Three mule deer—one doe and her twin spotted fawns—drank from a creek skirting the park. I stayed statue-still. The deer romped near the park's swingset. As the mother nuzzled one baby, the other excitedly tumbled to the grassy earth, bouncing upright like a rubber ball. I envied that agility.

Much later, when stars winked brilliantly in a clear black sky, I could not sleep. I crept from my tent to Henry's cage. The captive was curled in a ball atop the den Hugh had fashioned out of logs, snoozing with his brown shiny nose poking out from between his massive front paws. I sighed, unsure which fate—training for a movie career or the deputy's bullet—was best for such an elegant but compromised animal. That wasn't my decision to make.

Watching Henry, I realized how like a caged bear my father must have felt twenty-nine years ago. It was late August 1971, and our family was driving east to Philadelphia after our exhilarating ten-week summer adventure in Oregon. At a campground near Albuquerque, my father told only my mother that he had found a new, black, sinister-looking growth halfway up his left forearm.

My sisters and I didn't know anything was amiss until school started in September. My mother told us that our father wouldn't be teaching any classes yet. A biopsy confirmed that the growth was cancerous—his third occurrence of malignant melanoma since 1955. He needed another operation. Once again, the doctors decided they needed to dig deep, beyond the visible cancer. My father recovered in a Philadelphia hospital for close to a week. Absurdly enough, children were not allowed to visit patients—even a parent—in the early 1970s. My mother's way around that rule was to drive us to the hospital parking lot. The four of us would line up on the asphalt, waving to a distant figure clad in a hospital-issue gown and a bathrobe standing at the window of his upper-story room. We could just make out his smile.

Looking at that crown of stars in Mitchell almost three decades later made me wonder what thoughts flashed through my father's mind as he gazed at his four waving daughters, ages twelve, ten, eight, and six. After the surgery, he rested at home until he had the energy to resume teaching about three weeks later. He turned thirty-nine that September. I think that's when he began to feel as if the cancer that had dogged him during his adult life was on the verge of winning. The disease didn't birth his anger, but it certainly stoked it. He had the sword of Damocles poised over his head. It could be lowered gently, one scalpel slice at a time, leading to death by a thousand cuts. Or it could fall like a mighty sling blade, chopping the life out of him quickly. Either way, cancer stalked him relentlessly. That burden, combined with feeling trapped in the city by a job that he'd had for eight years, was making him antsier than usual. His inner wildness, the freedom that gives humans wholeness, was being tamed, and I don't think he could stand it another minute. Like that caged bear in Mitchell, my father needed an exit plan.

My father's newest distinctive scar looked as though surgeons had scraped out a sizeable hunk of tissue with an ice cream scoop. Determining how deep the melanoma might have penetrated was still a guessing game of sorts. Doctors erred on the side of caution. As a child, I thought that half-moon scar on my father's arm seemed perfectly shaped for balancing a baseball or a peach. No wonder that missing piece drew startled looks from strangers and whispered queries from my curious friends. But my father never stopped rolling up his sleeves to his elbows and fielding their questions graciously. I admired him for that simple act of courage.

By 1973, my father started hatching an escape plan. Early that spring, he and my mother headed to the Pine Barrens of southern New Jersey for a long weekend of camping. It was basically a retreat to allow them to figure out the logistics of leaving the city behind. They parceled us kids out to a neighborhood family while they brainstormed.

They were not interested in returning to their roots in the Midwest. New England, particularly western Massachusetts, was on their radar screen because of a remote connection. Stuart Rice McGowan, my father's adoptive father raised in Cleveland, had given us a series of tattered volumes that documented his family's history. Some Rices, on his father's side, had lived in the tiny Massachusetts village of Conway, which poet, Librarian of Congress, and Harvard University professor Archibald MacLeish put on the map when he lived there.

In June 1973, our family traveled to western Massachusetts for an exploratory visit. Our budget being pitifully small, we used a campground as a home base by night and tagged along behind a real estate agent by day to look at houses in this region of hill towns south of Vermont and east of Albany, New York. By July, we had decided to leave Philadelphia. My parents resigned from their teaching jobs and put our house up for sale. My father obsessed about how much our family could afford to cart north because the moving company charged by the pound. We had to jettison school projects and papers, along with toys, clothes, and books. The model trains we had set up in the basement became yard sale fodder. Each of us was allowed a single box of personal items. Our move date was set for August 21.

Some Philadelphia friends and neighbors thought we were bold and brave to launch such an adventure. Others told us we were crazy. The country was mired in a deep recession, we were moving to an unfamiliar place, and neither parent had yet lined up a job. Still, by late August, we were arranging our belongings in a rambling nineteenth-century Massachusetts farmhouse that had once served as a roadside inn. It was in Ashfield, a town of twelve hundred, adjacent to Conway.

My parents soon discovered what they seemed oblivious to, or in denial about, while plotting in Philadelphia. Employment options in rural Massachusetts were never plentiful, even during economic booms. Our household budget had always been far from exorbitant—teaching and tutoring at Quaker schools was not lucrative—but we lived on a sharp edge for those first six months in Massachusetts. We shopped at thrift stores and counted on a health clinic instead of a primary care physician. In Philadelphia, we had attended private schools on scholarships and at deeply reduced tuition rates because of my father's teaching position. Our wardrobes were already quite small because we wore uniforms to school daily. In Massachusetts, that meant we barely had enough clothes to cover the week when we started at the regional public schools. Ironically, before we left Philadelphia, my mother had earnestly explained that we would be moving to a rural area where some children had only one pair of shoes. I joked to my older sister—she was fourteen and I was twelve—that it probably never occurred to my mother at the time that her four daughters would be the ones experiencing those wardrobe deficits.

After months of substitute teaching and diligence, my father finally landed a position with a small publishing house. My mother eventually enrolled in a training program at a local historical museum. Fortunately, they could commute together to a nearby valley town in the sole family car.

Even though the move and the job hunt had stressed my father, I know he didn't regret following his compass north on this shaky but liberating venture. He charmed all the neighbors and local leaders in our new town by engaging them in conversation and pitching in at community events. Townspeople welcomed a new citizen who was so gung-ho about serving on committees such as the Board of Zoning Appeals in a community that relied on volunteers to keep democracy ticking. Beyond his civic duties, he especially loved taking long walks on back roads where pedestrians usually outnumbered vehicles and exploring every angle of the five acres that surrounded our house.

His joy is captured in a small color photograph. Our property included an old two-story barn and a newer, three-bay shed with a corrugated metal roof built for storing vehicles and a winter's supply of firewood. The previous tenant had left behind an antique tractor that had probably been sitting unused for at least ten years. Ever the tinkerer, my father spent reams of spare hours between job interviews in the fall of 1973 beating on its metal parts and ordering them to submit to his cuss-loaded demands.

Serendipitously, my mother had a camera poised to capture the magical moment when the mechanical beast fired up like a dormant dinosaur belching back to life. Seated on its ancient metal tractor seat, my father is pumping his fist and smiling his treasured smile. He looks like a young boy with his life ahead of him and without a worry in the world. Every time I peer into that photograph, I find myself wishing he could have had hundreds of other days just like that.

CHAPTER 10
EASTERN OREGON: AN EASY-BAKE OVEN

E arly on August 25, I nodded a sad farewell to Henry and climbed out of Mitchell toward 4,357-foot Keyes Creek Pass on Highway 26. That seven-mile ascent was easier on the eyes than the legs. Refreshingly, wildlife on the yawning high desert was uncaged. I spotted at least a dozen bounding mule deer and then three bighorn sheep, partially hidden by juniper bushes. It was also a haven for turkey vultures, wild turkeys, ravens, quail, grouse, and magpies.

At the peak of the pass, I stopped to admire the dry beauty. Realizing too late that I had foolishly forgotten to unclip one cleat-clad foot, I tumbled to the ground, jouncing my already-compromised left elbow and rescraping my scabbed knee. Medicine for those aches was the long, satisfying drop of at least fourteen hundred feet from Keyes Creek Pass into John Day country. Still, that steep descent reminded me that it's possible to experience too much of a good thing. The sheer drop-off to rocky oblivion on my right made me grip the handlebars so tightly that my limbs were fatigued by the time I reached the bottom.

Mitchell bills itself as the gateway to the Painted Hills. What a treat to meander through a geologic maze of carved cones, prismatic basalt, steppes, and buttes, their hues of usually subtle pinks, oranges, reds, and browns exaggerated by rays of the rising sun. High rock walls on both sides of the mostly car-free highway near Dayville gave me the sensation of zipping through a flume on a raft. Shooting through Oregon's Picture Gorge—a spectacular geographical melding of South Dakota's Badlands and Arizona's Painted Desert—was the closest I would ever come to spelunking on a bicycle. An unfazed doe and her spotted fawn, both hoof-deep in the John Day River, stared up at me with big brown innocent eyes as I crossed a bridge.

Seemingly endless swaths of timber, promising gold strikes, and the opportunity to seek one's fortune in livestock lured white settlers there in the latter half of the 1800s. I concluded that a fellow named John Day must have been among them because since leaving Mitchell I had passed a dam, a river, two towns, a hotel, a valley, and fossil beds named for him. But a few sentences in a brochure I discovered at the John Day city hall proved me wrong. Day was indeed a real person, a hulking Virginian hired as a hunter in 1810 by the Pacific Fur Company. Mysteriously, however, he never set foot in this part of Oregon, which eventually became Grant County.

Prairie City, my destination that day, rests at thirty-six hundred feet on the Columbia Plateau. The bank thermometer that afternoon registered in the high nineties, more than double the morning temperature in Mitchell. I smeared aloe lotion on my poor ears, which felt as if they had been sizzled on a charcoal grill. Mileage-wise, I had achieved my longest day yet, eighty-four miles, but I cursed myself for neglecting to reapply my sunscreen at midday in that Easy-Bake Oven landscape. Locals at the Branding Iron restaurant told me ninety-something felt tolerable. Two weeks earlier, temperatures had topped a hundred degrees. At least I hadn't subjected my sore ears to that.

My makeshift campsite at the Methodist church positioned me perfectly for the next morning's climb of Dixie, Tipton, and Sumpter, a triplet of five-thousand-plus-foot passes in the Blue Mountains. It wasn't clear how Tipton fit in, but local lore hinted that Southern sympathizers christened Dixie and Sumpter, spelled with a *p*, in the 1860s.

I left Prairie City early the next morning. The sun hadn't yet warmed the western slopes when I overcame my first obstacle of the day, 5,277-foot Dixie Peak. My gloved fingers felt like talons, curled and frozen to my handlebar grips, when I steered toward a one-gas-pump store at an isolated crossroads called Austin Junction. The store was a mecca for hunters donned in camouflage. "I'm sorry," I overheard the proprietor telling a motorist desperately in need of gasoline. "The oil truck hasn't come up the mountain yet." I scooted inside, seeking edible fuel.

The storekeeper, an older woman, was kind enough to let me heat water in her personal microwave. As I lingered with my tea, she regaled me with stories about her favorite cyclists. "A few months ago, I had a father and his daughter stop in here. I thought it was beautiful they were riding together. And they were headed to Virginia, like you are." The father, in his early seventies, wanted to reconnect with an adult daughter he barely knew because his peripatetic military career had caused him to miss so much of her growing-up years. That story touched the most tender part of my heart. It made me crave my father's physical presence—something I hadn't felt for twenty-four years. Maybe I was a bit jealous of that daughter because all I had was my father's spirit with me. But I like to think he would have jumped at the chance to bond with me on such an adventure.

As I completed the second and third climbs—Tipton and Sumpter,

5,124 feet and 5,082 feet, respectively—of the morning triumvirate, I wondered what it would be like to ride with the sixty-eight-year-old version of my father. Most of the one-on-one time I had with him came when I was in first grade and we walked to Penn Charter School together. I had him to myself that year because my older sister was in third grade at the neighborhood public school. My two younger sisters hadn't started school yet, but they would wave goodbye to us each morning from the living room window.

On one particular winter morning, doing my usual skip steps to keep up with my father's lanky frame was a bit more difficult because I was wearing my favorite but clunky chocolate-brown rubber boots. They were lined with bread bags to keep the zippers from leaking. To the clomp, clomp, clomp of my boots smacking the wet sidewalk, I carefully recited each syllable of the word *chrysanthemum*, hoping I wouldn't forget it by the time I reached Mrs. Yocum's classroom. Per usual, my father was carrying his tan briefcase in his left hand. But in his right hand, he was carrying an ornate sword that was about as tall as I was.

It was my morning for show-and-tell. My father had given me permission to show off the sword he had bought in Japan during the Korean War. He had gone ashore during several of his rest-and-recuperation breaks when his navy ship was positioned in Korea Bay in the Yellow Sea. As one of half a dozen girls in my class, I figured I needed such a bright and shiny object to hold the attention of all those boys.

The previous night, I had breathed deeply before knocking on the door of the third-floor study where my father spent hours each weeknight holed up and prepared his lesson plans. He created his entire curricula from scratch, refusing to use textbooks because he felt that would be shortchanging the high school boys he was entrusted with educating.

Instead of shooing me away, he listened. Then, he walked the few steps to the wall where the golden sword hung from a silky yellow cord. He let me grip the solid handle and run my hands over the intricate metal scabbard, textured with dozens of carved chrysanthemums. He explained that the Japanese so revered this sacred flower that it had evolved into a symbol for the emperor. That night, we rehearsed saying the word *chrysanthemum* together. My father was unusually patient. "That's OK, Elizabeth," he told me. "If you get up in front of the class and can't remember the whole word, just say they are mums. That's the flower's nickname."

That's the version of my father I wanted pedaling by my side as I completed a sixty-nine-mile day into Baker City. The city of more than nine thousand is on the Powder River, which had been my constant and beautiful companion for the last twenty-seven miles. Baker City's history is all about cattle and pioneers because its heritage is the Oregon Trail. Travelers' hardships are recognized on a bronze plaque mounted on a slab of granite that proclaims to be the offering of eight hundred Baker City schoolchildren honoring "the memory of these pioneers whose suffering and death brought Oregon under the American flag." That tribute is dwarfed by a giant granite salute from the Cattlemen's Association to the prized cows, horses, and sheep herded east on the Oregon Trail to points in Wyoming and Nebraska.

Leaving Baker City early on August 27, I figured it would be my last full day in Oregon. Navigating was easy. All I had to do was head mostly east on Highway 86. It was a treat to pedal through the gorgeous Powder River Valley, most of which hovered under 3,000 feet. Still, some of those downhills were daunting, especially when I noticed strands of barbed wire fencing that would tear me to shreds if I veered too far right. Conical hills formed the backdrop for lush green irrigated valleys that supported thousands, if not millions, of cattle. It's not likely that steers and bulls outnumbered the sagebrush. It just seemed that way.

When I rolled into Richland, a sweet town of 175 on Eagle Creek, I was tempted to stay overnight. But it wasn't yet eleven a.m., so I looked for lunch instead. I skipped the dollar-a-dozen deal on worms and opted for a chocolate milkshake at the only café. Pedaling on, I realized why I had been tempted to camp in Richland. My maps showed me that services were extremely limited until the Idaho border. I figured I'd take my chances. Something would work out. The only convenience I needed was a phone to call the Milwaukee radio station the next morning for another interview.

When I saw the pay phone in front of a little grocery store in Pine Creek, Oregon—just thirteen miles from the Idaho border in an area known as Hells Canyon—I figured I'd better stop, even though it was only about three p.m. Pine Creek was a narrow spit of a town in a little gully divided by Highway 86, with no parks, campgrounds, or churchyards. The community consisted of maybe a dozen houses and a hunting-and-fishing outfitting business, so I would have to be creative. I checked the outfitter off my list when I saw the lone pickup truck near it was plastered with a "Ted Kennedy has killed more people with his car than I have with my gun" bumper sticker. I was indeed in the land of extremes. The rivers and streams were alluring. Yet the dry, rocky, and exposed landscape dominated—and shade was as scarce as a Democrat.

Hanging out on the store porch, I schemed. I decided to approach a kind-looking, grandfatherly man wearing red suspenders I had seen puttering in his front yard. I knocked on the door of his trailer and explained my dilemma. After accepting a brochure, he smiled. "That would make an excellent campsite," he said, pointing to a nearby silver maple. "Let me know what else you need."

His graciousness made me realize how much I missed conversation and connections. Yes, I had talked with plenty of people about Heals on Wheels, but lately my encounters were brief. I'd had no substantive talks since visiting with my friends in Madras several days before. Eastern Oregonians weren't unfriendly, just standoffish. Unless I engaged with them first, they didn't seem curious. Maybe they just thought bicycling was a frivolous pursuit. The man who introduced himself as Ken Alexander turned out to be my antidote.

"You've certainly got your work cut out, doing this alone," he said, setting out two lawn chairs near my tent site. He didn't rush away, so I mentioned the disturbing bumper sticker.

"Well, it's a small world around here and people are attached to their guns," he said. "And I've done my share of hunting too."

"I know all about small towns," I said. "I lived in one for a long time in Massachusetts."

Ken had retired a few years ago as owner of the nearby Hells Canyon Inn. He was also a brother-in-law to one of the two clerks tending the grocery store.

"What I don't tell most people is that I don't have the heart to hunt anymore," he confided. "I've become attached to mule deer. They are beautiful to watch. I just share the goodies in my vegetable garden with them."

Later, while I was sipping chocolate milk and cobbling together bologna sandwiches, Ken appeared with a bottle of mustard and a pile of just-picked tomatoes.

"Oh, this makes for a perfect dinner," I said, cutting thick, juicy wedges of tomato with my Swiss Army knife. "Thank you."

"You sure don't need much to make you happy. Let me know if you need anything else," he said, then retreated to his trailer.

I balanced my sandwich and pen while jotting a script for next morning's radio spot in my journal. It was open to the page where I had stuck the fortune saved from the cookie I ate at a Chinese restaurant in Baker City. "You will enjoy good health," it read. "You will be surrounded by luxury."

CHAPTER 11
BONDING OVER BASEBALL

By Christmastime 1973, our family's little adopted town in the hills of rural western Massachusetts was feeling more like home. Heating oil was exceedingly expensive because of an embargo by foreign suppliers, and it would cost a fortune to warm our less-than-airtight, sprawling two-story house. So our thermostat stayed at fifty-five degrees. We wore extra layers and stacked blankets on our beds. Our newest rituals included stapling sheets of heavy-duty insulating plastic around the foundation of our clapboard house and stacking cord after cord of wood in our shed and cellar to fuel a fireplace and woodstove.

My father had retrieved a rickety wood-burning stove from the barn behind our house and installed it in the kitchen. The fact that it didn't measure up to his demanding safety standards was likely a concession to not having money for extras. At full blast, its cobbled-together sheet metal body glowed red and spewed a noxious odor—a mix of creosote and the paint-like substance that kept it black.

On New Year's Day in 1974, my father was on his knees building a fire in that stove. While wadding up sheets of newspaper, he noticed a lump the size of a marble on his left wrist, mere inches from the deep scar on his forearm. It was skin-toned, not black. A visit to a local doctor proved it wasn't a harmless bump. The biopsy confirmed that the cancer that had consumed bits and pieces of him in Ohio, Connecticut, and Pennsylvania didn't have geographical boundaries. I don't think he had expected to outrun it by moving to Massachusetts. He was just looking for room to breathe, for enough air to keep from suffocating in sameness.

As usual, my father didn't relay the news about his newest cancer to his daughters directly. That wasn't because he lacked courage. It was likely too heartbreaking, even for a teacher accustomed to delivering tough lessons. My mother handled that task in February. That night, it felt as if the cancer had pulled its own horrible chair up to the dinner table as the wretched and uninvited seventh member of our family. It was always hovering, waiting to shoehorn its disgusting and rampant self into every layer of our lives.

"Girls," my mother told the four of us when my father was out of earshot. "This time, the surgeon is talking about amputating his entire left arm. He thinks it's the only way to stop the cancer."

The beef and noodle casserole became a cement ball in my stomach.

A few days later, my ten-year-old sister was in her second-floor bedroom. From her window, she watched my father alone in the shed, lifting his ax over his head—and repeatedly slamming it down on logs set on the chopping block. He was using only his right arm, practicing for what seemed inevitable.

Within weeks, the surgeon changed his mind. He decided my father's case was too complicated for his small practice. Instead, he referred my parents to the large cancer clinic affiliated with Dartmouth College in Hanover, New Hampshire. It was about two hours away from our home. Distance aside, the experienced doctors at the clinic were a better fit. After weighing the medical options, the surgeons opted to carve more tissue from around my father's wrist where the latest melanoma had been removed. He was able to keep his arm, but he was required to return to Hanover for regular checkups. After that, his disease seemed to go dormant.

The cancer scare had not dimmed my father's obsession with projects. By May 1974, the first spring in our new home, our family gathered around the dinner table, this time for a more joyful reason. It was time to design our first backyard vegetable garden. A generous neighbor plowed the monstrous plot when the threat of frost passed. My sisters and I were the built-in labor force who would not only plant, weed, and harvest the garden, but also serve as his interior deconstruction crew. That spring, he had unilaterally decided to expand our cramped but serviceable kitchen. We knew it was usually impossible to change his mind once he became fixated on an idea. His half-baked plan called for creating a giant kitchen by removing the walls and shelves from the three capacious pantries that separated our kitchen from the dining room. The wood floors in that space were so sloped that, with a running start, you could slide downhill in socks. What he tore out, we carried outside in buckets. We carted so many loads of plaster, lath, and wood to a pile behind the barn that my parents joked our arms had been permanently lengthened.

Later that spring, another generous neighbor mowed most of an expansive hayfield between our houses that kids on our road used for our summer ritual—evening softball games that ended only when it was too dark to see the scuffed ball. We set up makeshift bases and pooled an odd assortment of softballs, baseballs, mitts, and bats. The black wooden bat our family had ordered with S&H Green Stamps was heavy, but when you connected on its sweet spot it made that perfect cracking sound. Balls that soared into the unmowed area usually became home runs because outfielders had to hunt for the ones they didn't catch.

Those games triggered my interest in professional baseball. Until then, the little I knew came mostly from my maternal grandfather in Ohio, a Cleveland Indians fan. He preferred the insights of the radio announcers, so he would listen to games on the radio while watching the muted television. He had been a three-sport athlete in high school and a catcher for his college baseball team at Ohio University in Athens.

In seventh grade, my first year of school in Massachusetts, I saved up enough allowance money to buy my own AM/FM radio. Our town was a two-hour drive from Boston, home of the Red Sox and fabled Fenway Park, but my antenna was strong enough to pick up Red Sox broadcasts from a station in southern New Hampshire. I listened every night, even when swings up and down the West Coast meant games didn't begin until ten thirty or eleven p.m. on the East Coast. My sisters joked that they could tell whether the Red Sox had won or lost by my mood the next morning. When junior-high boys talked baseball in the early mornings with our geography teacher, I lingered just outside the scrum. A hunger to absorb the history and the intricacies of the game led me to libraries and used bookstores.

One Saturday afternoon in the summer of 1975, my father was watching a baseball game in our living room. He had been cancer-free for more than a year, was satisfied with his job, and seemed to be adapting well to country life. I wandered in, noticed how relaxed he seemed, and sat down near him.

"Hey," I piped up after a double play. "That batter should have bunted to move the runner to second base. Why did the manager let him swing away?"

My father looked incredulous. "How did you know that?" he asked.

"I don't know," I responded. "I guess from reading and talking to Ben," referring to my best male friend who was a star pitcher for the local Little League and school teams.

We watched the rest of that game together.

By September, all of New England was frenzied because the long-forlorn Red Sox were playoff bound. Luis Tiant, Denny Doyle, Rick Burleson, Rico Petrocelli, Dwight Evans, Bill Lee, Jim Rice, Fred Lynn, Carlton Fisk, and my favorite, Carl Yastrzemski, or "Yaz," became household names as the team clinched first place in the American League East Division with a respectable 95–65 win-loss record. In early October, the team shocked the Northeast and California by trouncing the formidable Oakland Athletics in three straight playoff games to claim the American League pennant. Then the Red Sox surprised even themselves by catapulting into a World Series matchup—their first since 1967—against manager Sparky Anderson and his talented National League champions, the Cincinnati Reds.

My father and I watched every inning together on a tiny black-and-white television perched on the corner of an antique blanket chest in our living room.

"Look at that old guy play!" my animated father would yell joyously when Yaz—at thirty-six, ancient in baseball years—pounded another hit or somersaulted to snag a line drive. "He's been playing forever, and he just doesn't give up."

Yaz had started in left field since 1961, the year I was born. He took over that position from the incomparable Ted Williams, the last player to hit for an average higher than .400. Yaz, a native of the potato-growing region of Long Island, made the position his own with grit and drive. He complemented his natural talent with intense winter workouts.

By 1975, Yaz had moved to first base to open up left field and its famous Green Monster outfield wall for a graceful and powerful rookie named Jim Rice. However, manager Darrell Johnson had to play Yaz in left field late in the season because Rice was sidelined with a broken leg. My father and I erupted after midnight on Tuesday, October 21, when Boston catcher Carlton Fisk deployed body English in the bottom of the twelfth inning to will his solo home run to the fair side of Fenway Park's left-field foul pole. He jubilantly circled the bases, giving Boston a 7–6 victory and tying the seven-game series at three apiece.

The Red Sox sputtered to a 4–3 loss in Game Seven. Yaz made the final out. Boston dropped one of the most memorable and dramatic World Series to Johnny Bench, Joe Morgan, Ken Griffey Sr., and the phenomenal "Big Red Machine." My father and I would have to wait until next year to find out just how resilient these Red Sox were.

After that World Series, my father spent evenings and weekends with other parents to make toys, games, cheeseboards, clothing, and crafts for the annual Christmas gift fair at the elementary school that my two younger sisters attended. The tradition gave students access to affordable presents. Those group sessions inspired him to experiment in the workshop he had cobbled together in the back of the barn.

That Christmas, my family tore into his uniquely wrapped packages and discovered that he had cleverly turned castoffs into thoughtful gifts. For me, he transformed a misshapen piece of wood with a large screw jutting out at an odd angle into a foot-tall apple that he painted gold. He also painted the threaded metal protuberance to look like the tail end of a worm, and carved the worm's head of wood so it poked out near the apple's stem. I loved it.

As winter enveloped New England, we took brooms to the frozen ponds behind our house to clear the snow from what became the neighborhood skating rink. A steep hill beyond served as our skiing and sledding slope.

Navigating that slope was tricky because you had to shoot for a four-foot-wide opening in a barbed wire fence near the bottom. Getting off track meant bailing out and bracing downhill, feet first, so the wire didn't shred your skin or clothes.

I taught myself to ski on that mini-mountain. At twelve, I was thrilled to uncover a pair of beat-up wooden cross-country skis in our barn. The leather bindings were so cracked and stiff that I lashed the skis to my boots with makeshift buckles and pieces of clothesline. My poles were mop handles my father helped me cut. It was liberating and exhilarating to rip downhill, knowing I had to rely on strength and wits to remain upright through the barbed wire opening. My parents sometimes talked about enrolling me in ski lessons. But I wasn't counting on that luxury. We barely had enough money for clothes, groceries, and keeping one car operating.

One day in early January 1976, while our parents were in New Hampshire for my father's regular doctor checkup, I was out on that hill skiing alone. When I saw my older sister walking toward me, I suspected she wanted help with dinner. "Elizabeth, you need to come right away," she said. "Something didn't go well with Daddy's appointment."

It wasn't that cold, but I couldn't stop shivering. We trudged home silently in the twilight. The only sound was the crunch of our boots punching holes through the crust of ice that glazed several feet of snow. I knew I wouldn't be signing up for ski lessons. What I didn't know was how much longer I would have a father.

CHAPTER 12
IDAHO: TAMING WHAT'S WILD

MILES RIDDEN: 648
MILES TO GO: 3,602

E arly on August 28 in Ken Alexander's yard, I tucked my remaining trio of tomatoes into a sort of pannier nest feathered with a T-shirt. Then it was off to the pay phone to tell the Milwaukee radio station that I was 13.5 miles from the Snake River and my second state, Idaho. Unlike Oregon, my time in Idaho would be short. It would be 286 miles of a meandering, river-hugging route in the lower part of the state's panhandle between Oregon and Montana.

The temperature hovered in the mid-seventies, and riding on Highway 86 proved to be delightfully easy. The area is burdened with the name Hells Canyon, but the contrast between stark shades of brown mixed with bits of green vegetation was strikingly beautiful. I was enchanted.

That mesmerization ended abruptly as I approached the ugly concrete scar of Brownlee Dam on the Snake River, the Oregon border with Idaho. It was one of my Edward Abbey moments. I so wanted the author's mythical and mischievous characters, George Hayduke and his Monkey Wrench Gang, to miraculously appear and set things right by obliterating this man-made eyesore. Humans are a strange and contradictory lot. We can stare goggle-eyed at a river's pulsing beauty and almost simultaneously scheme to selfishly harness that coursing power, other species be damned. My head, of course, understands the potential economic and clean-energy benefits of hydropower. But my heart believes rivers were meant to roll unharnessed so fish and other aquatic creatures can feed, breed, and freely follow other natural cycles of their watery worlds. Taming a river is like putting a leash on a lion.

My head also knows that any dam is only a temporary fix for reining in the wildness of water. No matter how advanced the engineering, water always wins. It might take centuries, but chokepoints eventually will be vanquished. I'd been schooled in water's power the day before while pedaling past still-stark evidence of a landslide that had started sixteen years prior. Some eastern Oregon residents became isolated on an island of sorts in September 1984 when a monumental movement of Earth covered

Highway 86 west of Richland. What's called Hole-in-the-Wall Landslide started when rainfall lubricated a layer of wet clay under fractured basalt blocks. Simply put, gravity overcame forces of friction, pushing ten million cubic yards of soil and rocks downward. It blocked the Powder River and created a half-mile-long reservoir. A highway bypass around the mayhem was completed for residents in 1987.

Brownlee Dam is named for John Brownlee, who operated a nineteenth-century ferry service for gold and copper miners crossing the Snake. For me, the dam generated more ill will when I noticed thumbtack-like thorns stuck in both bike tires shortly after crossing it. I plucked them out and was relieved my tires continued to hold air as I began a fourteen-mile climb on Highway 71 that lifted me from two thousand feet in elevation to forty-three hundred feet. I had been dreading that ascent since Don and I had driven it on our way to Astoria. It's a long, desolate stretch where you wouldn't wish a flat tire on anybody. Wild turkeys were my only company.

My first face-to-face conversation that day wasn't until noon in Cambridge, an Idaho community of about 375 near the Weiser River where Highway 71 merges with Highway 95. After eating the last of Ken's tomatoes on a patch of lawn in front of the library, I wheeled to the combination gas station/farm cooperative to check my air pressure. "What lovely helmet hair," said the jovial man who loaned me his tire gauge. My once light-brown hair was becoming blonder by the day.

"Thank you. I'll take that as a compliment," I replied, laughing. "I like to think this sculpted look will soon be all the rage." A sales clerk who overheard our banter asked for a brochure. Seconds later, she mentioned her husband's recent surgery for skin cancer—and handed me a five-dollar donation.

Those encounters, plus my talks with Ken, confirmed that I had emerged from the grumpy stretch of trail. The kindness continued east of Cambridge when I stopped at a roadside sign marking a historic apple farm. There, I met a clutch of four westbound bicyclists who had christened themselves the Cabooses because they were consistently at the tail end of their tour group. "We're eating our way across the country," said one, recommending I stop for free pie at a town in Illinois whose name escaped her. "You'll know it when you see it." They also warned me that Kentucky's bicycle-chasing dogs were fact, not fiction.

In Idaho, most dogs just barked from pickup trucks. But larger mammals were a concern. Barn-size mounds of hay, which dwarfed any bale I had ever seen, and bold yellow-and-black "Watch for Stock" signs, which had nothing to do with the perils of Wall Street, were reminders of agricultural abundance. Cattle, an introduced species, are hoofed mowers.

They roam on expansive grasslands where bison once ruled before the fences of immigrant Europeans became commonplace. Near Council, I was jarred by the sight of an intimidatingly large bull charging up the shoulder, straight at me. Even though he was a vegetarian and I was not much of a carnivore, I surely would be on the losing end of a collision with this big hunk of red meat. I stopped first. He halted. We stared. Then, wide-eyed, he daintily sidestepped me and hurried toward his four-legged companions.

On August 29, I pushed myself 89.5 miles from Council to White Bird, my longest day yet, tracing Highway 95 along the Weiser, Little Salmon, and Salmon Rivers. I wanted to be fresh the following day for eleven miles of low-traffic switchbacks in Nez Perce National Historical Park. On my contour map, the climb was pictured as an intimidating isosceles triangle.

Logging trucks were my constant roadside companions out of Council, so seeing the Evergreen Forest Products lumber mill in the tiny settlement of Tamarack wasn't a shock. The fresh, tangy scent of newly sawed lumber was so surprisingly appealing that I stopped for a few extra sniffs. But that pleasantry was short-lived. Soon, the odors of smoke and, periodically, charred wood penetrated my nostrils. Some forty miles later in Riggins, streams of smoke hovered over the town of four-hundred-plus on the Salmon River. Tiny black pieces of ash twirled around in smoky clouds. A hand-lettered sign taped to the door of a small store summed up the situation: "Closed: Everybody Out Fighting Fires."

The postmistress in Riggins told me the smoke would be even heavier in White Bird. She also directed me to the restaurant a few doors down renowned for its blackberry milkshakes. Fortunately, the waitress didn't mind that I spent an inordinate amount of time in the restroom scrubbing away layers of dirt, sand, and other grit that had adhered to my sunscreen- and sweat-coated skin as I pedaled through a six-mile construction zone. I hadn't realized what a mess I was until I saw my face reflected in the napkin dispenser.

Much of the twenty-nine-mile ride from Riggins to White Bird should have been a cinch because it was downhill, but I expended any extra energy the milkshake provided by wrestling with a fierce headwind that seemed powerful enough to scrape away my freckles.

Those westbound cycling "Cabooses" had told me both restaurants in White Bird were full of characters. I discovered their insights were spot-on after sitting on a Silver Dollar Inn barstool next to Lonnie Lee, who introduced himself as a White Bird native. Even a television blaring *Jeopardy* wasn't going to keep him from broadcasting his family history. Very loudly. He barely breathed between sentences. I figured he must have been telling the truth about being a descendant of the Remingtons, of rifle fame, and

Robert E. Lee, of Confederacy infamy, because I doubted anybody could concoct such fiery heritage that quickly. As I ate the burger and onion ring special accompanied by a few one-dollar draft beers, Lonnie prattled on about an annual fundraiser called For the Hill of It, organized by the local hospital. Participants bicycled some hellacious route that included the ascent out of White Bird on through the Nez Perce National Historical Park, the same climb I faced the next day. I knew I was no match for that year's winner, who had completed the race in an unfathomable forty-eight minutes.

I retreated to a quiet, carpet-like patch of grass in front of the white clapboard Sacred Heart Church, where I had left my bike. I pitched my tent, temporarily boosting the population of White Bird to 151 souls.

Close to one thirty a.m., I was awakened by a soft something on the other side of my nylon tent butting my head with fierce determination. *Oh no*, I blearily wondered. Was it a diseased raccoon or opossum, or worse yet, an angry skunk ready to let loose? White Bird could not possibly stock enough tomato juice to remove the skunk stink from my tent. But when I folded back the tent fly, I stared into the sweet face of a white kitten with extra-big paws. He barged in, fearlessly examining every square inch of my digs and purring unceasingly before nestling into my sleeping bag.

Cat people must have a special scent to a feline nose. Surely this little green-eyed guy sensed that I had grown up in a cat family. We always joked that our long line of cats—Huntley and Brinkley (a tribute to the Chet Huntley and David Brinkley NBC news team of the late 1950s and 1960s), Marmalade, and Pierre—provided male companionship for my sorely outnumbered father.

At dawn, I noticed a gray smudge shaped like a drunken circle atop the cat's head. It matched the ash from a forest fire that had dusted my tent and gear overnight. I half-expected to hear somebody calling for his pet, and perhaps accuse me of cat-napping. But nobody came looking, and I felt like a negligent parent when I kissed him on his little pink nose before starting the much-anticipated climb.

As I huffed and puffed upward, I laughed about the natives referring to this forty-two-hundred-foot peak as a hill. It would have been the equivalent of Mount Everest in Wisconsin. Signs at a roadside pull-off at the very top explained how a coalition of ecologically minded groups was trying to rid the Salmon River Canyon of exotic plants such as spotted knapweed, leafy spurge, and yellow star thistle that were displacing native species. I celebrated my successful ascent by peeling an orange I'd been carrying since Baker City.

While savoring its nectar, I spotted a cyclist coming uphill from the east. He was a fit young man on a lightweight racing bicycle. Usually, I didn't know what to say to those types of super-athletes, but he seemed eager for conversation, so I engaged. It turns out he was a wildfire-fighting smokejumper based in Idaho for the summer. It was his day off, so he'd ridden the ten miles from Grangeville to try to break his personal speed record.

"What is it so far?" I asked.

"Fifty miles per hour," he said. "I want to top that. But I need more weight."

"Well, daredevil, you could use my panniers, but I'd need them back," I joked, revealing that my stomach started somersaulting when I cranked up beyond thirty miles per hour, and that my downhill speed-demon record thus far was a blazing thirty-five miles per hour.

"Isn't jumping out of airplanes to put out fires enough?" I asked. "I mean, don't you just want to read on your day off?"

"What I usually tell people is that I'm afraid of heights," he replied. "The reason I jump from planes is so I can get back to Earth as quickly as possible."

I laughed but wondered if there was more to him than that pat answer. He asked why I was in White Bird, and I recited my elevator speech, the thirty-second version of my well-rehearsed spiel. He probed a bit, so I told him about my cancer and how every time I thought I wanted routines and regular patterns, I ended up embarking on an adventure.

He grinned.

We agreed that the thought of a predictable nine-to-five job was alluring, but often it seemed like a conspiracy designed to squelch people's sense of adventure and curiosity.

"See, you're like me," he said, accepting an orange slice. "I couldn't bear to have a job that required me to wear a necktie. It would feel like a leash."

I nodded as he cinched his helmet strap and pedaled away, in pursuit of fifty-one miles per hour.

CHAPTER 13
THE RELENTLESS STALKER

E arly in 1976, I fished a red-white-and-blue sticker from a box of breakfast cereal and stuck it on my bedroom door. The flag-shaped decal was a tiny salute to our nation's two hundred years of independence. I thought we would be celebrating both our nation's birthday and my father's improving health.

His January cancer scare was alarming on one level but routine on another. Once again, the doctors in New Hampshire carved out another malignancy in that troublesome area on his left forearm. They continued to monitor him on about a monthly basis because of his sketchy medical history. Everything appeared to be normal at his May checkup. But that didn't last. In early June, my parents returned from New Hampshire—with the frightening news that the doctors wanted them to return to the clinic in a few days.

My mother came home from that second appointment alone.

I knew something was horribly wrong, but she volunteered only minimal information about some follow-up tests. I think it was too hard for her to talk about what had happened. All I could gather was that my father's melanoma was no longer confined to his arm. My sisters and I didn't see him for the rest of that month.

That spring I had turned fifteen. My sisters were ages eleven, thirteen, and seventeen. In June, my mother was balancing her full-time job as a museum guide and historian with almost daily trips to the hospital by herself. She was exhausted and distraught. I had always been able to make her laugh with my jokes and humorous stories. But those were no longer working. I wanted to fix her sadness, but I didn't know how.

In early July, my mother answered the ring of the green, wall-mounted telephone in our front hallway. As she listened, she stretched the long cord into the adjacent living room. I heard her gasp, then speak briefly and very quietly. I peeked into the living room and saw her slumped on the couch, gripping the big plastic receiver. The caller had clearly hung up, but my mother was just sitting there, staring at the floor. I knew it was something awful about my father, but I didn't know what to do. I stayed where I was, frozen in place.

For the next several days, my mother didn't say anything about that call. I realized I would have to ask questions if I wanted to know the truth.

On Saturday, I approached her in the first-floor master bedroom where she was sorting clean clothes in a wicker laundry basket. Her bulky bathrobe made her look smaller than usual, and the whites of her brown eyes were streaked with the squiggly red veins that appeared when she wasn't sleeping well. She managed a pitiful smile as I perched across from her on the edge of a green-gold wing chair.

"I know Daddy's cancer has spread," I said in a monotone. "And I need to know: Is he going to die?"

She stopped mid-fold, and the tears began.

"Elizabeth, they called from the hospital the other day to tell me the cancer has spread to your father's brain," she said, her entire body drooping. "He's almost afraid to look at any part of his body, for fear he'll see the lumps, the melanoma, growing everywhere."

When I heard *brain*, I reeled and dug my fingernails into the chair's nubby fabric to steady myself. This was one of the biggest rooms in our house, yet there wasn't enough oxygen. I felt as if I were on the high end of a seesaw, and my playmate had just gotten up and walked away, leaving me desperate for breath after crashing back to Earth.

I knew this much from the science I'd had through ninth grade: The brain controls the lungs and heart. When those organs shut down, life ceases. You whirl away into that sinkhole of nothingness forever. There, clinging to that wretched chair, was when I grasped the cruel terror of the word *never*. Death meant I would never, ever, ever see my father again.

Wasn't this something that happened to other families? Weren't we somehow immune? After all, this was my indomitable father. Couldn't he sustain his life, keep his heart pumping and lungs inhaling and exhaling, on sheer will?

I bit my bottom lip to keep my entire mouth from quivering.

"That means he is going to die," my shaking self whispered. My eyes focused on the pair of polished, barely creased, black loafers lined up neatly under my father's chest of drawers in the narrow dressing room. *My father can't die*, was the irrational thought my fifteen-year-old brain conjured up. *He hasn't even worn out his shoes*. I desperately needed a lifeline, a small voice of hope, to penetrate this Goliath-like crush of despair.

If I had grown up in the sort of family I read about in books, saw on television, or visited after school, this would have been the point in the conversation where I hugged my mother. But we weren't practiced at comforting each other. Instead, affection was implied, not demonstrated. Embraces were rare, and none of us girls remember ever hearing an "I love you." Intellectually, I knew what questions to ask my mother, but emotionally, I was at a loss about how to respond. That's when I wished the perfect daughter I figured my mother always pined for would make her grand entrance and do the right thing, whatever that was. I berated myself for not knowing how to offer solace to my own heartbroken mother. My awkwardness seemed amplified. Those double hurts—learning my father was dying and not knowing how to fix everything for my mother, who was watching her partner of twenty-two years fade away—sank into my gut like a stone wrapped in barbed wire. Lacking the will to move, I just sat there with those aches. Then I picked up the folded laundry and carried it upstairs.

The neatly planted rows of bright-green sprouts in the field across from our house were just starting to be recognizable as the sweet and field corn they would become later that summer when the doctors decided that my father was stable enough to come home. He had begged for time away from the hospital bed, where his back hurt so much that lying down was torture.

He wasn't able to go to work regularly, but he could take short walks, putter around in his barn workshop, and organize papers in his office. One day, one of my younger sisters and I were goofing around on one of the bicycles we had pulled out of the hulking brown barn at the end of our dirt and gravel driveway. We laughed uproariously as we wobbled along the speckled hardtop of our country road, me pedaling while my younger sister sat first on the front handlebars and then on the rack over the back tire. Both of us sobered up in a heartbeat when we looked up and noticed our father leaning out of my sister's second-floor bedroom window.

"Hey girls, come up here," he called to us, beckoning with one hand.

"Uh oh," we whispered simultaneously, our bodies tensing reflexively as I steered the bicycle past the tulip tree and leaned it against the basketball hoop pole. Sister telepathy told me we should both be ready for a scolding. Surely we were going to hear his lecture about never doubling up on a bicycle or riding without an orange safety flag affixed to the rear wheel.

Obediently, we scrambled up the rock steps that led to the side door, then hurried through the living room, up the front staircase, and into my sister's room.

My father turned to us. And smiled. "What you were doing out there with that bicycle, that sure looked like a lot of fun," he said. "I wanted to tell you how happy that makes me. You need to know that."

My sister and I, having instinctively prepared our defense, stood in amazement. I was afraid to make direct eye contact with her, so I concentrated on the wallpaper pattern of chirpy yellow flowers. Who in the world was *this* man? Instead of erupting like Mount Vesuvius, he was telling us he wanted to be out there with us. My sister and I, caught off guard, just smiled back at this impersonator. I wish I could have marked this unexpected moment with gestures grander and more sweeping than a sigh of relief. But maybe two grinning daughters were all that my father needed to see. I was afraid to speak.

I studied the peaceful, serene man standing in front of us. I knew him, yet I didn't. He was still tall enough to loom over me, but his pants and his button-down shirt hung loosely on his usually fit frame. He had cinched his skinny black belt at least one notch tighter. Those were still his piercing hazel eyes flecked with gold, but they weren't shining with hate, resentment, or frustration. It was something else. Gentleness? Adoration? His smile highlighted his beautifully straight white teeth. But the harsh cancer treatments had thinned his thick mat of black hair to a few untamed wisps. His once-angular face was pale and puffy, leaving little trace of the reddish whiskers that usually emerged when he went a day or two without shaving. A slightly faded red line circling the top of his head, a tattooed crown of sorts, marked the points where a technician aimed the powerful beams of radiation that were supposed to shrink the melanoma tumors in his brain.

He was still in there. But he looked so tired. Perhaps those beams, evidently unable to prevent the cancer cells from multiplying, had instead shut off the switch that controlled his anger. Had the fire and fury exited, defusing the time bomb that usually ticked inside him, leaving him just too damn tired to shout anymore? Maybe looking at the two of us from that window had reminded him of a similar joyful moment from his childhood in rural Ohio. He'd had the freedom to roam the countryside with his friends, play near the Kokosing River, and explore the college campus in his backyard. Or perhaps he was just trying to savor pieces of that summer of 1976, knowing deep down that it would be his last.

My father never wanted sympathy or pity. Maybe he cried when he was alone or with my mother, but I never saw tears when he was with us. The only time he mentioned the anguish of his cancer to me was when he joked that "the doctors were taking me one piece at a time." "Eventually," he added, "they will probably carve out enough to make a whole other person." On that summer day, he had to be aware that the cancer was strangling him, but I don't know if he recognized the emotional changes that my sister and I perceived.

When he turned to leave the room, continuing what seemed to be a slow, self-guided tour of our entire house, I realized I wished that the father I knew, the one I'd learned to read and anticipate so well, would reappear. If he criticized and yelled, that meant he was robust enough to live for years and years, right? I ached for the familiar comfort of sameness and routine.

Even if it wasn't the healthiest sameness and routine, it was mine and it was what I knew. On that day, I grasped, on some rudimentary level, one truth about fear. I realized that the chaotic circumstances upsetting our daily lives are a thousandfold more vicious and terrifying than the monsters we imagine are lying in wait beneath our beds.

My sisters and I were always surprised there were four of us because babies and young children set my father on edge. Our unpredictable behavior—bouts of crying, wet beds, fights, skinned knees, and spilled milk at the dinner table—upset his need for order. But he also was terrified that something awful and out of his control would happen to one of his four girls on his watch. He was haunted by a fear that he wouldn't be able to protect us from a lurking evil.

"Your father would refer to you four girls as a flower garden that he helped to plant," my mother told me years later. "He wanted you to grow up to be strong people who were givers, not takers."

In his mind, that required extraordinary discipline. He didn't mention any of that to my sister and me that summer day in 1976 when he called us up to the second floor.

He also didn't tell us what he had recently shared with my mother: "It's not so much that I'm afraid of dying and not existing anymore," he told her during one of their frank discussions. "What I can't stand is that I'm going to miss you and the girls so much."

CHAPTER 14
IDAHO: LOST AND FOUND

MILES RIDDEN: 803
MILES TO GO: 3,447

After bidding goodbye to my smokejumper acquaintance on August 30, I pedaled through Grangeville and then on to my campground destination off Highway 12 in teeny Lowell. It was a bumpy ride over the small wooden bridge leading to the campground, which I attributed to the boards being warped and uneven. But the peculiar *thwump-badump-thwump* noise during the crossing seemed extreme.

I anticipated a flat tire, which would have been my first, and easy to fix because I carried extra inner tubes, a pump, and tools. I wasn't prepared for what I saw instead: an odd bulge protruding from the rear tire, a factory-issue model with no visible wear. Its compromised sidewall had sprouted a carbuncle the size of a fifty-cent piece. Extra tires were too cumbersome to lug along. I was 127 trail miles from the closest bike shop in Missoula, Montana. I still had plenty of daylight, so I headed to the campground store to see if I could scrounge up a solution.

On my walk over, I was greeted by Jake, a good-natured Idaho Department of Transportation employee. When he saw my compromised tire, he insisted I roll over to his campsite.

"I never go anywhere without my mountain bike," he told me, pointing to the fancy two-wheeler leaning against his state-issued pickup truck. "I can give you one of my tires. It's much easier for me to find a replacement."

Unfortunately, his tire size didn't match mine. But I couldn't shake this robust, enthusiastic problem-solver.

"OK, if we can't trade tires, we'll just make a big Band-Aid for yours," he said, hoisting a roll of duct tape from his gear-laden truck. "This is the bombproof stuff we use to tape those thick cables to the asphalt. If it can stand heavy traffic, it can fix your tire."

We tore strips of silver tape with our teeth and layered them on the tire's interior, creating a temporary brace. "Thanks for healing Heals on Wheels," I told him.

By the next morning, the taped tire still looked stable. I became yet another do-it-yourselfer who worshipped at the duct tape altar as I headed east to Powell Junction. The annoying *kathunk, kathunk, kathunk* of the taped spot slapping the asphalt became my metronome. That was fine on level ground, but my first steep downhill gave me second thoughts about the temporary fix. My overactive imagination conjured up vivid, macabre disasters that involved broken teeth and mangled body parts. I tried to command the evil storyteller lurking in my brain to knock it off. But twelve miles out of Lowell, I pulled over on Highway 12 and stuck out my thumb.

Traffic was scarce, but as a fancy black sport utility vehicle approached, the driver surprised me by pulling over. "I'm Carmen," she said, taking the last drag of her cigarette. "I never stop for hitchhikers, but I really did need to find out why you aren't riding the bike."

"I'm Elizabeth, and I really need a ride for my gear, not me or the bike," I said, explaining my predicament and then giving her a minute to read my brochure.

"Wisconsin!" she exclaimed. "My parents are from Ladysmith."

"Oh sure, Up North," I replied. She joined me laughing because anybody with a Wisconsin background knows "Up North" denotes a rural getaway that isn't marked on any map but begins somewhere north of Madison.

Carmen and I loaded all but a few of my worldly possessions into the back of her pristine vehicle. We studied my map. She agreed to haul the load fifty-four miles up Highway 12 to Powell Junction, my destination that day. Before she pulled away, we double-checked the exact drop-off location. These tiny towns could be confusing, and she didn't have a map.

When I remounted minus my panniers, I felt as if my bike had undergone a liposuction treatment. Wow! I was soaring without that extra weight. But I also began to feel like a moving target. This stretch of Highway 12 was a scenic byway tracing the Lochsa River (Salish for "swift water") and sections of the Selway-Bitterroot Wilderness. But my map noted that truckers were aggressive. What an understatement that was. I felt as if drivers were aiming for the orange-and-yellow luminescent safety triangle attached to my rear rack.

The highway is a major grain-hauling route, and truckers not only beeped loudly but also hogged the single, skinny eastbound lane. Often, I was just inches from their mammoth loads. I feared being sucked into their slipstream and pulled into a metal maw that could reduce me to unrecognizable pulp within seconds. What was this, the Idaho 500?

Ironically, a highway sign proclaimed that the beauty of the Lochsa River was a secret to everybody but the most hardy until 1962 when the highway was completed. I wondered how Nez Perce chiefs such as Joseph, White Bird, and Looking Glass would react to this modern-day calamity.

81

To escape pedaling purgatory, I would periodically take respite in the woods along the river. There, I sometimes let out a primal scream just to vent my frustration. I interpreted the squawks from talkative Steller's jays and ravens as sympathetic votes of support. The same swift river currents that swallowed my outbursts also soaked my feet and filled my water bottle. The Lochsa is just one sliver of wild riparian expanse that supports a bounty of ducks, herons, geese, bald eagles, and ospreys in Idaho. Tracing my index finger along the meandering blue lines on my map revealed a ballad of river and creek names: Weiser, Little Salmon, Salmon, Clearwater, Slippy, Sheep, Little Elk, Boulder, Rattlesnake, Lightning, Fiddle, Hazard, Grizzly, Cottonwood, Threemile, Maggie, Sally Ann, Suttler, Snowshoe, Otter Slide, Tumble, Tomcat, Bimerick, Pete King, Old Man, Coolwater, Big Stew, Postoffice, Sponge, Badger, Indian Grave, Little Tinker. Skookumchuck, a feeder creek to the Salmon near White Bird, won the award for most musical.

I was relieved to arrive in speck-on-the-map Powell Junction by two p.m., way ahead of schedule. I attributed my early arrival to being pannier-free and to being chased like a rabbit on a greyhound track. My patched rear tire had performed valiantly. Now I would have plenty of time to pick up the gear that Carmen had dropped off, scope out a campsite, catch up on my journal, and maybe even free up valuable pannier space by reading, and leaving behind, one of the magazines I carried.

Soon, however, relief turned to panic. Nobody at the store, the lodge, the ranger station, or the campground had seen—or smelled—my belongings. And, unless there was some weird rabbit hole, those were the only places to check in this remote outpost. It wasn't the friendliest of settlements. The clerk manning the store was grouchy, and I felt as if I were being filmed for *Candid Camera* when a US Forest Service employee told me my last "hope of ray" was to check with the store's morning shift employee the next day. Brilliant, but where was I supposed to sleep in the meantime?

Self-doubt gnawed at me. Had my unshakeable belief in my own altruistic venture made me too naïve and trusting of strangers? My reporter instincts about people were usually spot-on, but could I have totally misjudged Carmen's character? She seemed honest, sympathetic, and eager to assist. And we had that Wisconsin bond. Besides, what would she want with a pile of stinky clothes, an old tent, a bare-bones bag of toiletries, a travel mug, a torn plastic tarp, and a stack of brochures? How embarrassing would it be to tell people tracking my journey that I had to quit my trip because I had willingly turned my belongings over to a stranger in an effort to relieve the strain on a compromised tire? I felt like an idiot.

I took stock of my sad situation. I could probably muster the energy and resources to re-outfit Heals on Wheels, but I was already operating on a shoestring budget, and just the thought of it was overwhelming. I cursed myself and I cursed Carmen.

Needing to burn off nervous energy, I hurried to the ramshackle "campus" designated for seasonal cooks, cleaners, and maintenance workers. Victoria, an employee I met in the store, suggested I check with her later. She invited me into the trailer she shared with another employee and listened to my pitiful story. Victoria said she was convinced that I would never see my gear again because, as she framed it, "too many people carry out too many cruel acts for no reason at all." Her negative view shocked me. She was only in her twenties and had moved west from North Carolina to find a job and have an adventure. Despite her pessimism, she was sympathetic enough to proffer her sleuthing services. She offered to drive me to a few hidden places where she thought Carmen might have mistakenly stopped.

We climbed into her rumbling beater of a sedan and chugged to a Department of Transportation barn just two miles up the road. Nothing. But a staffer there suggested we try the closed visitor center at Lolo Pass at the Idaho-Montana border. No luck there either. My optimism was quickly draining. "Well, now that we've come this far, we might as well check out Lolo Hot Springs over in Montana," Victoria suggested. My mind raced a hundred miles per hour as she punched it up and down about ten miles of steep mountain passes toward the now-deserted resort. As Victoria idled her car, I sprinted into the empty restaurant and spilled my pathetic tale to a waitress sorting silverware. By then, it was about four thirty p.m.

"I haven't seen anything," she said, and my spirits deflated yet again. "But let me check in the bar," she continued as she walked several feet, then disappeared around a corner. I paced back and forth, knowing I was out of options after this. A tense minute later, she re-emerged, clutching my sleeping bag. My heart did a double-time jig.

"Is this what you're looking for?" she asked, leading me to the corner where my items were neatly stacked with one of my trademark yellow brochures on top. "Best of luck!" Carmen had scrawled across the front.

Never have I been so elated to be reunited with an assemblage of inanimate objects. I babbled to the bartender, bear-hugged the waitress, and triumphantly bolted from the restaurant. Victoria's eyes popped like a cartoon character's when she saw me with my belongings. She wouldn't accept money I offered to cover gasoline, so instead I thanked her about a thousand times on the drive back to Powell Junction. Silently, I hoped that the reunion she had witnessed had restored a bit of the faith and trust she seemed to have lost in her fellow human beings.

That night in my journal, I wrote an apology to Carmen for even thinking she wouldn't follow through on her promise. I couldn't send it because I didn't have any contact information. I didn't even know her last name. I just needed to pour those pent-up thoughts onto paper. She had merely made the innocent mistake of stopping at the wrong drop-off point. Lolo Hot Springs in Montana, where she had left my belongings, is 24.5 miles beyond Powell Junction in Idaho. By imagining I could pedal 90.5 miles that day, instead of the sixty-six I actually did, Carmen clearly had more faith in my bicycling stamina than I did.

I pitched my tent near the Powell Junction campground that night and thought about how my friend Noreen would have reacted to that day's debacle. She lived in Portland, Oregon, and Don and I had stayed with her for several days after our three-day drive from Wisconsin with my bike. I hadn't seen Noreen since the spring of 1991 when we first met.

She, too, had begun hiking the Appalachian Trail in Georgia that April. But, unlike Don and me, she never made it to Maine. Frustrated by an uncooperative boyfriend/hiking partner, the rain and cold of the Georgia mountains, and the vicissitudes of life in the woods carrying forty-plus pounds on her back, she turned for home just a hundred miles up the trail. By then, though we'd known each other for only five or six days, she and I had formed an unbreakable bond. After we said goodbye at a trail campsite in North Carolina, we exchanged letters, telephone calls, and emails over the next decade.

Noreen, who adopted Oregon as her home after leaving her native Kentucky, was one of the sweetest, warmest, and most unpretentious people I had ever known. She had an innate ability, probably enhanced by a childhood that spared no hardship, to turn a negative into a positive. I have no doubt that if her home had been engulfed by a tornado, she would scope out the damage and say, "Well, I needed new dishes anyway."

About the time I was loading my gear into Carmen's truck, Noreen was strapping on a parachute near Portland. To celebrate her birthday, she had taken that day off from her animal shelter job to skydive for the first time. While I was pedaling along the Lochsa River, she had bravely stepped from an airplane and dropped thousands of feet to earth. I fell asleep imagining that sensation.

CHAPTER 15
AN EMPTY AMBULANCE

On school picture day in September 1976, I sat in the passenger seat of our pumpkin-orange Dodge Aspen station wagon as my mother stomped on the accelerator, trying to compress a two-hour drive into one-and-a-half. I had just started my sophomore year but wasn't headed to the high school that morning.

The previous afternoon, a desperate doctor from the New Hampshire hospital had made an urgent call to my mother at work. My father had slipped into a coma after suffering a stroke. He had been in the hospital most of that month. Our family had visited him a few weeks before, on the weekend closest to his birthday. The cancer was devouring him. Now, his doctors figured he had hours or days, not weeks, to live.

One of my mother's co-workers insisted that she not make the trip alone. My mother wasn't sure where to turn on such short notice. She asked my older sister, a high-school senior, to go. That sister declined, saying the visit would be too emotionally draining for her. One look at my pale, traumatized mother, however, prompted me to speak up. I volunteered to go. Now it was just the two of us in the car.

"Please, Daddy. Keep breathing," was the mantra I pleaded repeatedly, while clutching my knees and rocking slightly in the front passenger seat. "We're on our way. You just have to keep drawing air into your lungs and pushing it back out."

The night before we left, I couldn't sleep, thinking about how lonely my father must feel. I grappled again with that word *never*. He would probably never be coming home. I might never see him alive again. He would never be part of our lives again. The terror of that inherent truth, that he would be gone, gone, gone forever, kept me awake all night. I reminded myself to breathe.

When we reached his hospital room, my father was on his back, his mouth agape. Each breath made a grating, raspy sound so common with the elderly in nursing homes. But at least his lungs were functioning. I smelled the distinctive odor of the Keri Lotion that always reminded me I was in a hospital. The nurses had that doleful look that made me cringe. I knew they were intent on comforting me, but I didn't want their sympathy or sorrowful gazes. Didn't they know I felt awkward enough?

I stiffened when they hugged me, and I greeted their smiles with polite, mumbled words, then clunky silence. What I wanted to tell them was that this swelled-up, pale man with the sallow skin, the one with a few days' growth of red scratchy stubble on his chin and the wispy black strands of hair that no longer hid the jarring red radiation lines painted on his head, was not my real father. This was a stunt double filling in while the original one recovered. My real father had a thick head of black hair and an honest smile that made people want to tell him their secrets. He could hit a softball so far into the pasture of our makeshift baseball diamond that everybody had rounded the bases by the time outfielders caught up to the ball. And he could still execute a front somersault off the diving board decades after the cancer surgeons had cut through the muscle tissue of his neck and shoulder.

My deep-sleeping father did not acknowledge my mother or me. But I wanted to believe that he at least sensed our presence. "Go ahead and talk to him," one nurse prodded. "We're sure he can hear what you say." I felt too embarrassed and ashamed to open my mouth while the adults were hovering. Only after they'd dispersed could I find my voice and begin a quiet, albeit stumbling, monologue about baseball. It was a safe topic I could cover without choking on my words. I summarized the latest Boston Red Sox game and lamented the team's dim-to-nonexistent chances of even claiming a spot in the American League playoffs that fall after almost winning the World Series a year ago. My father's scratchy breathing continued. I touched his hand, relieved it was still warm.

My mother and I spent that night in bunk beds at a nearby hostel for patients' families. By the next morning, my father had stabilized, shocking the doctors. He was still comatose, but his condition wasn't deteriorating as rapidly. Still, they could not predict if he would drift off into death or emerge from this deepest of sleeps.

That slight improvement allowed my mother and I to drive home late that night. On the hour-long bus ride to school the next morning, my regular seatmate asked where I had been. I tried to tell her, but my mouth trembled too badly, so I asked about the Spanish homework instead. When a friend at school inquired about my brief absence, I managed to croak, "Oh, my father is sick so I went to visit him," before burying my head in my locker, pretending to hunt for a textbook. It gave me a minute to cry alone.

A few days later, my mother was back at the hospital with my still-comatose father. She was sitting by his side talking when suddenly he began muttering, and then he woke up.

"I really need to go home," he announced. "Can you take me home?"

The shocked medical staff obliged. By then, the cancer had no Off button. He was no longer receiving any treatments, only pain medication. Though he was weak and incredibly tired, he came home later in September. My mother and her sister, a nurse who was visiting from Ohio, talked about setting up in-home hospice care for my father.

Unfortunately, his pain was so excruciating that he was never comfortable, whether standing, sitting, or lying down. Within a week, he was back in the hospital. By then, it was early October. My father continued to insist to his doctors that he be allowed to go home as soon as he regained some of his strength. He had specifically stated that he wanted to die in familiar surroundings. Everybody promised to help.

My mother coordinated a plan with the town's ambulance crew for October 11. They had generously volunteered to drive her to New Hampshire in the ambulance so my father would not have to ride home in our uncomfortable station wagon. On the evening of Sunday, October 10, my mother called the hospital and talked to my father about bringing him back to Massachusetts. Although he was heavily sedated, she had no doubt he grasped that she would be coming for him the next day.

Monday, October 11, dawned as a lung-cleansing, cloudless day in New England. It was the Columbus Day holiday, so we had the day off from school. That morning, I waited around in the living room, peering out the windows periodically for signs of the red-and-white ambulance. Later that afternoon, our high school football team would be playing a home game that had been rescheduled because of a Saturday rainout. I had volunteered to sell tickets at the game and would be headed there with friends as soon as my father was settled into his downstairs bedroom. One of my younger sisters was running in a track meet, and the youngest and oldest ones were home.

When I heard tires crunching on our gravel driveway, I sprinted out the side door and down our rickety wooden steps, wanting to be the first to welcome my father. But I knew something was terribly wrong when I noticed tears in the eyes of the driver, a barrel-chested emergency medical technician who had attended to his share of tragedies. His mouth started moving, but no words were coming out. My mother, seated next to him, seemed paralyzed. I looked in the back of the ambulance and spotted the empty gurney. "Nooooo," I screamed silently, grasping for a different truth. *This can't be. They must have left my father at the hospital because he was too exhausted. That must be it.* But I knew my horrifying "never" had arrived.

When the ambulance had arrived at the hospital early that morning, my mother was startled to find my father's bed empty. His oncologist apologized and guided my mother to a tiny room where attendants had wheeled him just minutes beforehand. His body was still warm. She hugged and kissed him goodbye for the last time. I never had the chance to say goodbye to him.

My exhausted father had died alone in a hospital bed about fifteen minutes before the ambulance arrived. Hospice workers will tell you that terminally ill people often choose when to die. They decide when they've had enough. Some wait until their families are gathered around them, and others, perhaps not wanting to disappoint, die when they are alone. I don't know if my father could not bear for his family to see him in that state, or if he was just too worn out to hang on for another minute.

After the ambulance pulled away, our next-door neighbors came over. They were an older couple who had been beyond kind to us in our three years there. I sat on the living room couch next to the husband, quaking. Wordlessly, he wrapped his hands around mine.

My older sister called a friend and headed to the football game. I stayed home. My tears wouldn't come until much later that afternoon when I walked by myself on back roads.

That fall, baseball became more of a refuge. It was my escape to some sort of normalcy where three strikes meant you were out, four balls meant you walked, and if you made it all the way around the base paths, you got to go home. After that miracle year in 1975, the Red Sox hadn't even come close to contending for a playoff spot in 1976. The team had lost its spirit, stumbling to a third-place finish in the American League East with a mediocre 83–79 record. My father wasn't around to watch the World Series with me in 1976, as he had been the year before. Those autumn days were gloomy and rainy. It seemed as if all of New England was in mourning.

Half-heartedly, I watched the New York Yankees, the longtime nemesis of the Red Sox, take on manager Sparky Anderson and his indomitable Cincinnati Reds, back for their second consecutive World Series title.

Seven days after the Reds thrashed the Yankees 7–2 in Game Four, to complete a four-game sweep as Series victors, my mother received a letter from Dr. Herbert Maurer, my father's oncologist. He was the same doctor who had apologized profusely to my mother for that phone call she had received about my father's cancer spreading to his brain. Delivering that news via phone, instead of face-to-face, had been a dreadful mistake made by an unsupervised underling.

Dr. Maurer's letter confirmed that the autopsy results showed the melanoma had spread throughout my father's body. But it also confirmed that he had taken the time to know my father and his spirit, not just his disease.

"I am glad that Ronald did not linger very long, as I know this was his wish, and I am sorry that the end did seem to drag on so long," the doctor wrote in his one-page note. "It is quite surprising to me, in view of the examination of the brain, that he lived as long as he did because there were large and multiple deposits of tumor in many areas. It is clear that the strength of your husband was what kept him going so long."

CHAPTER 16
MONTANA: WHERE THERE'S SMOKE, THERE'S FIRE

MILES RIDDEN: 947.5
MILES TO GO: 3,302.5

A swirling, sooty dome of mist and smoke capped Lolo Pass early on September 1 as I pedaled into my third state, Montana, on Highway 12. The westbound Lewis and Clark expedition had crossed that same 5,235-foot landmark on that same date, 195 years earlier. I wondered if they had heard the same raucous calls and squawks from resident ravens and Steller's jays.

Historical markers spelled out how Meriwether Lewis, William Clark, and their ill-fed crew endured a grueling detour to reach this point. Unable to cross the Salmon River, they had traded goods for packhorses south of here and hired a Shoshone woman named Sacagawea to guide them over this mountain pass. This geographical impediment is often cited as the Corps of Discovery's most formidable obstacle. Long before white settlers arrived, Indian tribes had traversed this pass in the Rocky Mountains to access buffalo hunting grounds in what are now Wyoming and Montana. Lewis and Clark trekked through Lolo Pass again in 1806 on their return trip from the Pacific Coast.

Both times, downed trees and a lack of game made those journeys far more arduous than my puny effort on a paved highway. I also felt spoiled having access to resealable plastic bags to keep my stowed gear dry. Those oft-soaked travelers of yore had to count on oilskins and animal pelts to protect their vital necessities.

Soon, I gazed at acre upon acre of recently scorched Douglas firs and lodgepole and Ponderosa pines, my first sighting of the destruction wrought by large-scale wildfires that I thus far had only smelled. Firefighters' tents dotted the blackened landscape. I zipped down the mountain, past rounded rock formations that looked like they'd been formed by beach giants squeezing wet sand between their massive fingers. About eight miles later, I was the only bicyclist eating breakfast at the Lolo Hot Springs restaurant— the same place where Carmen had mistakenly left my gear the day before. Firefighters from the nearby ring of camps huddled at tables, strategizing.

One reason I had started my trek in August instead of June was to avoid peak wildfire season. That summer, some cyclists either pedaled on Interstate 90 in Montana or skipped the state altogether because smoke-choked air had intermittently closed the bicycle route. Yes, 1988 will be remembered as the year that Yellowstone—the cornerstone of this country's park system—burned to a crisp. But 2000 was another Year of the Wildfire. Conflagration reigned.

When I left the restaurant to make the 33.5-mile push into Missoula, a gauze-like coating of smoke and ash muted the sun's usual brilliance. My first stop in Missoula was the Bicycle Doctor. "Hey, look at this weirdly wounded tire," the mechanic marveled as her colleagues examined the oddity. "Pretty impressive that it held up for more than a hundred miles. You're just lucky." I contemplated shipping the misshapen tire home as a souvenir, but decided it would be a waste of postage.

Rain had made the city of forty-three thousand soggy, so I spent much of the late afternoon and evening in the spacious waiting area at the hospital's cancer center. It was a relief to catch up on my journal and reading, and pick up a new batch of brochures at the post office. Unfortunately, the heralded hostel for cyclists had abruptly closed the year before, so I set up a makeshift camp under the overhang of a downtown high school that had been converted to a day care facility. A bed, or at least a foldout couch, would come soon enough. I was only fifty-four miles away from Hamilton, Montana, where I planned to spend a few days with Jane and Joe, transplanted friends from my newspapering days in Wisconsin. Near nightfall, the sky put on a riveting lightning show. Rain-starved locals seemed so thrilled by the downpour that they cast aside their umbrellas and jumped around joyously in the puddle-laden streets.

The next day, September 2, I roughly paralleled the Bitterroot River as I forged through a lowland valley of the same name toward Hamilton via Highways 12 and 93. Although the sight of blackened patches of forest was unnerving, I was surrounded by mountains and often immersed in green explosions of pines, firs, spruces, hemlocks, and junipers, the currency of southwestern Montana. Snowy icing atop distant peaks accentuated the gorgeous geography.

Clearly, the setting was a magnet for two-legged creatures because so much of what I pedaled past had been parceled out solely for human habitation and agriculture. One area we Homo sapiens *had* managed to share with other creatures was the Lee Metcalf National Wildlife Refuge, just north of Stevensville. There, I watched an osprey clutching its piscine prey, just plucked from the river, in its talons. The bird squawked boisterously, as if gloating that it had lunch, and I, alas, did not.

I might have been in the land of conifers and big sky, but Montana's nickname could just as easily be "Pickup Truck Haven." So many truck beds came equipped with dogs that I wondered if car dealers made canines part of the package. These balletic dogs, however, seemed to have strains of Rudolf Nureyev or Mikhail Baryshnikov in their genes. How else could they stay upright at sixty-five miles per hour? Back in Wisconsin, friends had dispensed reams of advice about how to keep pursuing dogs at bay. Blowing a whistle, spraying mace, squirting lemon water, and issuing a solid thump with a tire pump were among the suggestions. But practice is more difficult than theory when you're balanced on two wheels. And besides, if I had lemon water, I was not going to waste it on a mangy dog. Thus far, I had found that barking back with an authoritative "NO!" was a viable solution for my few dog encounters.

In Stevensville, a community of eleven hundred about thirty-three miles beyond Missoula, I watched my odometer click to a thousand miles. That meant roughly one-fourth of the trip was behind me. Just beyond, rain that had lingered in Missoula caught up to me that afternoon when Mother Nature doused my sorry self. Fierce headwinds made the branches of the roadside cottonwood trees sway and forced me into overdrive just to stay on the shoulder of Highways 269 and 203, also known as the Eastside Highway. I was able to laugh only because I conjured up an image of the most convincing wicked witch of all time, Margaret Hamilton, riding her old-fashioned bicycle in that classic scene from *The Wizard of Oz*. A refrain of *doot doot doot doot doot doot, doot doot doot doot doot doot* played in my head as T-shirt temperatures retreated into the fifties. My rain pants stuck to my legs like tights, and my shoes took on water like a sinking canoe. When it lifted, the storm yielded one of the most vibrant rainbows I had ever seen.

"Well, I vowed I would deliver rain to your valley," I told Joe when I met him at his furniture store in Hamilton and we loaded my gear into his pickup. "And I don't like to break promises."

"We'll take it all," said Joe, noting that a pitifully scant 2.48 inches had fallen in the Bitterroot Valley since March. "We're so terrified of these fires," he continued as we bumped up the rutted road to their cabin, "that Jane put her wedding dress, family pictures, and other valuables in off-site storage."

Over dinner, Jane, a reporter for the local newspaper, confirmed that wildfires like the ones my bicycling smokejumper friend was fighting in Idaho had burned at least eleven western states that summer, but the most ferocious ones were in the Bitterroot Valley. Of the seven hundred thousand acres consumed by fire in Montana that year, more than half were in the valley.

After two days off with Jane, Joe, and their menagerie of six cats and dogs, I was back on the bicycle on September 5. My destination was seventy-four miles away—a tiny speck called Wisdom, along the Big Hole River. Almost half of that route on Highway 93 traced the Bitterroot River. By now, the rain had blown in cooler weather. That contrast to the boiling heat of the high desert of Idaho and Oregon forced me to forage deep into my panniers for thermal tops and leggings. Temperatures dropped to the thirties and forties at night and did not rise much above sixty even with the sun shining.

Splitting away from the Bitterroot River near Sula, I climbed 6,990-foot Lost Trail Pass, then 7,241-foot Chief Joseph Pass, my first crossing of the Continental Divide. Fire had scorched large swaths of forest near both passes, and I was pelted with an unpleasant mix of sleet and rain. The stinging precipitation was perhaps a gentle slap from the Nez Perce chief, reminding me of who was still in charge in this part of Montana.

I was shivering when I rolled into Wisdom, a community of 160 roughly 130 miles southeast of Missoula in the heart of the Big Hole Valley. The temperature was in the low forties when I wrapped my hands, which felt like frozen stones, around a mug of hot tea at Fetty's Bar & Grill. I drank what felt like enough tea to fill the spacious Big Hole Valley. A rancher at an adjoining table told me the weather always rolled in from the north and the west, so everybody was accustomed to being cold. He also educated me about the town's name being linked to the Lewis and Clark expedition. The explorers named a nearby river in honor of Thomas Jefferson, then christened its three tributaries Philosophy, Philanthropy, and Wisdom to honor the virtues of the president who had sent them on their mission.

Wisdom also touts itself as the Land of 10,000 Haystacks. I didn't count, but I believed it. From a distance, the massive piles resembled pale green palaces. I christened it the International Falls, Minnesota, of the West because it also sets record-low temperatures. Wisdom rests in the deceivingly high Big Hole Valley, with elevations above six thousand feet. Out here, populations rarely exceeded altitudes.

I spent that frigid evening in a forlorn little bed at a drafty bunkhouse, the Sandman Hotel. Even though the owners were reluctant to turn on the heat, being inside was still preferable to camping at the American Legion Park a half-mile outside town. Being cold and wet in a tent is not only unpleasant but could lead to hypothermia. Why risk it? Bunkhouse co-owner Tina revealed that business was slow because the wildfires had closed forestlands to hunters. Of course, she didn't mention that she was probably making twice as much as usual off the firefighters in need of lodging. The thin bunkhouse blankets were more suited for summer, but I made do by cocooning in them, all of my extra clothes, and my sleeping bag. I'm sure I looked like some sort of sausage with a skin condition, but I didn't really care. This was about comfort, not beauty. My room didn't come equipped with a phone. Before nodding off, I had convinced Tina and her suspicious husband to allow me to use their office phone the next morning to call the Milwaukee radio station. I could tell they weren't quite sure what to make of a woman riding solo. Early the next morning, I noticed Tina hovering near the doorway until she heard with her own ears what I had patiently explained to her beforehand—that she wouldn't be charged for a long-distance call because I was making a collect call and the radio station would be picking up the tab.

From Wisdom, I followed the Big Hole River for sixteen miles along Highway 278 into Jackson. Serendipitously, I arrived when the restaurant and spa, the only functioning business in town, opened at noon. While I sipped soothing hot tea alone in the lodge-like great room under the watchful eyes of dozens of mounted elk, deer, pronghorn, moose, and other critters, the second and third customers of the day walked in. They introduced themselves as Diane and John.

"Is that your bike out front?" Diane asked. I nodded and handed her a brochure.

"Wisconsin!" she practically yelled after skimming it. "Talk about a small world. You must know where Racine is, on Lake Michigan. That's where I live."

"I not only know where it is," I responded, "I was a reporter at the newspaper there in the mid-1990s."

Diane had started working as Racine's public health administrator a few months after I left. They invited me to their table and bought me lunch. She and John were in Jackson as part of a whirlwind vacation that included picking up his custom-made hunting rifle. My time in an off-the-beaten-path town with a population of thirty-eight had turned into more of a family reunion than a gathering of strangers.

After hugging the friendly couple goodbye, I prepared for a forty-eight-mile trek to Dillon. However, two significant bumps on my map made me wonder if I was biting off a bit too much that afternoon. At 7,360 feet, Big Hole Pass would be my highest climb yet. And the second uphill, Badger Pass, at 6,760 feet, was no slouch either. But what a reward awaited me on the other side. If a lump doesn't well up in your throat upon taking in the Beaverhead Valley and the purplish majesty of the Pioneer Mountains, then your DNA test probably would reveal that you are not a human being. Wow, just oh wow! I am ordinarily not much for sentimental schlock, but verses from Woody Guthrie's "This Land Is Your

Land" spilled spontaneously from me as the wind whistled through the vents in my bicycle helmet. I half-expected to find out the stunning scenery was painted on a giant cloth curtain that somebody would yank back and teasingly announce, "Just kidding!"

I surprised myself by arriving in Dillon in just three hours, meaning I averaged sixteen miles per hour. Unintentionally, I had also set my all-time speed record for a fully loaded bicycle at a don't-try-this-at-home thirty-six miles per hour. Wheeeee! The downhills were remarkable, and Highway 278 was so devoid of traffic that I could hog the entire lane without worries of becoming a hood ornament on a passing car. Still, with 360 degrees of beauty, I had to focus on balancing my load. I didn't want to end up as roadkill dinner for turkey vultures.

Early September 7, I followed the Beaverhead River out of Dillon along Highway 41, past prosperous sheep and cattle ranches. Overhead, flocks of snow geese flew in V formations. My goal for the day was seventy-four miles away in Ennis. Southwest Montana was a mix of scene-stealers, and I was treated to the whole mélange that day: flatlands, mountains, lush green forests, and sagebrush deserts. Gussied-up communities such as Nevada City and Virginia City were tourist-trap versions of Gold Rush times, while quirky Twin Bridges and Sheridan *hadn't* been painstakingly restored and still looked to be from the Gold Rush era.

Piles of mine tailings—waste left behind after valuable ores are siphoned off—along Alder Gulch on Highway 287 were the ugly legacy of that mid-1800s frenzy for gold, and of Montana's colorful and reckless past. The gulch yielded gold valued at an estimated $10 million in 1863. At what cost, I wondered?

I reached Ennis early enough to spend some time in the library roughing out a journal entry before eating dinner. It was the only library I have ever visited where fishing poles and life vests were rented by the hour. When I told the Ennis librarian that her town was windier than Chicago, she replied, "People around here don't know how to stand up if the wind isn't blowing." I waited for those strong winds to slacken before pitching my tent in the city park.

The librarian's humor proved true again on September 8, when I battled fierce winds for most of the seventy-three miles between Ennis and West Yellowstone. I couldn't outsmart a strength-sapping headwind that entire morning. Even when I dropped to granny gear, designed for easier pedaling, I couldn't propel myself faster than five to eight miles per hour. All the aspen trees around me were shaking down to their roots, and gusts kept birds aloft as if they were feathered kites.

I struggled to keep the bicycle upright in buffeting crosswinds. That turbulence didn't deter dozens of fly fishermen bedecked in their Orvis gear from braving a Madison River covered with whitecaps.

About twenty-five miles shy of West Yellowstone, in far southwestern Montana, I felt as if I had parachuted into a Salvador Dalí painting when I broached Earthquake Lake. As the name suggests, it was created on the evening of August 17, 1959, when a temblor knocked part of a mountain loose. The disastrous landslide killed twenty-eight people. Dead-tree totems, a tribute to nature's wrath, stood upright in the water like petrified ghost soldiers. Everything seemed lopsided. It was the only time I'd ever been able to stand at ground level and peer down into an osprey nest—cobbled together with large sticks—perched high in the branches of a woody snag.

I experienced an even odder sensation a few minutes later. The swirling wind had spun around 180 degrees. A headwind miraculously became a tailwind. Powerful gusts pushed at my back just as my father's hand had more than three decades earlier as I learned to ride a clunky blue two-wheeler with shiny metal fenders in our Philadelphia neighborhood. It seemed crazy, but my grateful legs settled in, and I practically coasted toward Hebgen Lake at twenty-five miles per hour. Of course, that gift didn't last long.

The fickle wind switched direction yet again a few miles later, forcing me to regroup at a picnic table at the edge of a somewhat washed-up resort called Kirkwood Ranch. I needed to recharge before pedaling the final twenty miles into West Yellowstone. The ranch featured a marina, a motel, a small grocery store, and a campground for recreational vehicles. While I studied my map, a man approached, announced that he was a transplanted Californian, and wanted to know what I was doing. I explained. "Maybe you should stop in the next large city you come to," he joked. "I'm sure a psychiatrist there could help you with your 'cycling condition.'"

I was thinking maybe I wasn't the one who needed to see a doctor, when a second man approached. He'd been tying flies in front of a nearby cabin and intervened by introducing himself as Michael and showing me his vest, laden with an assortment of flies and other fishing accessories. "I guess it needs a washing," Michael said sheepishly in an accent flecked with the drawl of his native Georgia. "But you don't have to smell good to fish for trout!" I assured him that you don't need to smell fresh as a daisy to ride cross-country either.

"I understand your motivation," he said. "My grandmother survived breast cancer." Minutes later, he showed me a nasty scar above the elbow bend on his right arm and explained that a knife attack at a construction site prompted him to flee Atlanta five years ago. Here in Montana, he said, he could earn a living as an electrician, and also hunt, hike, hear elk bugle, and pursue his beloved fly-fishing. He was headed to "West," the local nickname for West Yellowstone, that evening to meet friends at a bar and offered to give me a ride in his truck. "That would be cheating," I said. "Wind or no wind, I have to ride the whole route." If I wouldn't take a lift, I should take food, he insisted. He disappeared into his cabin.

I waited. Minutes later, he emerged in a different outfit. He had carefully folded his spotless white socks in just-so fashion over his hiking boots. "I'm a perfectionist about these things," he said after seeking reassurance that the checkered flannel shirt he was wearing over a T-shirt matched his green shorts and would be appropriate for a night on the town. I approved. He handed me a can of Bud Light and a paper plate covered with Pringles and a tortilla filled with pressed turkey and cheese. "Well, this is all I had. But it's yours." I smiled and bit my bottom lip so it wouldn't quiver. Souls like Michael were what long-distance travelers, even those with an atheistic or agnostic bent, refer to as "trail angels." His small, thoughtful act stoked my stomach and my heart, and gave my legs the boost they needed to fend off the wind for a few more hours.

CHAPTER 17
YELLOWSTONE NEVER DISAPPOINTS

Uncharacteristically, I slept until seven the next morning, September 9, in West Yellowstone. How decadent. Finding a campsite the night before had been a hassle. "West," a popular gateway to Yellowstone National Park, is a jumble of hotels and a blare of neon signs pointing tourists toward food and trinkets. Underground sprinklers in the only park available had shot off in succession until at least eleven p.m. Their pattern wasn't predictable, but I eventually found a not-too-soaked spot adjacent to a picnic table.

The only other camper at the park was a fortysomething man who spoke in snippets from the Bible. Between swallows from a large cardboard milk carton, he introduced himself as Slow Ken and explained that he had relinquished his driver's license after twenty-five years because tailgaters exhausted him. His noble goal was to backpack around the country encouraging deliberate and thoughtful behavior. "Everybody is in a hurry," he lamented. "People need to think how their actions affect the natural world."

That morning, I ate breakfast at the Silver Spur Café. Debbie, the waitress, was quick to alert me that half an inch of snow had dusted Yellowstone's Old Faithful overnight. As I lingered over my eggs, tea, and toast, we talked about what it meant to be a Westerner and the long school bus trips her children endured in these wide-open spaces. She looked at one of my brochures and told me that her mother had died of breast cancer recently. Debbie then revealed that cysts periodically appeared in her own breasts. "Don't worry," she said, responding to my anxious look. "I'm vigilant about having my doctor monitor me. I want to see my two children grow up." When I returned to the counter after changing my clothes in the warm bathroom, Debbie told me I owed her nothing for breakfast. "Use this for your ride," she said, pressing a wad of bills into my hand. "I believe in what you're doing. Please be safe." A croaked "Thank you so much" was all I could manage through trembling lips.

Minutes later, I was pedaling on Highways 20 and 191 along the Madison River, under a cerulean sky etched with pleasing puffs of clouds. What I hadn't told Debbie was that my father would have turned sixty-eight that day. I celebrated his birthday by cycling into the fourth state of my journey, Wyoming, and its glorious Yellowstone. My very first trip there had been during our family's 1971 continental camping adventure.

Yellowstone—larger than Rhode Island and Delaware combined—was still an exquisite jewel twenty-nine years later. Even if I couldn't ever visit each of its 2.2 million acres spread out over Wyoming, Montana, and Idaho, just knowing that this incomparable haven existed was a balm for my heart and soul. Our mistake-prone country did the right thing in 1872 by designating this wonderland as its first national park.

Yellowstone is a refuge for a veritable bonanza of wildlife. I gazed with wonder at trumpeter swans, bison, elk, and coyotes. Thank goodness conservationists had the foresight to rescue a few of the thousands of bison that once thundered across the Great Plains. My stomach churned when I thought of the pieces of the natural puzzle we had cast aside and stomped on with impunity in the name of Manifest Destiny. This was one of the few places where the top three predators—wolves, grizzly bears, and cougars—were still allowed to roam in a habitat not despoiled by strip malls, subdivisions, and big-box stores. What a relief to know that less than 2 percent of Yellowstone was developed with roads, trails, parking lots, buildings, and campgrounds.

At one roadside sign, I read the 1834 perspective of a white traveler named W. A. Ferris, who wrote about his visit: "I had heard in the summer of 1833, while at rendezvous, that remarkable boiling springs had been discovered, on the sources of the Madison. I determined to examine them myself. I parted with the company after supper, and [the next day] reached the vicinity of the springs about dark, having seen several small lakes or ponds on the sources of the Madison. From the surface of a rocky plain or table, burst forth columns of water, of various dimensions, projected high in the air, accompanied by loud explosions and sulphurous vapors, which were highly disagreeable to the smell."

Magmatic heat that powered volcanic eruptions 2 million, 1.3 million, and 630,000 years ago continues to fuel Yellowstone's geysers, hot springs, fumaroles, and bubbling mud pots. Remarkably, the park is home to almost a third of the roughly one thousand geysers around the globe. Magma roiling deep in the earth's bowels at an estimated fifteen hundred degrees still warms the rainwater and snowmelt that seep underground. That heat builds pressure, forcing the water to escape through rocky fissures. By studying precipitation patterns, scientists have theorized that the intervals between Old Faithful's regular eruptions are dictated by the amount of rain and snow that falls each year. A drought means fewer gushes.

Of course, I needed to take a side trip to be dazzled by Old Faithful, as our family had been in 1971. Visiting Yellowstone and not watching

101

this reliable landmark spout off is akin to leaving turkey, cranberries, and pumpkin pie off the Thanksgiving menu. This time, about a hundred of us oohed and ahhed while watching the geyser shoot plumes of steam and water some eighty feet upward at 2:23 that afternoon. It was uplifting and reassuring to stand with those strangers and know that no matter if it was our first or our hundredth visit, this natural wonder left us gaping and gasping in awe. Witnessing such beauty allows us to be our true, vulnerable, innocent human selves with all protective armor stripped away. I walked to my unlocked bicycle comforted by the thought that we are never as jaded or cynical as we might think.

I laughed out loud when I remembered how excited my father would get during that long-ago summer trip. With his left elbow propped on the sill of the open window of our station wagon, he would exclaim, "Look at the view, kids, look at the view!" as we wended our way down the California coastline near Big Sur on a narrow scenic highway with limited guardrails and sheer drop-offs. Yes, the ocean was beautiful, but we all feared we would be treading water in it if he didn't focus on driving. I carried his enthusiastic spirit with me as I feasted my eyes on Yellowstone's lakes, rivers, waterfalls, and hillsides of lodgepole pines, mountains, and talus slopes.

That magical summer of 1971 was when my ten-year-old self likely began to piece together a conservation ethic. But one of the most indelible lessons about my potential impact on the natural world had come from my father several years beforehand—in the city. On a warm day sometime in the mid-1960s, I was squatting on our Philadelphia backyard patio, watching a tiny train of black ants carry bits of detritus across the red bricks to their homes in our adjacent yard. When a big red ant emerged, I lifted my sneakered foot and announced that it was ugly and I was going to kill it. "Why?" my father asked. "Well, because," I started, realizing I didn't have a good reason to use my shoe as a weapon. "That ant is harmless," he told me. "Try to think about its life and how you would feel if somebody had the power to snuff you out with a stomp." I felt so ashamed that I lowered my foot slowly, letting the red ant march away. I have never looked at ants, or almost any other insect, in the same way since.

On that September day, I saw plenty of totems, burned-out trees standing as monuments to the much-ballyhooed Yellowstone fire of 1988. Though labeled tragic at the time, that carnage schooled us about the dangers of fire suppression. Tree ring records from Yellowstone indicated that the region's forests burned every two hundred to four hundred years. Periodic fire, as Native Americans knew, and as the rest of us are coming to realize, is a valuable tool in maintaining a healthy ecosystem.

Evidence lay in the bounty of conifers bending in the breeze as I reached the highest elevations thus far on my ride by crossing the Continental Divide twice, first at 8,261 feet and second at 8,391 feet. The second crossing was exceptional because it was straddled by snow-fed Isa Lake. Isa, covered with lily pads, might have small beginnings, but it leads to big places. The geographical surprise is that the lake drains in two separate, and backward, directions. Its west arm follows an easterly route by feeding the Firehole River, which leads to the Madison River, the Missouri River, and the Mississippi River before emptying into the Gulf of Mexico. Isa's east outlet runs west, first trickling into Yellowstone's Shoshone Lake and Lewis River before wending to the Snake River and the Columbia River, then pouring into the Pacific Ocean.

At dinnertime, I pulled into Grant Village, a Yellowstone campground. Only a few sites were occupied because temperatures were expected to dip below freezing. Plus, most people had said goodbye to summer travels, transforming to their post-Labor Day lives. I approached a park ranger, who was locking up the visitor center. She tried to discourage any inquiry with an I-just-want-to-go-home-can't-you-bother-somebody-else look when I gave her my spiel and begged to use a park computer to write a journal entry. Her face softened when I told her more about my trip, handed her a brochure, and mentioned how much I'd learned a few years prior as a volunteer intern for the National Park Service at Northern Arizona's Petrified National Forest/Painted Desert. "We'll see," she said. "Meet me here at nine tomorrow morning."

Before walking the half-mile from the campground to the combination restaurant/store, I pitched my tent, bundled up in most of my clothes, and locked my belongings in the heavy-duty bear-proof box. At the restaurant, I realized my queasy stomach could handle only fruit, crackers, and generous offerings of steamy tea. My father would have called this intestinal upset "the galloping crud." Fortunately, I had just a minor case.

Sleep was spotty, and I awakened very early. I sought refuge in the only campground building—a two-stall bathroom that was warmed briefly every ten minutes or so when a clanging heater belched a welcome blast of hot air. A wall-mounted diaper-changing table served as a makeshift desk where I penciled the outline of a journal entry I hoped to email to the Wisconsin hospital with the ranger's help. I still couldn't fully extend the left arm I had injured during my Oregon tumble, but at least the appendage was functional enough for daily camping chores. I had mostly weaned myself off over-the-counter painkillers because I figured my liver was compromised enough by melanoma surgery. I treasured the internal organs I still had.

A camper who entered my temporary writing refuge to brush her teeth

103

told me in a heavy Irish accent that just the idea of bicycling in this weather made her shiver. She and her companion had forsaken their tent for their car the previous night to try to escape the freezing cold. They weren't sure how much longer their planned camping vacation would last.

Fortunately, the ranger kept her promise and greeted me at nine on the dot. She cheerfully mentioned that she had stayed up well past her bedtime because she had become so immersed in reading my online journal entries. When I reported that somebody had delighted the area ravens by dumping a fish near my campsite, the ranger told me I had earned all the computer time I needed in her office that morning. She immediately radioed a campground employee to remove the fish before it attracted a hungry black or grizzly bear. Bears, of course, are fine. So are some people. But the rangers are absolutely justified in taking measures to keep the two species apart.

While typing my journal entry that morning, I remembered how little my father expected on his birthdays. As unpredictable as he could be, one less-than-mysterious part of him was his ability to appreciate the smallest of gifts from his children. Our meager allowances never allowed us to buy much, but he could make us feel as if we had handed him the moon when we presented our handmade birthday cards and a carefully wrapped package of felt-tip markers, a bundle of pipe cleaners, or an oddball animal or pot shaped from clay in art class. I beamed when he hung my "Safety First" mobile in his Massachusetts study. I had spent hours crafting it with cardboard, colored markers, and sewing thread as a birthday tribute to his new job writing safety literature for corporate clients.

I think all that my father had wanted for his forty-fourth birthday in September 1976 was to be home. But he was back in the New Hampshire hospital because his pain became unbearable. What was unusual about that hospital, I learned later, was how the doctors and nurses acted much more like hospice workers, long before such principles spread nationwide. They grasped the fact that a dignified death was part of life, not an act of failure that they hoped would happen on somebody else's shift. Their goal at this stage was to minimize his pain. My father's oncologist was not in denial about his impending death, and the two of them apparently had frank conversations about it. My father wasn't able to have that same candid talk with his children. Maybe that would have been just too excruciating for a parent, even one who was borderline obsessed with truth and honesty.

On the Saturday closest to what turned out to be his last birthday, our family traveled to the hospital with a picnic lunch. We had even made a birthday cake. My father was so weak that he couldn't walk very far on his own, so my sisters and I took turns pushing him slowly around the hallways in a wheelchair. It started raining so hard that we couldn't go outside. Instead, we ate in his hospital room. I don't remember him eating much. But I do remember the nurses joining us to sing "Happy Birthday." My father didn't have quite enough breath to blow out the few candles on the cake. So we all helped.

CHAPTER 18
WYOMING: BUTTES AND BATHTUB RINGS

MILES RIDDEN: 1,375.5
MILES TO GO: 2,874.5

My serpentine route out of Grant Village on Yellowstone's South Entrance Road early on September 10 was mostly southeasterly, with strong headwinds whipping up whitecaps on Lewis Lake and the Lewis River. At nearby Lewis Falls, I met Jan, an oncology nurse, and three other short-term touring bicyclists from the Washington, DC, suburbs.

"Wow, great story. Will you please pose right here with your bike?" Jan asked, pulling out her camera. "I'm always looking for ways to inspire my cancer patients. I can hardly wait to tell them I talked with you."

I thought Yellowstone had exhausted my quiver of superlatives, until I glimpsed the craggy, snow-covered peaks of the Grand Tetons looming over Jackson Lake. Say what you want about the legacy of John D. Rockefeller Jr. and his family's robber baron propensities, but the country owes him for having the foresight to preserve this grandeur. Fearing that development would despoil these heart-achingly gorgeous views, he surreptitiously purchased thirty-five thousand-plus Jackson Hole acres in 1927 as part of his under-the-radar Snake River Land Company. He then prompted the federal government to establish Grand Teton National Park, a link with already-protected Yellowstone, by donating his holdings.

The Tetons are mere babes in the Rockies, just nineteen million years old. The range rises at least seven thousand feet above the valley floor, with spectacular Grand Teton almost double that at 13,770 feet. What's disconcerting is the lack of foothills. Peaks rise abruptly from a plateau of sagebrush, willows, cottonwoods, and aspens.

In the Buffalo Valley framed by the peaks, aspen leaves tinged with yellow merely hinted at the full golden crescendo due in autumn. I felt fortunate to catch sight of a bull moose. I wished for a rearview mirror when I pedaled beyond the Tetons along Highways 26 and 287. I sneaked backward peeks regularly, mourning the mountains' quiet strength and exquisite elegance when they disappeared from sight.

In Montana and northwestern Wyoming, I crossed the Continental Divide half a dozen times in the span of ten September days. One 9,658-foot crossing on Highways 26 and 287 between tiny Moran Junction and Dubois was named Togwotee Pass, after a Shoshone Indian guide. It is the second-highest summit on the TransAm Trail and requires an eighteen-mile, circular climb. No shoulder meant bobbing and weaving in a single uphill lane to avoid potholes and traffic. But I forgot about the cold and my aching lungs at the apex when I tipped into a thirty-mile downhill on the other side. A backdrop of clear blue sky made profiles of rock fortresses such as Pinnacle Butte and Ramshorn Peak even more majestic.

Roads beyond Yellowstone, the Grand Tetons, and Togwotee propelled me into jarringly different but equally striking territory. This part of Wyoming revealed a chiseled splendor of red-and-brown-banded badlands and undulating hills covered with sagebrush and juniper. From a distance, some rock formations resembled ancient cliff dwellings. Such geography reminded me of the Painted Desert in Arizona, a terrain that's also simultaneously unforgiving and sensual. Flat-top buttes and cuestas—ridges with a steep face on one side and a gentle slope on the other—ruled. Clearly, the twin agents of erosion—wind and water—have industriously plied their trade on surrounding rock. It's that third agent, heat, that wears down humans. When temperatures soared into the mid-eighties, I peeled off thermal layers. It was hard to believe that snow had dusted Yellowstone's Old Faithful just a few days beforehand. Nooks and crannies provided plenty of hiding places for the prairie grouse, jackrabbits, pronghorn, mule deer, elk, and bighorn sheep that roamed here. Fortunately, gusts blow constantly along the appropriately named Wind River and Wind River Mountain Range, keeping foothill vegetation exposed for overwintering wildlife that otherwise might starve if snow covered the basin.

Just shy of Dubois on September 11, curiosity caused me to investigate the roadside Tie Hack Historical Monument. Yes, that's tie hack, not tack. I learned that a hack was a beefy man, usually of Scandinavian extraction, who worked for the Wyoming Tie and Timber handcrafting lodgepole pines into railroad ties for the Chicago & North Western Railroad. Each tree yielded about three ties. Employees churned out twenty-five hundred ties for each mile of railroad track and were paid about ten cents a tie. The monument included a handsome stone sculpture at the top of a mammoth staircase fashioned, of course, from railroad ties. Tie hacks went the way of Pony Express riders in the early twentieth century when machines elbowed them aside.

107

It seemed appropriate that a Sacagawea coin I received in change near Yellowstone still jingled in my pocket as I approached Fort Washakie, home of the Shoshone Cultural Center. Sacagawea, of course, was the Shoshone Indian guide who had been kidnapped by another tribe and was instrumental in leading the Lewis and Clark expedition out of peril with her baby strapped on her back. She is supposedly buried nearby, next to her two sons and Chief Washakie, the legendary Shoshone chief.

"I can give you directions to her marker, but that doesn't mean she is buried there," Floyd, the cultural center's environmental agent, told me, adding that some Indians claim her final resting spot is deep in the mountains. "I guess that's our way of protecting her, just in case."

"Thank you," I said. "I don't mean any harm. I just think she's a forgotten piece of American history, and I wondered how she is remembered here."

I found her marked gravesite easily enough and was fascinated by the curious assortment of items visitors had left there. The sage bundle, feathers, beaded necklace, and bouquets of plastic flowers seemed to be appropriate tributes. However, the hair clips, coins, sugar packets, pencils, pens, cigarettes, lighters, and red plastic Safeway grocery store discount card mystified me. Why would people empty their pockets at a sacrosanct site?

More than fifty miles beyond Sacagawea's marked grave, Sweetwater Station featured the junction of three famed trails—Oregon, Mormon Pioneer, and Pony Express—which all overlaid original Native American pathways. It's where Highway 135 feeds into Highway 287/789, which my route followed through much of Wyoming. The Sweetwater River, supposedly so named because it's where a stumbling mule spilled some long-ago travelers' precious sugar supply, also crosses here. A campground, a gas station, and restrooms with flush toilets now mark the historic juncture. Divergent opinions from early nineteenth-century travelers plodding for at least a week through a stretch of sand and sage that should have been nicknamed the American Sahara are spelled out in a neatly lettered sign.

"How I long for timbered country," one pessimistic soul wrote about his trip west. "In a thousand miles I have not seen a hundred acres of wood. All that comes near to arborification is a fringe of cottonwood and willows along the banks of the creeks and rivers. These everlasting hills have an everlasting curse of barrenness."

Another traveler from a long-ago summer offered a glass-half-full perspective, noting that the river was low and clear for crossing, grass for livestock was plentiful, and the days were bright and mild. "Still by the Sweet Water," this unidentified optimist wrote in a journal. "The valley is becoming more narrow and the stream more rapid. In advance and a little to the north of our trail, we can see the Wind River Mountains. Their lofty summits are covered with snow, and in their dazzling whiteness appear truly sublime."

The river at the heart of the Sweetwater Valley provides a veritable salad bar for creatures great and small—from a thousand-pound moose to a quarter-ounce pygmy shrew. Willow roots that stabilize its stream banks sprout the bark, stems, and leaves that provide shade for breeding and feeding fish; dam and lodge material for beavers; and the staple of the moose diet. Sandhill and whooping cranes flock to the river to fatten up during migratory flights.

Split Rock, a dramatic cleft in the Rattlesnake Mountain Range, was another prominent navigational landmark for Indians, and eventually trappers, emigrant families, and deliverymen on the Oregon, Mormon Pioneer, California, and Pony Express trails. I spied it about fifty miles outside of Rawlins, my destination for the evening of September 14. I half-expected to spot a family lumbering west in a Conestoga wagon or a Mormon pushing a handcart through the desert sand.

A marker explained why the Pony Express, an integral piece of Western lore, lasted just eighteen months. Officially christened the California Overland Mail and Pikes Peak Express, the Pony Express galloped into history on April 4, 1860, just before the Civil War. It was doomed by the October 1861 completion of the more reliable and less dangerous transcontinental telegraph line. An advertisement to recruit riders for the sixteen-hundred-mile route from St. Joseph, Missouri, to Sacramento, California, bluntly states: "Wanted! Young, skinny, wiry fellows not over 18. Must be expert riders, willing to risk death daily. Orphans preferred. Wages $25 per week."

That afternoon, I took refuge in a Rawlins motel operated by a family from India. The town had been whittled down to about ninety-three hundred after peaking at twenty thousand several decades before, when copper mines churned full bore. In 2000, the school district and the oil refinery were the biggest employers.

A long soak in hot water was just what my bones needed after nine days of pedaling and camping. Sunscreen and sweat were wicked magnets for roadside grime. Plus, my oiled chain had covered my calves with greasy black "bicycle tattoos." I was encouraged that my injured left arm was strong enough to scrub away the filth. When I hoisted myself out of the tub, I realized I had left behind a distinct dirt ring—something I hadn't managed to do since childhood.

A friendly teacher at the Carbon County Higher Education Center gave me unlimited access to a library computer. I told him that for all of Wyoming's natural beauty, the landmark that captured my heart was a no-frills sign I'd spotted a couple of days earlier in front of a Wind River Indian Reservation elementary school. This perfect tribute to public education read: FREE KNOWLEDGE, BRING YOUR OWN CONTAINER.

That message reminded me of how my father, a born teacher, approached lessons with his own children. His favorite saying, "Look it up," meant just that. Although he would guide us to resources where we could find answers, he wasn't going to spoon-feed us anything. However, if I displayed curiosity about a topic, whether it was the proper uses of *who* and *whom* or how to best summarize an article about soldiers dying in the Vietnam War for a current events presentation, he could display saint-like patience to be certain my grasp exceeded the superficial.

His intensity and insistence on deep dives led to a standing joke between my older sister and me, especially as our homework loads became heavier and more difficult. When we asked our mother a schoolwork-related question that she couldn't or didn't want to answer, she would suggest, "Why don't you ask your father?" My sister and I would smile at each other knowingly. Then one of us would say, "Maybe later. I don't need that much information right now."

CHAPTER 19
CHOOSING MY NEXT POISON

By Thanksgiving 1987, I was a few weeks shy of completing my yearlong experimental regimen with the interferon immunotherapy. A final set of scans and exams in December showed my body continued to be melanoma-free. Of course, no doctor would definitively say that the interferon had prevented the cancer from reappearing. But then again, nobody could tell me what might have happened without the treatment.

Either way, I felt liberated to execute my long-incubated plan to jump-start my reporting career in a new environment. As much as I loved Vermont and the idea of remaining in New England, jobs were limited. I was fixated on Wisconsin because the essence and history of the state appealed to me. I didn't have family there, but I had been offered a job there out of college that I regretted not taking.

Between interferon injections, I mapped out a move-to-the-Midwest strategy. In the pre-internet world, that involved mailing resumés and cover letters, and following up with phone calls to line up in-person interviews with editors. By November 1987, I was thrilled to have accepted a reporting position with a newspaper in Janesville, south of Madison. I would be covering local governments and writing features for a newly launched Sunday edition. My start date was January 1988. A moving truck carted away my worldly belongings, enough to fill a small bedroom. One of my younger sisters offered to drive west with me if I picked her up at my mother's house in Massachusetts. Snow had enveloped the Northeast, but in late December, my sister, my cat, Wilbur, and I squeezed into the cab of my jam-packed pickup truck, intent on outracing yet another storm. When ice overwhelmed the windshield wipers, we made an emergency stop with relatives in Buffalo. Still, we arrived in Wisconsin in time for my sister to fly back for her New Year's party.

Fittingly, my first feature story assignment at my new job was to test and grade the region's sledding hills. I traipsed all over town bundled in hat, mittens, and scarf, zipping downhill on my stomach and backside, and interviewed a full range of sledders. I created a "McGowan yahoo scale" to rank each hill's attributes. My editors loved it. As I dove into my reporting beat, I churned out more enterprise stories and delved into breaking news and investigative pieces. I was convinced I had the best job in Wisconsin. My goal had been to regain traction in journalism and put my episodes with melanoma behind me, and I was on my way.

Still, I had to be diligent about checkups. I had shipped my Vermont medical records to University Hospital in Madison because it was a leading research facility and a relatively easy commute. My first appointment, in the spring of 1988, was with an oncologist who appeared to be reassuringly avuncular.

During my quarterly appointments, I became accustomed to that doctor's Lurch-like pale face, his chin and cheeks always sporting a five o'clock shadow. An unruly mass of black hair topped off his disheveled look. His spidery fingers, long enough to palm a basketball, allowed him to probe for signs of swollen lymph nodes or other trouble as I sat ramrod straight in the classic tie-at-the-back, less-than-dignifying hospital-issue "gown" on a stainless-steel examining table covered with thin white crinkly paper. Afterward, he and other specialists would review the results of the X-rays or CT scan I had undergone before the appointment. I insisted on waiting around until he could share the results in person. I didn't want bad news delivered on the phone.

Clean reports that first year in Wisconsin lulled me into the luxury of what I labeled "normal mode." I could comb my hair without worrying I would discover a bump on my scalp or neck, and I would not cringe when fellow reporters uttered the word *terminal* when referring to newsroom computers.

Then, just when I was adapting to that new normal, I was reminded of how we are all hanging by a thread. On a winter day in early 1989, I waited in an exam room for my oncologist to return with my scan results. I knew something was wrong the moment he walked in.

"We've found some dark spots in both of your lungs," he said flatly, without looking at me. "We can't be sure what they are without a biopsy, but they are making us nervous given your history."

He left the room.

It's jarring enough when melanoma can be seen with the naked eye or felt with experienced hands. But how do you take it on when it silently creeps into your internal organs? I felt desperate enough to scream. However, making a scene in a doctor's office would be un-Elizabeth-like. Nobody, after all, was ever supposed to know how I really felt because exposing a weakness would be just, well, wrong.

I was too stunned to cry. I focused on controlling my trembling fingers so I could button my shirt and tie my shoes before a nurse escorted me to a waiting area. There, I sat alone in a small spartan room furnished with hideous yellow-and-green vinyl-cushioned chairs. Periodically, my long-fingered oncologist scurried by. His hunched-over posture and inability to make eye contact revealed an intensity and frenzied nature I had not noticed before.

I felt small and overwhelmed. Nobody was there to smooth my hair, hold my hand, and tell me the lie we all crave to hear when terrified: "Don't worry, it's going to be OK." How would I explain this mess to the higher-ups at the newspaper where I had worked for a little more than a year? Would this be the constant cycle of my life? A few months of good health sandwiched between surgeries and chemical treatments? No wonder my father seemed on edge so often.

My mind raced. Would this accelerated pace mean that I, too, would lose one step and then another and another, thus allowing the drooling, ravenous cancer beast to catch me in its claws? Was the fault with me? Was I doomed by my genetic makeup, or did I have what some researchers called a "cancer personality" that made me weak or incapable of healing for the longterm? Was there something wrong, or ugly or spiritually unclean about my internal core that made me a magnet for disease? Or was I so pitiful that I wasn't even worth saving?

After a half hour or so, my awkward oncologist interrupted my bleak reverie by sitting across from me, smiling his sad smile. He didn't offer comfort, but he did have an idea. My lung masses were too dispersed and numerous to be removed surgically. But one spot in my right lung was close enough to the surface to be biopsied by a skilled surgeon. I put on my inscrutable reporter face and tried to listen.

That doctor seemed unaware of my inability to stop shaking. All he could see was melanoma. I didn't dare share my frightening, rambling thoughts. Instead, I hung onto the hope that he was like other doctors who gravitated to medicine because of an overwhelming urge to fix what was physically wrong with patients. He might not see the whole me, but that wouldn't stop him from toppling hospital hierarchies, insurance dilemmas, and government regulations to help. After all, he wasn't about to let a twenty-seven-year-old die on his watch, right?

Within weeks, a modicum of order emerged from what felt like non-navigable chaos. I set a date for in-patient surgery. My newspaper editors were kind and supportive. Friends offered to transport me to and from the hospital in Madison. My older sister, married and living a few hours away near Chicago, agreed to come to my Janesville apartment to look after me as I recovered.

By March 1989, I was admitted. Two of my ribs had to be separated to reach the spot in my right lung. When the anesthesia wore off, I felt as if I had taken successive punches from Joe Louis, Rocky Marciano, and Muhammad Ali. And I did not consider myself a pain weenie. I didn't miss a day of work after I dislocated my left elbow playing soccer. In a separate incident, I broke my left ankle in an ice-slick parking lot. Hobbled, I then drove twenty miles, operating the clutch pedal with that injured foot. After the lung surgery, I spent several excruciating days in the hospital. My doctor delivered the pathology report in person: malignant melanoma. Left alone, the black blobs were likely to grow or break away. Something needed to be done, but what?

On a return visit, my oncologist laid out four options. Two were traditional chemotherapy pills. The other two were types of immunotherapy. They were supposed to beat back the cancer by harnessing my immune system. Both were similar to the experimental interferon treatment I had undergone in Vermont, but considered more cutting-edge. Of course, none of the proposed treatments guaranteed a cure and no answer was right or wrong.

I told my doctor I needed time to evaluate. Choosing a treatment that day seemed a ridiculous eeny, meeny, miny, mo exercise.

Chemical and biological treatments available for melanoma in the late 1980s seemed the equivalent of crapshoots—because they were. Interviewing specialists and reading study results offered me guidance but no definitive solution. Success rates with the two oral chemotherapies were abysmal. Believe me, the idea of swallowing a cure-all sounded appealing—even if side effects included losing your hair and your appetite. I eliminated both as little more than placebos, narrowing my choices by half.

My oncologist riffed eloquently about monoclonal antibodies, convinced that nascent research would soon position these proteins as a miracle cure. Treatments called for injecting my veins with the antibodies so these biological molecules could bind to specific target cells. In theory, they would either attack my tumors directly or shuttle toxins to selected cancer cells.

To create monoclonal antibodies back then, scientists injected human cancer cells into mice. In response, the mouse immune system created antibodies that could fend off these cancer cells. Then, the scientists removed the mouse plasma cells that produced the antibodies and fused them with laboratory-grown cells to create hybrid cells. Hybrid cells can indefinitely produce large quantities of pure antibodies. One risk was that the mouse "signature" could trigger an immune reaction that could block the monoclonal antibodies' action and sometimes cause a life-threatening form of immune shock in a patient. Today, cultured human cells can make

115

monoclonal antibodies, but the mouse option was the only one available in the late 1980s.

My oncologist's idea was to craft monoclonal antibodies specific to the antigens on the surface of my melanoma cells. Simply put, an antigen is a substance introduced to stimulate the production of an antibody. In theory, the monoclonal antibodies would help boost my immune response by either interfering directly with melanoma cells or delivering poisons such as anticancer drugs or radioactive substances to my cancerous growths.

I wanted to believe that monoclonal antibodies were magic, the type of silver bullet that cancer researchers had pursued for decades. But literature on results was very thin. Plus, I learned that my oncologist had real skin in the monoclonal antibody game. His research centered on that science, and he needed numbers, results, and willing participants to justify pursuing it. Realizing that a vulnerable patient could be manipulated was quite a wake-up call. Naïvely, I had believed that my oncologist would search nationwide for a cure, not funnel me toward his personal research project. I crossed monoclonal antibodies off my list.

The other immunotherapy choice was interleukin-2. Evidently, my body already naturally secreted interleukin-2. It's part of the body's immune system, a messenger molecule designed to alert other cells about infectious invaders. Interleukin-2, one of many interleukins, was prized as an anti-melanoma weapon because it stimulated the growth of two types of white blood cells. Specifically, these are known as T and B lymphocytes. They are supposed to be powerful enough to topple melanoma. The interleukin-2 for my treatment would not come from my body. Instead, it was mass-produced at a medical facility that deployed genetic engineering to mimic the natural version.

My oncologist gave me a videotape about interleukin-2 that I watched at home. It opened with an active young woman about my age looking straight into the camera and telling her heartbreaking cancer story. Her will to live impresses me to this day because I can still see her hopeful face in my mind's eye. By the end of the video, however, this poor courageous woman had died in spite of her valor. My hand quivered when I tried to punch the recorder's eject button. It was difficult to detect whether the melanoma or the interleukin-2 had killed her. To me, this was a case of the cure being worse than the disease.

My options had dwindled to zero.

Needing a fresh approach, I did what any sensible woman would do. I called my mother. I felt guilty burdening her with more melanoma worries after all she had endured with my father, but I had no doubt she would do everything in her power to keep me breathing. We'd had conversations that nibbled around the edges of how my father died, but I wasn't yet able to formulate the questions I wanted desperately to ask. There were too many layers of hurt, doubt, and insecurity to peel away before I'd be ready for that task. I also didn't want her to know how scared I was about the trajectory of my life, and she probably didn't want to admit her fears either.

In addition to all of that, the rewind button in my brain kept getting stuck on a vignette from 1986, when the melanoma had jumped from my skin to my lymph system and I was preparing for my year-long interferon treatment. My mother had invited me to her house for a long weekend, and at the last minute, I had invited my friend and co-worker along—the one who helped me with the injections. What stuck in my mind about that weekend was how my mother worried about dinner. She was planning to serve lobster and was fretting because there might not be enough with an extra person at the table. I appreciated her efforts to prepare a delicious meal, but I really didn't care if I had to split a lobster seventeen ways. I just didn't want to feel sad and isolated. I needed to feel loved and embraced. How could I build a bond and talk about what mattered most with a mother so intent on maintaining order and formality? It made me feel distant from her.

Despite those strains, we were allies in 1989. From my apartment in Wisconsin and her house in Massachusetts, we hunted and gathered information about melanoma treatments and vaccines by calling cancer centers nationwide. We were hounds on a trail, and we compared notes regularly. Responses were sincere and supportive. I was astounded to discover how eager nurses and doctors were to supply information via fax, phone, and snail mail to a twentysomething woman with melanoma in her lungs.

Still, it was unsettling to read studies about cancer treatments that laid out patient outcomes. Even though they are about people, they lack humanity. Statisticians boil a human life down to a number to give a snapshot of survival odds. But numbers are just that—numbers. Lumped together, they don't provide a full picture of the participants. Are they deteriorating octogenarians or robust athletes? Is this their first treatment or last in a long string? Are they involved in their own treatment decisions or leaving those up to doctors?

Ironically, after several weeks of research, our most promising lead came from the cancer clinic in Hanover, New Hampshire, where I had gone when I lived in Vermont and where my father had been treated before he died. It was a chemotherapy treatment devised by a team in the 1980s, and the survival rate was higher than any other treatment we found. One contributor was Dr. Paul LeMarbre, an oncologist and Dartmouth

117

College graduate. Referred to as the "Dartmouth regime," it called for a cocktail of three chemicals to be administered intravenously. It had one unusual twist. In tandem, the patient also swallowed a dose of tamoxifen in pill form. To me, the prescribed drugs sounded like a pharmaceutical alphabet soup—cisplatin (DDP), carmustine (BCNU), and dacarbazine (DTIC). Tamoxifen, which acts as an anti-estrogen agent, is recognized as a treatment for breast cancer. Surprisingly, LeMarbre and the other researchers had noticed the presence of estrogen receptors in melanomas. They hypothesized that tamoxifen mixed with other chemotherapy drugs could shrink or eliminate any melanoma tumors.

I latched onto the encouraging results of the Dartmouth regime study like the proverbial bee to a nectar-filled flower. I wanted those damn tumors—floating in my lungs like spilled corn flakes—out of my body. Dr. LeMarbre spoke with me on the telephone about his protocol. What struck me was his calmness. He answered all of my questions and acted as if being on the telephone with me was the most important task of his day. He was optimistic, he told me, but he couldn't guarantee success. I knew that, I replied, but I wanted to sign up anyway, as long as the drugs could be administered in Madison. I needed a treatment I could believe in. After all our research, his was the only one that offered me real hope. I figured nothing was wrong with that.

My skeptical side wondered if I was being a bit too rash, jumping at a therapy because the numbers looked convincing and the doctor sounded so kind. After all, that same hospital in New Hampshire hadn't been able to save my father's life. But I didn't want to discount it for that reason. My Madison doctor was surprised I chose a treatment he hadn't suggested, but he assured me he could administer it.

After settling on a treatment, I felt relieved and tranquil. A few weeks before my first round of chemotherapy that spring, I drifted off alone in the bed of my Janesville apartment. It was the entire first floor of a large two-story Victorian house. In the earliest gray of morning, before the first bird had started to croon, I had a very unusual experience. Groggy but awake enough to be cognizant of my surroundings, my relaxed body felt enveloped in what I can only describe as a safe, silky cocoon. Granted, I was covered with a sheet, but this wasn't just the soft brush of cotton.

I detected the presence of a being—a benevolent one—hovering over the entire length of me, just inches away. It wasn't applying enough pressure to immobilize me, but I was pleasantly paralyzed. That comforting sensation of utter safety lasted maybe a minute or two—I wasn't counting—but I was coated with warmth. Not wanting to spoil the sensation, I remained motionless.

CHAPTER 20
NORTHERN COLORADO: OPULENCE AND NATURAL RICHES

MILES RIDDEN: 1,758
MILES TO GO: 2,492

Mother Nature's ferocious dryer blew me into Colorado—my fifth state—near the North Platte River on September 17, where Highway 230 morphed into Highway 125. Pitching a tent in that wind was trying. If rebar weren't so heavy to carry, I would have used it to replace my flimsy aluminum tent stakes. Why do forecasters even try to predict what the skies of the Rocky Mountains will deliver? Don't they know these giants just scoff at such predictions by manufacturing their own weather?

Though the landscapes appeared pristine from a distance, closer examination revealed property altered significantly by hordes of pick-and shovel-wielding money-grubbers seeking their share of gold, silver, lead, copper, and whatever else they could extricate from Mother Earth. The region on the Wyoming-Colorado border now called North Park had once been home to giant herds of American bison nourished by lush grasses of the valley, as well as to beaver, muskrat, elk, deer, and bobcat. While horses and cattle now reign in this land of ranches, where beef is indeed what's for dinner, I was pleased that North Park High School in Walden still claimed a wildcat as its mascot. *Park*, I learned, is an English bastardization of the French word for game preserve, *parc*.

At my lunch stop in tiny Cowdrey, a friendly storekeeper warned me that traffic would increase dramatically in sixty or so miles at Highway 9. Unfortunately, he was right. Traffic might have been light when this central Colorado bike route had been mapped in the 1970s, but it had exploded in tandem with subdivisions and strip malls. Hundreds of cars whizzed by.

"Route 9 is a suicide mission," a well-sculpted trainer/physiologist told me when I stopped to do outreach at a wellness center near Kremmling. "I reroute every bicyclist I see." When I protested that I was a purist who had vowed to ride every foot of trail as marked on my maps, he just rolled his eyes and sketched an alternate route. "This will add eight or ten miles to your day but likely prolong your life." I relented when I found out he had been a finalist for Olympic rowing and cycling teams.

And I was glad I did. I encountered only half a dozen vehicles on the trainer's recommended detour on a rustic dirt road through the Arapaho National Forest. Plus, I felt like the queen of speed when I passed four riders on horseback. Lack of traffic allowed me the luxury of drinking in 360-degree views of craggy peaks and conifers. The only hazard was the occasional maw of a metal cattle guard, where dismounting was a wise move.

Pedaling through the opulent Colorado ski towns of Silverthorne, Frisco, and Breckenridge was a shock to my minimalist and tragically unhip makeup. Fortunately, about fourteen miles of that section was on an oasis of a bike trail, but busy roads were sprinkled with "shoppes," starter mansions, and all manner of trendy accoutrements designed for the beautiful people. These communities seemed so otherworldly that I found it fitting and funny that until relatively recently, Breckenridge wasn't sure it was even part of this country. Northwestern Colorado was originally part of the Louisiana Purchase, but because boundaries were unclear, some land was evidently overlooked when the Colorado Territory was sliced into counties. In 1932, the US Land Office confirmed there was doubt about the legality of a claim to a section of Colorado measuring ninety miles by thirty miles, which included Breckenridge. After multiple legal gyrations, the US Attorney General's office suggested that Congress annex the territory in question. The parcel was proclaimed part of the Union at an August 8, 1936, ceremony in Breckenridge.

I, too, was relieved to know I was officially in these United States on September 20, when I neared the apex of the TransAmerica Trail. Reaching that highest point required an eleven-mile, lung-pumping elevation gain of 1,500 feet from Breckenridge to 11,542-foot Hoosier Pass. The last four miles featured a series of strenuous switchbacks with hairpin turns. To complicate matters, the shoulder on Highway 9 was about as wide as a bolo tie and the asphalt was regularly usurped by a phalanx of dump trucks hauling gravel from a quarry in nearby Alma.

At the top, I took a few swigs of sparkling cider to reward my titanium nerves and celebrate my final crossing of the western Continental Divide. I also read a plaque that answered one of the moment's most pressing questions: Why was a pass deep in the Colorado Rockies named for people from pancake-flat Indiana? Evidently, some Indianans had "discovered" and mined gold from nearby Hoosier Gulch starting in 1860. The only gold I noticed was on the leaves of shimmering aspen trees, which had traded their drab summer green for a bedazzling autumn wardrobe.

Preparing for the Hoosier Pass descent, I felt downright giddy anticipating a rip-roaring downhill that would allow my legs and lungs to relax. "If you could be anywhere in the world right now, Elizabeth, where would you want to be?" I yelled to myself as the wind whistled an odd tune through the vents of my red helmet. "Right here," I answered. "Right here." I was thirty-four days and nineteen hundred miles into my exhilarating adventure. A Wisconsin friend had referred to my trip as "cycle therapy," and she was correct. Out here, it was just me, my resolve, and the bicycle. I had stripped life down to its barest essence of muscle and bone by shedding all the extraneous and complicating layers. I didn't need a compass or road sign to tell me which way north was. Lying in my tent on starry nights, I scanned the sky for the reliable and expansive Big Dipper. Two stars at the end of its ladle pointed directly to the North Star. That North Star, or Polaris, anchored the tip of the bent handle of the harder-to-find Little Dipper.

Corny as it might sound, I could not pedal through this part of Colorado without a certain John Denver song echoing in my helmeted noggin. Talk about feeling dwarfed. These "Rocky Mountain Highs" were a resplendent blend of rugged snow-covered peaks that served as a backdrop for a mosaic of willows, aspens, and bristlecone pines.

On the other side of Hoosier Pass, South Park unfolded. The Middle Fork of the South Platte River courses through a region that was once a mining hotspot. South Park is also the inspiration behind that cable television comedy with the weird-looking, smart-alecky cartoon characters. I scooted into the tiny settlement of Alma for lunch at a natural foods store.

The store owner, who good-naturedly took the recyclables I had been hauling for miles, asked me if I had lost weight on the ride. "Well, I know there's less of me because my freckled McCheeks seem smaller," I told her, pointing to my face. "And I have to cinch the drawstring on my cycling shorts tighter."

When I asked about her life there, she revealed that she had been treated like a heretic for initiating a recycling program. "This area has a lot of Rush Limbaugh thinking going on," she explained. "People see all these trees out there and know there are more minerals underground, and ask why they have to reuse anything when they can just go out and cut or dig more."

From Alma, it was just another six miles to Fairplay, supposedly named by miners seeking equal opportunity. Though it boasted a population of eight thousand during the silver- and gold-mining heyday of the 1860s, that number had plummeted to about four hundred when I arrived.

Sage, a well-worn local I befriended in the dining room at the rustic Fairplay Hotel, was a cowboy in the summer and a ski bum in the winter. He informed me that the town was quirky and loaded with characters.

When I told him I didn't have time for a deep dive because I was just passing through, he replied, "That's the best way to see it." I wasn't sure if he was encouraging me to enjoy the scenery at a slower, two-wheeler pace or if I was lucky to be a short-term visitor in a forlorn town. I must have been a little punchy because I couldn't stop laughing when I told Sage about two signs I had seen earlier that day indicating the area had too many lawyers. One was in the bathroom of my campground in Frisco. "For your own safety," it warned campers, "please do not sit on the sink." The second was attached to the sliding board at a playground in Kremmling: "Caution, slide might be hot." Fortunately, for those not paying attention, the hospital's emergency room was right across the street.

The miners might be gone, but Fairplay maintains a link to their beasts of burden by promoting itself as the world's Burro Capital. A burro is the mascot of South Park High School, and Fairplay's annual Gold Days Celebration has had an annual 29.5-mile burro race since 1949. Racers can walk, run, or carry their four-legged friends, but they are not allowed to ride. Winners' names are listed on a shrine to burros.

Fairplay's elevation is close to ten thousand feet, and that was the last night I would be spending at such heights. The next day, September 21, I roughly traced the Middle Fork of the South Platte River on Route 9 as I aimed for Cañon City. That morning, cold wind and rain chased me up 9,404-foot Currant Creek Pass, but blue sky emerged early that afternoon and temperatures hovered in the upper seventies as I plunged down, down, down through Mack Gulch. I felt a tinge of sadness leaving the Rocky Mountains behind, but I welcomed the rich, earthy pungency of fall just a few days shy of the autumnal equinox. The uplifting mix of dark-green junipers, flaming berry bushes, and the scarlet and orange scrub oaks on the rock-strewn canyon walls fooled me momentarily into believing I was immersed in the fiery fall foliage of my native New England. A buoying tailwind propelled me the last three miles to a place called Buffalo Bill's Campground, at the intersection of Highways 9 and 50, about eight miles west of Cañon City. I had pedaled sixty-eight miles and dropped about forty-five hundred feet since Fairplay.

Plenty of daylight allowed me to explore a nearby ecological wonder, Royal Gorge Park. I was reminded that lush mountains were indeed behind me as I meandered through a dry landscape sprinkled with piñon, juniper, and prickly pear cactus. Soon, there loomed the Arkansas River's spectacular Royal Gorge, deep enough to induce vertigo. The ribbon of river looked like a trickle at the bottom of a schism carved out over thousands of years in the surrounding gneiss and schist, both types of metamorphic rock. I toured a tiny, newly opened, state-operated nature center that showcased minerals, birds, and mammals of the region. Signs also explained the dangers of poaching, how to identify animal scat, and the difference between horns and antlers. From an outside deck, I savored the sight of a soaring peregrine falcon. Colorado had recently reintroduced the species to this ideal bird-of-prey habitat.

Not so savory were booths peddling overpriced food, an attraction promoted as the world's highest suspension bridge, and a tourist train chugging to the bottom of the gorge. These man-made elements were managed by the same outfit that operated a chain of amusement parks. Unfortunately, that jarring juxtaposition lent this geographical gem a circus-like atmosphere. Royal Gorge, I thought sadly, was now more like Royal Gouge.

CHAPTER 21
YOU CALL THIS A CURE?

The earnest student nurse patted my wrist repeatedly, attempting to stimulate a promising vein. Meanwhile, I channeled every ounce of my fading energy into transforming that vein from the pitiful, quick-to-retreat specimen I knew it was to the ropy and prominent sort sported by the likes of tennis phenomenon Martina Navratilova. It was a rare medical professional who could start an intravenous drip on me with one try, but this June 1989 experience bordered on absurd.

While I was propped up on a pile of pillows on a bed at University Hospital in Madison, principled Chinese college students protesting government oppression had been massacred during a horrific confrontation in Tiananmen Square. Those noble demonstrators, many close to my age, had died bravely. I felt like a coward. I was facing a nurse wielding an IV catheter, not a military tank. She had me on the verge of tears after four failed attempts to stab veins in my hands and wrists. I was trying to be a patient patient in this teaching hospital but was ready to bolt when she suggested to her late-to-arrive supervisor that maybe she should resort to a vein in my foot. That was my limit.

"No, that's enough," I said in my best authoritative voice. "I know you're learning, but I can't be a pincushion. I told you my veins were problematic. It's time to find somebody who can handle this."

I earned a small victory when the supervisor ordered the trainee aside. Minutes passed before an older nurse arrived.

"You shouldn't have to tolerate all of that," she told me as she expertly jabbed my most reliable vein, the one inside my right elbow, layered with scar tissue.

"That's the one I pleaded with her to use," I responded, wiping my eyes. "But she thought she knew better. Thank you for listening."

Within seconds, a saline solution in a bag hanging on a steel pole was drip, drip, dripping through loops of plastic tubing and into my arm. Two of my loyal Wisconsin friends, Barb and Anna, entered the room with my mother, and pulled chairs up to my bed. They shared a bag of popcorn from the cafeteria. I nibbled on a few kernels even though I wasn't hungry, just nervous.

Weeks earlier, I had called my mother in Massachusetts to tell her I could muddle through the chemotherapy on my own. "Wild horses

wouldn't keep me away," she replied. "I'm buying an airplane ticket now."
She and I drove from Janesville to the hospital very early on the day my
chemotherapy was scheduled to begin.

That morning, the four of us discussed the news, our families, and
our jobs—anything but the ominous plastic bags of chemicals with
unpronounceable names hanging just a few feet away. We grew accustomed
to the constant interruptions from entourages of doctors, nurses, and
students who paraded through my room to poke me, study my chart, take
my vital signs, and pepper me with a rat-a-tat-tat of repetitive questions:
How old are you? "Twenty-eight." What are you here for? "Chemotherapy
to treat melanoma." Do you smoke? "What? No, never." My idealistic side
revered the idea of a teaching hospital, but my practical side wondered if I
really needed this extra layer of torture.

Cancer veterans had warned me about the brutal toll of these chemicals,
but I was an optimistic rookie. I envisioned the poison cocktail as medicine
for my ailing lungs, figuring I could persevere through a couple hours of
anything if it meant a cure.

Once the clear liquid of the Dartmouth regime began coursing through
me late that afternoon, I could hear the nearby conversation but could not
speak. I felt miles distant from people just five or six feet away. I could see
lips moving, but I could not make out what was being said. I felt paralyzed.
If my eyes were open, why was the light fading? I had the urge to grab the
walls, to keep from being dragged into a dim, looming tunnel. I couldn't
get my bearings. Disembodied voices floated around me. Images moved in
the slowest of motion. A force was tugging, tugging, tugging at my feet.
Why didn't somebody grab my torso and pull me back into the world?

I panicked when what felt like a foam ball lodged in my throat. I tasted
dreck as the few handfuls of popcorn rose from my stomach. Or maybe it
was someone else's body? I could no longer distinguish between what I was
watching and what I was experiencing. I don't know where that mess from
my mouth landed, and I felt so sick and disconnected that I did not even
care. "Is this what it feels like when you die?" my loopy brain asked. "No,"
came the answer, "this is how you feel when you want to be dead."

When I woke from my stupor hours later, the only visitor remaining
was my mother. It was close to midnight, and my friends had already driven
home. I had conked out before the fluids had drained from the plastic bags.
The nurses had said chemotherapy affects everybody differently. I felt jittery
and itchy, as if tiny ants were crawling all over me. I ripped the bandage
off my arm.

"Can't we open the windows?" I yelled. "I feel trapped. I have to get out
of here. I need to go home immediately."

127

My mother, alarmed by my unfiltered behavior, said she would check with the nurses.

Frantically, I awaited her return. If they wouldn't let me go, I thought about tying the sheets together to escape, even if it required breaking a window.

"The nurses let me sign you out," said my mother as she crept back into the room. "You can change, and I'll pack your belongings."

"I can't wait that long," I said, hurriedly pulling my jacket, pants, and shoes over the hospital-issue gown and socks. "What's the fastest way out?"

I bolted to the garage to track down my little red pickup truck, my mother trailing behind me. As she drove, I stuck my head out the passenger side window for the entire forty-minute trip home. The fresh air soothed my skin and cleansed the antiseptic hospital oxygen out of my lungs. We pulled into my apartment driveway at about two in the morning. It was a starry night.

That spring and summer, I endured three more rounds of those wretched treatments. After the first session, I insisted that the hospital administer subsequent rounds on weekends because I needed some sense of order. That way, I could maintain a semiregular work schedule. After each session, I had to wait two, three, or four weeks for my depleted red blood cell counts to recover enough to tolerate another blast. At least the hospital staff had the sense to give me anti-nausea drugs during the ensuing treatments. I don't know why they skipped that medication during my first round. I needed to retain all the calories I could.

Food tasted bad and smelled worse. The scent of coffee sent me to the bathroom to wretch or convulse with dry heaves. I punched extra holes in my belts because my clothes hung on my dwindling frame so loosely. A silver pinkie ring I had worn for years would not stay on my thinning finger. Miraculously, I did not lose my hair. But at that point I would have traded every hair on my body for my health.

One summer day between chemotherapy rounds two and three, a severe throbbing in my head prompted me to visit an oncologist at the clinic just minutes from my apartment. I had neither the time nor the energy to drive almost forty miles to Madison. That local oncologist didn't have my medical records but agreed to an emergency appointment. After listening to a synopsis of my cancer story, he announced officiously that I needed an immediate brain scan. The headaches had manifested "because the melanoma had probably spread to your brain," he told me coldly. "The scan will probably show lesions."

"How could this happen so fast?" I asked, shuddering in horror. "I thought I would have more time." I left his office feeling overwhelmed and dejected. A few hours later, I called an oncology nurse in Madison and relayed to her the episode with the local cancer specialist.

"You need to stay away from him," she said calmly but firmly. "The chemotherapy is causing your red blood cell count to drop. That's restricting the flow of oxygen to your brain and causing those pounding headaches."

Those symptoms would disappear once the chemotherapy ended, she told me, adding that any over-the-counter pain medicine would offer relief.

"Well, I wish somebody could have told me that when I was in Madison," I said. "This is all new for me. Sometimes I just don't know what to ask."

She was exactly right about the effect of the over-the-counter medicine. But when I felt better, I couldn't stop thinking about that menace of a local doctor. If he had scared me so, what was he doing to his regular patients? I needed to speak up, so I called his office. I was surprised he came to the phone.

"Look, you really frightened me yesterday," I said politely. "I don't understand how you could make such an off-the-cuff conclusion with so little evidence. Dealing with cancer is scary enough. Aren't you supposed to help people instead of making their situation worse?"

"I remember you," he said. "I made the most appropriate recommendation based on the evidence you provided. I didn't treat you any differently than I would one of my regular patients."

That was it. He wasn't going to apologize. And I wasn't going to back down.

"Well, I was the one with the headaches, but maybe you're the one who needs his head examined," I said.

"Do you need anything else?" he asked.

There was nothing else to say, so I hung up, elated that the treatments had not drained the fight out of me.

I finished my third, and what was supposed to be my final, round of chemotherapy in early August 1989. The follow-up X-rays and scans revealed that the tumors in my lungs had not budged. They taunted me from their unreachable recesses. Ugh!

After weighing the pros and cons with my oncologists in Madison and New Hampshire, I opted to undergo a fourth round. The data was based on three rounds, but adding another was a medically sound decision, not an indulgence for a desperate patient. Nobody knew what would happen—and it wasn't as if I had a whole list of other options. Double ugh!

That last round was administered in September. Scans showed it hadn't dislodged the stubborn tumors.

I was angry and disappointed. What was the point of abusing my body almost beyond repair for more than four months, and then having nothing to show for it? I wanted the cancer GONE. The longer it lingered, the more I feared breakaway cells would lodge in other organs. When melanoma traveled, whether to the lungs, the brain, the liver, or wherever, it didn't become lung, brain, or liver cancer. It was still melanoma. Now what?

One doctor tried to calm me by emphasizing that while my tumors hadn't shrunk or disappeared, at least they weren't growing—an encouraging sign with melanoma. That might have sounded comforting to him, but he wasn't the one waking up at two in the morning in a sweat-soaked T-shirt, panicking about what kind of a future he would be able to forge. Usually, the sharpest needle of worry pricked me awake in the wee hours. I was so fearful that any new bump on my leg or pain in my chest was cancer mocking me yet again. To soothe myself during those night terrors, I walked for hours in my neighborhood, seeking comfort in familiar landmarks.

I was haunted by questions nobody could answer: What if the lung tumors spread with abandon? How would I find health insurance if I lost my job? Would I have the luxury of making it to age thirty? I didn't want "stabilized" tumors. I wanted a pair of healthy lungs without black spots. And I didn't know where to turn.

CHAPTER 22
EASTERN COLORADO: FROM THE ROCKIES TO THE GRAIN RANGE

MILES RIDDEN: 2,009
MILES TO GO: 2,241

Bicyclists eastbound on Highway 67 take a sharp left turn onto Highway 96 near Wetmore, Colorado. That intersection is where the southerly trajectory from Oregon ends and a more straightforward easterly route begins. I arrived at that juncture on the morning of September 22, pulling on my rain jacket just as looming nimbus clouds wetted Wetmore.

While waiting out the worst of the cloudburst on the porch of a closed restaurant, I tempted four feral cats living under the house next door with cheese pretzels. They seemed content to accept the human snacks as their breakfast. Temperatures tipping between the high sixties and low seventies made for comfortable riding despite intermittent showers.

Since leaving the Cañon City campground that morning, I had pedaled through rocky canyons and past an array of buttes. Cholla cactus, prickly pear cactus, and sagebrush reigned. Wetmore marked more than a distinct topographical transition from the Rocky Mountains to the plateau of the Great Plains; one day I had been staring affluence in the face near Vail, and forty-eight hours later I was shaking hands with Hardscrabble, USA. Mountain ranges formed naturally from rising rock were replaced with man-made peaks that I had christened the Grain Range. Residents must either be hard of hearing or merely immune to the steady, day-in and day-out, irritating whine of these ubiquitous grain elevators. Maybe to them, it sounded like money.

Just twenty-eight miles beyond Wetmore lay Pueblo, a city I always associated with those public service announcements broadcast on long-ago late-night television. They touted an assortment of federal government information packets free to any alert citizen who dialed a toll-free number or wrote to a post office box in that Colorado city. I had long pictured the city as a settlement flush with acre upon acre of identical Quonset huts that served as repositories for millions of those pamphlets. On my ride, however, I found no such structures. But I did note that Pueblo served as the physical halfway point of my journey. It's roughly where I started to tabulate miles to go before miles already pedaled. Yes, I still had more than twenty-one hundred miles ahead of me, but it was a psychological boost.

Pueblo had humble beginnings in 1842, when three fur traders built a fort at the confluence of Fountain Creek and the Arkansas River. The community was dubbed El Pueblo because buildings were made of mud and logs, mimicking the adobe dwellings of Indians of the Southwest. A village soon prospered because of its proximity to the gold and silver mines of South Park, to the north, and to coal mines to the south. Later, mineral reserves and the hydroelectric potential of the Arkansas River attracted smelting operations.

Unfortunately, the outskirts of Pueblo, now a community of almost a hundred thousand, sported strip malls and the same eyesore of urban sprawl consuming acres of this country's countryside and former farmland. However, unless it was just wishful thinking on my part, a river walk and a convention center signaled a revival in the heart of downtown.

Lingering storm clouds convinced me that Pueblo would become my temporary home after fifty-five miles of pedaling. Aware that rain was forecast for at least the next thirty-six hours, I opted for indoor accommodations at a budget hotel. When September 23 dawned damp and cold, I stayed another night. I was delighted to be holed up in the Pueblo library pounding out a journal update. The library had only one public-access computer, and the charge was a dollar an hour, so just on principle, I wrote my speediest entry yet.

Temperatures sank into the low forties as an iron-colored sky shed sheets of rain all day. I figured the bicycle goddess, a creature I chose to believe in at times like this, must have been lurking nearby, because while raindrops were plentiful, I had thus far been able to sneak between the snowflakes. *The Denver Post* I read in the library informed me that I had missed—by just one day—a blizzard, which dumped fourteen inches on my route over the Rockies. The parts of Wyoming I had pedaled through just a week before were now covered with at least eight inches of the white stuff. Timing, as they say, is everything.

I might have avoided the snow, but not the cold. I left Pueblo on September 24 bundled in layers. Pedaling along those plains reminded me of just how thirsty the West was. In eastern Colorado, grass crunched like Shredded Wheat cereal, and the drought made life dicey for crops of wheat, milo, millet, corn, melons, sunflowers, and soybeans. Squint and squint as I might, I couldn't slit my eyes enough to transform the beef cattle littering the landscape into American bison. The government's wholesale slaughter of these noble beasts in the nineteenth century, and the simultaneous positioning of railroad tracks to divide bison herds, ultimately altered

133

Native Americans' existence forever by stripping them of their livelihood. Only handfuls of bison remained by the early 1880s. Never mind that constant warfare with white settlers and the US government had already diminished the Plains Indians numbers.

While I didn't spot any bison, I did spy one last herd of pronghorn in eastern Colorado that gracefully raced me along Highway 96. If not for the impediment of a fence, they would have out-scampered my bipedal self in a few heartbeats.

I felt like a tumbleweed blowing through dusty, dilapidated, and barely existent towns of eastern Colorado, where empty homes and vacant stores, some with inventories still intact, were caving in on themselves. People had apparently voted with their feet and left for more prosperous environs, opening the way for restoration of the Buffalo Commons of the Great Plains. It seemed right to let Mother Nature reclaim what had always been hers, replenishing it with native plants and animals. Aren't there some places where human beings should be visitors, not permanent residents?

In Kiowa County along Highway 96, a campaign sign for a county commissioner candidate announced: "Elect a man with drive to keep this county alive!" *Why bother?* I thought. Very few people had evidently heeded the advice of a sign stenciled on a caved-in building: "Welcome to Olney Springs. A Place to Invest the Rest of Your Life."

I was shocked, yet pleased, to happen upon one very much alive creature as I neared Sugar City, where I planned to camp on September 24. A brown, hairy tarantula about the size of my palm crawled purposefully along the asphalt shoulder. Such pluck and tenacity. I stopped to track its progress for fifteen to twenty minutes, and remarkably, it seemed to be using the white line as a guide.

Sagging Sugar City was yet another community hanging on by its raggedy fingernails. Tiny homes where the town's last generation of retirees lived bordered a small municipal park. It was still open to bicyclists, though it offered neither toilets nor running water. The greeting party was a gaggle of semi-feral cats meowing for a head scratch or a taste of tuna. The map profile of my route through western Colorado had such a string of heart-challenging, severe ups and downs that it resembled an electrocardiogram. That flatlined in the plateau of eastern Colorado. The mapmakers hadn't bothered to include a profile of the terrain. A week earlier, I had been whipping down Colorado's Hoosier Pass, and now I was just above forty-three hundred feet—an elevation drop of seven thousand-plus feet in seven days.

"Welcome to what's left of Sugar City," said the woman who introduced herself as the chef, waitress, and dishwasher of the city's sole surviving, and empty, restaurant. "I'm Lynette. Sit wherever you want."

She was also willing to pinch-hit as historian when I prodded. In June, she explained, 252 residents had celebrated the city's centennial in the park where I was camped. A sugar beet factory, the city's namesake, had opened in November 1900. Back then, two thousand residents enjoyed saloons, drug stores, grocery stores, hotels, and even a bowling alley. The community was hollowed out when the National Sugar Manufacturing Company left in 1967.

I enjoyed the lilt of her Western accent, especially the way she pronounced "squarsh" and "warsh." In western Massachusetts, I told her, the natives leave the r off the end of certain words. So, "drawer" becomes "draw." Those extra consonants must have been shipped west just for her.

"That's not all that's funny about me," she said. "I don't like children, but I raised a son who is studying to be a teacher. And I really hate to cook, but I've been operating this restaurant for seventeen years. What about that?"

"It's OK," I told her. "All humans are a series of contradictions. I call myself a newspaper reporter, but I hate daily deadlines. Maybe that's why I'm really out here riding, to escape all of that, not to raise awareness about melanoma."

"One reason I keep cooking is because the other jobs seem so awful," she said, mentioning options in the livestock yard, road construction, the county jail, and the state prison. "When they built that new prison, my friend was so excited to earn a good wage with benefits."

Then, the monotony and day-after-day contact with violent offenders gradually consumed him.

"He started drinking and drugging like the rest of them," she said. "Then he and his wife divorced. It's all so depressing."

But it seems to be a never-ending cycle in these remote, run-down areas that are promised prosperity with marginal jobs. That prison Lynette talked about sounded like the modern version of mining. It left people and communities more broken than whole.

On September 25, I pedaled east on Highway 96 yet again. After about thirty-three miles, I stopped in Haswell (which I dubbed Hasbeen) to see what was billed as the nation's smallest jail. The defunct oddity built in 1921 measures ten by twelve feet. A bed and a commode were all that was visible when I peeked through the window of the whitewashed adobe building. Fortunately, nobody was on either. Turning old-fashioned lockups into museums seemed to be a trend. Rawlins, Wyoming, and Cañon City, Colorado, tried to lure tourists with the same fad.

I finally met another eastbound cross-country cyclist beyond Haswell.

All Heals on Wheels supporters received this post-ride thank you in December 2000.

Adventure Cycling's TransAmerica Bicycle Trail stretches 4,250 miles.

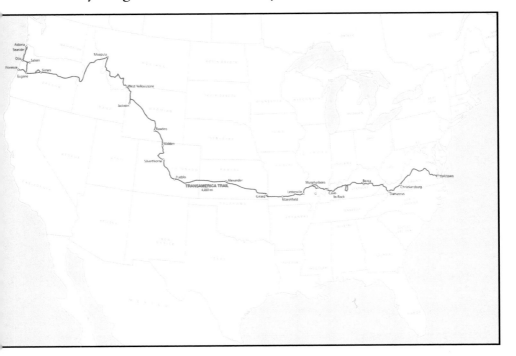

A young Elizabeth, left, pedals with her older sister, Jennifer, near their house in Philadelphia.

Ron McGowan with his four daughters at the Grand Canyon in the summer of 1971.

Susan McGowan with Carolyn, Jennifer, Elizabeth, and, in front, Gretchen, on Cape Cod, Massachusetts in 1968.

Ron and Susan McGowan bookend Jennifer, Elizabeth, Carolyn, and Gretchen in Philadelphia in the mid-1960s.

Ron McGowan sets up the "kitchen" at a Maine campsite in the summer of 1970; fires up the tractor at home in Massachusetts; and camps at Yellowstone National Park in the summer of 1971.

After graduating from high school, he served in the US Navy during the Korean War.

Susan and Ron McGowan in Massachusetts, February 1976.

The four McGowan sisters celebrate Carolyn's wedding in Ashfield, Massachusetts, 1994.

Elizabeth and Don revisit Springer Mountain, the southern terminus of the Appalachian Trail, in 1992, the year after finishing their thru-hikes on Mount Katahdin, October 8, 1991.

Don fixes the solar shower at Blackburn Trail Center.

Elizabeth with Don at Lulu Lake Preserve in Wisconsin and as a caretaker at Blackburn in Virginia.

Elizabeth summits Mount Katahdin in Maine, Oct. 8, 1991.

Elizabeth at Springer Mountain on April 13, 1991, before beginning her thru-hike.

start PACIFIC OCEAN

Elizabeth dips her bike in the Pacific Ocean on the Oregon coast before beginning Heals on Wheels.

WYOMING

Near the Wyoming-Colorado border, Elizabeth bucks her own bicycle bronco, wears zinc oxide to avoid a sunburned nose, and pedals through ranch country.

Scenery in Yellowstone National Park in Wyoming including Lewis Lake, right.

Powerful Wyoming winds slowed Elizabeth's pace, but also helped create the badlands in the Wind River region.

In a word, the Grand Tetons are mesmerizing.

This grave marker for Sacagawea spells her name with a "j" instead of a "g."

The Sweetwater Valley near present-day Rawlins, Wyoming, was a destination for white settlers headed west on the Oregon Trail.

COLORADO

Hoosier Pass in Colorado, the highest point on the TransAmerica Trail.

A peak near the Continental Divide at Muddy Pass in Colorado.

Colorado is laden with uphill climbs and blazing aspens that accentuate the Rockies.

Elizabeth bulks up on Wheaties, endorsed by a pre-fall-from-grace Lance Armstrong, in Frisco, Colorado.

Bison, horses, and cattle in Colorado are unfazed by passing bicyclists.

KANSAS

Visiting with tour guide Delillah at the Barbed Wire Museum in La Crosse, Kansas, was a trip highlight.

A handmade congratulations from Missouri's Blue Valley Bar; Kansas closeups of a post rock and curious livestock near Bazine.

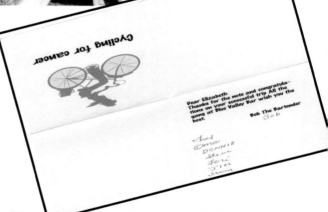

Cycling for cancer

Dear Elizabeth
Thanks for the note and congratulations on your successful trip All the gang at Blue Valley Bar wish you the best.
Bob The Bartender
Bob

MISSOURI

The regulars at the Blue Valley Bar in Missouri's Ozarks.

Bicyclists' legs catch a break along the Mississippi River flatlands.

ILLINOIS

A view of the Ohio River from the famous Cave-in-Rock.

Travelers to the Illinois cave have long left evidence of their visits.

A free ferry transports bicyclists across the Ohio River between Illinois and Kentucky.

Popeye welcomes bicyclists to Chester, Illinois, along the Mississippi River.

Shirley served every continental bicyclist a free slice of pie at Late Bloomers, her restaurant in Goreville, Illinois.

KENTUCKY

Kentucky roads were narrow, but the roadsides were flush with autumn color, patriotic hay bales, and barns near Berea used for drying tobacco and advertising tobacco products. Sonora is home to the Bucksnort Festival and the family-operated Brooks General Store. That's Delores in front of the soda machine.

An original BikeCentennial sign in Berea, Kentucky.

A National Park Service site near Sonora, Kentucky, tells the story of a young Abraham Lincoln.

VIRGINIA

Elizabeth at an overlook in the Appalachian Mountains, not too long before reaching Yorktown, Virginia, and its distinctive Victory Monument.

Transplanted Wisconsinites, Rick and Wanda, invited Elizabeth to stay overnight in Vesuvius, Virginia, adjacent to the Blue Ridge Parkway.

end
ATLANTIC OCEAN

After pedaling 4,250 miles, Elizabeth dips her bicycle tires into the Atlantic Ocean in Yorktown, Virginia.

He was standing next to a mammoth recreational vehicle equipped with everything, including the kitchen sink.

"My wife is following me all the way in this," said Bill, just retired from a career in retail. "All I'm carrying is a spare tube and a pump, so I rack up at least a hundred miles every day."

He was incredulous I hadn't been waylaid by the blizzards that had forced him to skip several hundred miles in Wyoming and Colorado. "But I live in Denver, so those will be easy to make up later."

For miles and miles near Eads, Highway 96 paralleled defunct railroad tracks. New telephone lines had been installed to my right, while the old poles, still equipped with greenish glass insulators that collectors cherish, stood to my left. The relics served as perches for hawks on the prowl and smaller birds I could not identify that sounded as if they were chirping "you can, you can, you can" repeatedly as my legs rhythmically propelled my tires.

Two prairie dogs poked their heads from a hole that was part of their extensive underground community. I wondered if they sensed the hungry coyote I saw preparing to pounce. I couldn't bear to linger long enough to watch how that predator-prey scenario played out. Besides, Kansas was beckoning.

CHAPTER 23
GEORGIA ON MY MIND

"Dying is part of life. It happens to everybody," my mother told me as we sat together on the honey-colored bottom step of the wood staircase in our Philadelphia house. "Everybody?" I asked. "So I won't be in this body forever?" This was not long after my grandmother, my mother's mother, died in Ohio. I had posed the question about death, but this wasn't the answer I wanted to hear.

The idea that death forever separated us from our parents and grandparents clawed me deep in the gut. I was a young child then, but I can still remember that distinct and raw fear. Coping without parents and that awareness of death as an adult must be terrifying. Why did anybody want to grow up?

Years later, my own cancer could reignite that same terror. And I knew I wasn't alone.

Mark Twain might have stated that death didn't frighten him because he had been dead for billions and billions of years before being born and had not "suffered the slightest inconvenience from it." It's a great laugh line. But as he aged, I doubt that was how he comforted himself privately.

That underlying fear of nonexistence crept up on me again late in the afternoon of September 13, 2000, as I pedaled into central Wyoming. Death doesn't have a ZIP code, but if it did, it could well be 82310—the five digits on the Jeffrey City post office. Options for food and shelter were limited along that stretch of Highway 287/789, and I had already ridden fifty-eight miles from Lander under a broiling sun.

Very little in Jeffrey City looked—or even smelled—alive as I surveyed the shriveled husk of a community about 150 miles east of the gloriously vibrant Grand Teton National Park. Its population barely broke triple digits, but the bleached bones of a patchwork of vacant buildings indicated a demise I didn't understand.

At the almost-deserted post office, I shed a few ounces by mailing home my first full journal and my Montana map. I also met Wallace, the longtime postmistress, who educated me with a short and to-the-point tour of Jeffrey City's spiral into Twilight Zonedom in an appealing drawl that exposed her Kentucky roots. Wallace unrolled a 1975 plat map on the counter as proof that Jeffrey City had once been a shiny boomtown without the word "no" in its vocabulary. With a manicured index finger, she showed me the neatly drawn grocery store, discount store, beauty shop, liquor store, bowling alley, motels, churches, houses, apartments, and schools that thrived when the nuclear industry was expanding and miners harvested uranium from the rocky peaks behind us. The population had whirred at five thousand strong when Jimmy Carter was elected president.

After the mines closed in the late 1970s, the remaining six grammar-school students attended classes at the former game warden's house, and middle- and high-schoolers were bused to Lander. Wallace, who had survived lung cancer seven years earlier, told me she would work until the post office shut down—any day now, she expected. At precisely five p.m., she locked the building and peeled out of the parking lot in a green pickup truck gasping for a new exhaust system. Like almost everybody else, she didn't linger. Part of me wanted to hitch a ride.

I walked around the remains, which included shabby homes, a service station, a restaurant/bar, and a Baptist church. Sagebrush covered a long-unused baseball diamond. Tumbleweeds rolled past abandoned behemoths labeled Bachelor Buildings No. 1 and No. 2, both abandoned dormitories for transitory miners. The high school, once home to the Longhorns—a fading but intimidating hand-painted mascot still visible—stood vacant next to an equally quiet elementary school.

A deteriorating Lions Club pavilion was the only shelter available, so I pitched my tent nearby. The wind, an airy broom, blew loose papers around in an adjoining clubhouse. They were typewritten minutes from decades-old Lions Club meetings. I felt like a voyeur of the past, imagining groups of earnest optimists plotting their next chicken barbecue or eyeglass collection drive for their cutting-edge town of the future.

A gargantuan orange moon, one waning day shy of full, crept above the horizon late that night, bathing the desert plateau in an eerie light. Its presence exaggerated a scene I half-expected Rod Serling to interrupt with a voice-over. My skin prickled late in the night, when I heard a wild chorus of tenors and sopranos. Coyotes were calling.

Even I, who usually did not mind vast stretches of solitude, was grateful to greet dawn. It wasn't yet light enough to ride, but I couldn't stay in my sleeping bag one minute longer. So I poked around some more in this void of a village that equally repulsed and fascinated me. This dark, abandoned place tugged at me. It wasn't cold, just windy. But I still got the shivers.

That strangeness made me think of the sincere young man I had met at a grocery store in Florence, Oregon, near the beginning of my ride. "Are you riding for the Lord?" he had asked upon seeing my Heals on Wheels T-shirt logo. I almost ignored him. But he had such a pleasing and earnest face that I felt obligated to engage. It never occurred to me that my logo had religious connotations. He explained that his wife had been treated for skin cancer recently and his sister had died of leukemia several months ago after receiving top-notch care in Seattle. I offered my sympathies. "That's OK, she's in heaven," he told me with conviction. To him, she was in heaven just as sure as he was here on Earth. A small part of me felt jealous that he had such undoubting, unbending, and absolute faith. "How is it that you do that?" I wanted to ask. "How do you believe so fervently in something you can't feel, see, or smell? If it's so easy for you, why is it so hard for me?"

On my ride, I lost count of the number of people who told me confidently that, of course, God and Jesus had healed me of cancer. They didn't discount the role of medicine but apparently thought it perfectly logical that God was the guide to survival. A woman in Idaho had asked if Heals on Wheels meant I could miraculously right people's physical wrongs by laying my hands on them. Caught off guard, I just joked to her that I didn't have that much power. Yet.

Since my first cancer diagnosis, it had always surprised me when acquaintances or colleagues told me they were praying for me—as if prayer came as easily to them as riding a bicycle did to me. It was such a foreign concept. I didn't grow up in a family that prayed for its own members, never mind non-relatives, so it moved me and relieved me that somebody thought of me that way. Catholics seemed to be the most verbal about it. I always thanked them because the offer seemed so generous and heartfelt. Even though I had come to define myself as somewhere between an agnostic and an atheist, religious faith and how people interpreted its meaning continued to fascinate me. Just because I had pretty much left organized religion behind at age twelve and didn't define myself as a traditional believer, why shut off a potential lifeline somebody was willing to toss my way?

Early on, I had wrestled with my own motives for my ride. I had made my reasons clear, but I always wondered if subconsciously other impulses lurked beneath the superficial ones. What really motivates any of us to act on what we think is a beneficial undertaking? Did I think that if I did this "good" thing, it would insulate me from being punished with more cancer? Had I convinced myself that I would be swaddled in a good-karma bubble if I deposited more positives into the universe than I borrowed? Or was I unconsciously trying to appeal to that billowy-bearded, light-skinned, kindly man who appeared as the framed image of an accepting Episcopalian God in the Sunday school classrooms of my childhood church? Was I some kind of imposter? I didn't think so, but I needed to ask the question. More likely, I discovered, I was motivated by doing instead of just hoping. Maybe

I figured performing physical feats was like a vaccine for cancer. After all, how could a disease kill me if it couldn't quite catch up with me?

Very few garden-variety cases of cancer exist. Survival usually depends on the type of cancer you get, the status of your immune system, and the quality and timing of your medical intervention. We all can take initiatives to navigate and secure our futures, but in the end, four variables probably hold sway: our environment, our genetics, our behavior, and our luck. And, of course, the world is full of oddities, like the smokers who live to be ninety-five. Then there are people like me, who are diagnosed with cancer in our lungs and have never smoked a single cigarette.

I didn't see the point in dwelling on making sense of my disease. The death of my father and having cancer early in my adult life taught me not to expect too much order and rhythm in what I interpreted as a free-for-all, clutter-filled world. Havoc seemed the rule, not the exception. Sometimes lame humor was all I had. That gave me a deep appreciation for a woman I befriended at the oncology clinic in Madison who also was undergoing chemotherapy. In our overtired state, we had devised what we nicknamed our "random chaos theory of appliances."

It went something like this: Metastasizing cancer fell into the major-appliance category. One day you're minding your own business, and WHACK, you're suddenly slammed with the equivalent of a refrigerator, a furnace, or a washer that has entered your orbit, hell-bent on doing irreparable harm. The heft alone could kill you, and nobody was immune. That awareness, the ability to have that perspective, meant we filed most any other problem with our health, jobs, or relationships into the small-appliance category—toaster ovens, microwaves, and blenders. Yes, small appliances were still a force to be reckoned with, but we figured we were nimble and resilient enough to recover from any damage an errant toaster oven could dish out.

Humor can be a coping tool that takes away some of the hurt. Of course, so can yelling. People often lavish praise upon patients who shoulder their cancers gallantly and serenely without making a fuss. No doubt being noble is all well and good, but what's wrong with cussing and screaming about a cancer diagnosis? Bursts of anger can be the force that powers a patient to rise up and figure out what defensive path to plot. Sometimes cancer patients need to vent, even if it's just a primal scream.

I cringe when people slip into military terms about cancer. Perhaps that violent vocabulary evolved in reaction to Richard Nixon's declaration of a "war on cancer" after he was elected to the presidency in 1968. Don't get me wrong, I was adamant about obliterating my cancer cells. But references to full-scale assaults, conquests, battles, invasions, arsenals, and bullets made me uncomfortable. Words matter. If I didn't want to wield such weapons, did I lack the killer instinct necessary to overcome cancer?

Perhaps. But I also was turned off by people telling me that positive thinking would cure me. So, if I thought about puppy dogs and rainbows all day—and then died anyway—I was a failure? That seemed like an unfair and impossible burden. Still, I needed something. I read plenty of well-circulated articles documenting stories of cancer survivors who claimed to have used guided imagery to heal themselves. Remarkably, they imagined their radiation treatments as a Pac-Man-like critter gobbling up malignancies, or pictured their chemotherapy drugs as a force of white light scouring evil from their bloodstream. Even though I wanted to be a believer, just to strip away some of my cancer angst, too many doubts plagued me. Such brain exercises seemed dangerous for a reporter prone to skepticism. I feared my gallows humor would intervene in some nefarious fashion, leading to self-sabotage. Some perverse part of me would somehow focus on a mantra of "dark" instead of "light" and I would just create more of a mess.

However, I knew the simple motion of walking had always helped clear my mind of those poisonous thoughts. Feeling a breeze on my cheeks and terra firma under my feet was usually enough to shake off the temporary terror of sheer nothingness. Moving helped me sort out problems and settle on answers. No matter how deflated my lousy health had left me feeling, climbing back up on my two feet had helped me achieve some semblance of serenity.

I realized it was a theme. After our family moved to Massachusetts in the early 1970s, we had a tradition of walking for hours on ample networks of country roads. When that ambulance didn't deliver my father to our Massachusetts home on that horrible October day in 1976, I had laced up my shoes and walked for miles to try to hash out this new fatherless world I had entered. And when I was trapped in a hospital, hooked up to an intravenous drip, I would push the IV pole along with me for hours as I circled the hallways.

Whether the surface was an earthen trail or a concrete sidewalk, I had always found that putting one foot in front of the other was the purest, most cleansing activity a body under stress could undertake. Part of my ambulating urge came from two childhood stories my mother told me. One of them had become a family joke of sorts. When my mother would complain about various aches and pains as a child, her mother used to tell her: "It's probably nothing that a good walk around the block can't cure." The other was a story my mother read in a science magazine. It hypothesized that the design of the human foot could eventually change as people relied more on cars. In elementary school, I used to worry I might actually see children without heels or toes before I became an adult.

It was that history, plus the fact that cancer was sending a tick-tock warning, that tipped me toward embarking on the granddaddy of all hikes: the Appalachian Trail. I had to live in the here and now. I didn't want to complete the trail in bits and pieces because that approach would stretch on into years I feared I wouldn't have. Instead, I wanted to walk all twenty-one hundred-plus miles from Georgia to Maine in one fell swoop. I needed to figure out a way to make it happen.

CHAPTER 24
WESTERN KANSAS: MORE THAN WHEAT AND MEAT

MILES RIDDEN: 2,190
MILES TO GO: 2,060

G reeley County was my first contact with Kansas, my sixth state, on September 26. That name alone did not trigger any connections until subsequent road signs on Highway 96 welcomed me to Horace and then, later, Tribune. As any journalist knows, three of anything indicates a trend, thus enough ammunition to pitch an article idea to an editor. And Horace Greeley certainly knew a story when he saw one. Greeley, of course, was a New Hampshire native and the publisher of the influential *New York Tribune* in the nineteenth century. What put him in the history books was his alleged advice about opportunity, "Go west, young man." Even if he didn't coin the phrase, he made it part of our lexicon.

By then, with two thousand miles on my odometer, I had compiled a nonscientific survey about how drivers shared—or didn't share—their cherished strip of asphalt. My anecdotal evidence rated passenger cars and vans as the most considerate of a bicyclist diligently hugging the solid white line denoting a shoulder. An estimated 95 percent of those drivers slowed down or pulled into the adjacent lane to give me plenty of leeway. Surprisingly, drivers with "God is My Copilot" bumper stickers were the most nerve-racking because of their less-than-skillful maneuvering.

With pickup trucks, however, it depended on who was behind the wheel. Women usually passed very cautiously. Do not, however, expect such cordial behavior from three young men riding abreast in the cab. As for tractor-trailers, recreational vehicles, and cars and trucks toting trailers or boats, I represented an annoyance to be beeped at for impeding their progress. I had been jeered at, but nobody had hurled any inanimate objects—something "The Cabooses" had warned me about back in Idaho.

Right or wrong, I admit to a strong bias against gargantuan recreational vehicles. What are people hauling in these shrines large enough to house a dozen families? I know, I get it, some folks always want all the comforts of home. But at what price? Each gallon of fuel pumped into the tank yielded single-digit mileage. These behemoths made me pause, glance at my panniers, and ask how many belongings we need to exist. People seemed oblivious to the irony of driving houses on wheels sporting names as absurd as Wilderness, Weekend Warrior, Arctic Fox, Eagle, Wildcat, Windsong, Montana Mountain, and Bambi. The only one I spied with an appropriate name was Intruder. At least that manufacturer deserved credit for honesty.

In Kansas, however, I realized I had to rejigger my theories. Kansans, no matter what they steered, must have all read the same Miss Manners manual about being cordial to bicyclists. Everybody, including tractor-trailer drivers and male teenagers in pickup trucks, moved to the left when approaching from behind. Sometimes they allowed me such a wide berth, even when traffic was barely existent, that I felt as if I were riding on the world's widest bicycle path. In construction zones, workers not only inquired about my trip but went out of their way to make sure I pedaled through unscathed. To top it off, almost everybody waved. A state trooper shocked me one day near Larned. I thought he was intent on citing me for some infraction when I saw him pull onto the shoulder. Instead, he asked about my travels. Unbelievable. Who taught this politeness, and is Kansas willing to share with the rest of the country? Funny, but even the few dogs that gave chase seemed appalled at their own behavior after I barked, "Go home!"

Bicyclists who had tried to convince me that Kansas was flyover territory, best passed through quickly with my head down, evidently weren't very inventive. My to-do lists had several musts. One was snarfing down at least one sugary, calorie-laden dessert at a local chain with a funny but fitting name: Frigid Crème. Another was visiting offbeat museums where the funky artifacts and specimens were as fascinating as the tour guides.

In Leoti—pronounce it "Lay-oh-tuh" or the natives will laugh at your funny accent—I met a melanoma survivor named Ron who gave me what he called the fifty-cent tour of the Museum of the Great Plains. I was captivated by a sequence of black-and-white photos depicting a 1935 dust storm roaring into Tribune. Early European settlers on the Great Plains had destroyed the deep roots of the native grasses by plowing up the sod to plant crops and build homes with the earthen blocks. That left the unrooted soil free to swirl away in the wind. When a horrible drought parched the region in the 1930s, huge clouds of that soil created the infamous Dust Bowl. News reports at the museum claimed that clouds darkened skies as far away as New York City and Washington, DC.

"But wait until you see what I've saved for the grand finale," Ron said, delightedly directing me to an ancient bicycle wheel with metal spokes.

"Oh my," I said, examining a well-worn and often-repaired rim fashioned from wood. I wouldn't have made it across Kansas, never mind the country, on that relic.

145

East of Leoti on September 28, I was disappointed when I saw a "Closed" sign on the door of the Barbed Wire Museum in La Crosse, but heartened when I noticed a tiny handwritten note that included a home phone number for Delillah.

"Honey, I've survived lung cancer, so I know what you've been through," Delillah told me when I called from a pay phone. "Let me finish my lunch and I'll be there in five minutes."

La Crosse became a magnet for such prickly fencing in 1966 when businesspeople formed the Kansas Barbed Wire Collectors Association, and they still have a swap and sell convention each May, Delillah explained after greeting me. Then, she turned me loose in the fifty-four-hundrred-square foot building.

I was uneducated enough to think just one type of barbed wire existed—the rusty kind that had punctured my thigh when I climbed over a farm fence long ago. Was I ever wrong. One display featured 2,066 sorts of barbed wire collected by two Nebraska ranchers. It was near an illustrated catalogue with the less-than-delicate title "Barbs, Prongs, Points, Prickers, and Stickers."

I learned how one inventor's ingenious wife created barbs by modifying her coffee grinder, how three early competitors in the nineteenth century fought to claim the "Father of Barbed Wire" title, and how one man's fight to prevent a barbed-wire monopoly escalated all the way to the US Supreme Court in 1892.

Other oddities included the Barbed Wire Hall of Fame, a 78 rpm record showcasing "Barb Wire Blues" played by the Mound City Blue Blowers, and a seventy-two-pound nest that ravens in Greeley County had built from the stuff. In the same county, nineteen miles of barbed wire had doubled as a telephone line in the early 1900s. Who knew?

Trees were so few and far between in this stark open landscape that farmers and stockmen stretched barbed wire between sturdy posts carved from stone quarried from limestone outcroppings. Dellilah explained that entrepreneurs delivered these "post rocks" via horse-drawn wagon for twenty-five cents apiece in the late 1800s. Thousands of miles of these unique tree substitutes still exist, but bicyclists won't be hauling them home as souvenirs—they can weigh up to 450 pounds apiece.

Back on the road, I dodged fleshy, yellow-green seed pods the size of grapefruits that dropped from Osage orange trees, the natural precursor to barbed wire. Early settlers planted them because the branches on these low-growing trees interlocked, forming a thorny barrier. A cousin to the mulberry tree, Osage oranges are also known as the horse-apple, yellowwood, hedge apple, and bois d'arc (French for "bowwood") tree.

While the arrival of barbed wire in the 1870s might have solved fencing problems for white settlers, it stifled that spacious feeling of the Great Plains. Along with fences, settlers' plows, roads, and irrigation ditches irreversibly reshaped those vast expanses.

Though folks racing through Kansas on interstate highways might dismiss it as simply the land of wheat and meat, it is unfair to sum up the landscape that succinctly. Yes, wheat dominates the western half, and no doubt corn and grazing cattle make the eastern half tick. Unless you poke around on blue highways and dirt roads, you won't have an inkling that what is now south-central Kansas is where once-continuous eastern and western prairies traditionally converged. A sprawling National Wildlife Refuge that I had the luxury of pedaling through near Hudson was called Quivira, the name Spanish explorer Coronado gave to the region when he sought gold there in the sixteenth century. Instead of precious metals, he found a treasure trove of wildlife. The refuge's lushness provides habitat for some 350 species of birds, mammals, amphibians, and fish. Bald eagles spend winters in the salt marshes, and endangered least terns nest in the salt flats. The dominance of modern agriculture made the creation of this twenty-one thousand-plus-acre refuge in 1955 even more vital.

Kansas, from the high plains of the west, to the Flint Hills of the east, and the valleys, ravines, and slopes in between, was birthed geologically to support myriad grasses. Each staple of the prairie—whether it's little bluestem, big bluestem, blue grama grass, buffalo grass, Indian grass, or switch grass—has adapted to flourish in a specific type of soil. Long-term survival also depends on altitude, the angle of the sun, and the amount of moisture absorbed.

Pedaling by crops of milo and wheat that benefit from this rich prairie soil, it was hard to square settlers' stories about losing cows in tall prairie grasses or touching grass tops from a horse's saddle. But botanists know that before the plow, grasses ruled the prairie, some reaching at least ten feet. Now, cattle "mowed" some of these same grasses before being fattened up quickly with grains and other products. Indeed, Leoti was home to the nation's largest livestock yard. It is adjacent to factories that pack meat and turn animal hides into leather.

Unfortunately, the cattle imported here generations ago by pioneers alter landscapes by vigorously chomping on all parts of the grass. Also, their stomping of stream and riverbanks has led to irreparable erosion. Even worse, overgrazing by cattle eliminates the midheight grasses, creating thousands of acres of sod dominated by short grasses. In contrast, bison and other native grazers do not gnaw grasses down to their roots, nor do their hooves trample stream and riverbanks. But those natives aren't big moneymakers, so they are few and far between. That's why I tipped my bicycle helmet to the schools in Cassoday—a trailside town of about a hundred in eastern Kansas off Highway 177—for making native prairies a focus of lessons about environmental vitality. It touts itself as the world's prairie chicken capital.

Two young brothers tumbled out of their nearby house to introduce me to their pet rat and hand me my tent stakes as I set up camp in Prairie Park on October 1.

"How do you fit in there?" Mick, a sixth-grader, and Jacob, a third-grader, asked in unison.

"I was the park's caretaker for the summer," explained a beaming Mick in his appealing drawl. "I saved up enough money to buy a stereo."

They showed me where the city had razed a deteriorating building to clear space for a park on the small triangle of land. They and their classmates had painted flowers on the park's trashcans, carried in a picnic table, and planted gardens full of native grasses and flowers. We sat at the table and talked about spiders and plants until their mother called them to dinner. I walked to the café that claimed to have "served food and gossip since 1879."

"My boys have told me all about your tiny tent and your adventure," the boys' mother told me close to bedtime. "If a storm rolls in tonight, please knock on our door, whatever time it is. There's no reason for you to be soaked when we have plenty of room."

Well, no storm roared into Cassoday. But the trains certainly did, and I was right by the tracks. Holy cow. All of that whistling and metal-on-metal grinding meant I slept in what felt like forty-five-minute increments. Those who romanticize trains have never tried to nod off within feet of active tracks. To Jacob, Mick, and their mother, those noises were as natural as the reveille of a songbird.

Early the next morning, I waved a reluctant goodbye to that sincere and authentic family. I had been tempted to scoop both Mick and Jacob into my panniers for the rest of my ride, but instead I rolled on alone.

CHAPTER 25
BOOTS ON THE GROUND

Once I became fixated on a Georgia-to-Maine walk, I was like the proverbial dog with a bone. I wouldn't let go. Yes, I was incredibly disappointed my fourth round of chemotherapy in autumn of 1989 hadn't extirpated my lung tumors, but was I just supposed to hope I didn't die at my newsroom desk? I figured an extended break from the daily demands of journalism and the needles, scans, and probes would be purifying. Weekend walks in the wilderness wouldn't suffice. I needed full immersion.

In 1990 and early 1991, between covering government meetings, writing feature articles, and plugging away on an exclusive investigative series about a child abuse scandal in the county social services department for the newspaper in Wisconsin, I began plotting my thru-hike. That was Appalachian Trail-speak for a continuous end-to-end trek. I dug into trail literature and began stockpiling a tent, sleeping bag and pad, stove, water filter, boots, backpack, and other supplies. I decided that my thru-hike should be a clean break. Sabbaticals weren't common at small daily newspapers, and I couldn't fathom returning to the same place and schedule. The few people who knew what I was up to told me I was courageous to embark on such a hike without knowing what would come afterward. Deep down, I didn't see myself as brave. If anything, I was afraid I was being cowardly by running away to an adventure in the woods instead of sticking with my chosen profession. But staying put seemed too safe. To save my life and sanity, I needed to move on.

In the fall of 1990, a fellow newspaper reporter had made tenuous plans to hike with me. She even drove to Virginia with me in late winter 1991 to attend a hands-on seminar taught by a quirky veteran Appalachian Trail backpacker. Despite that effort, part of me sensed her enthusiasm for a long-distance adventure was waning. So, I wasn't too shocked when she backed out two months before we were scheduled to start. Instead of letting that setback put the kibosh on my trip, I reshaped it into a solo venture. I traded in my two-person tent for a smaller and much lighter model.

On the practical side, I had to arrange for health insurance coverage during my hiatus and figure out how to distribute my few belongings. Although I hadn't commanded exorbitant wages as a reporter, I'd squirreled away what I calculated was enough money to support a shoestring hike. I left my job by mid-March and began doling out my stuff to willing friends. Wilbur, my delightful Maine coon cat, and I flew to Massachusetts because my mother had agreed to be his caretaker. Back in Wisconsin, I finished cleaning out my apartment and preparing my gear.

Fortuitously, a Wisconsin colleague who had recently moved to the South Carolina coast agreed to drive me from her new home near Charleston to the trail's southern terminus in Georgia. I just had to transport myself to her home in early April. I was pretty much a backpacking rookie when my South Carolina friend and I piled into her Jeep and headed to Springer Mountain in the heart of the Chattahoochee-Oconee National Forest. Yes, I had day-hiked and had tent-camped for years, but that was a far cry from carrying my entire house on my back.

On the afternoon of April 13, 1991—two days before my thirtieth birthday—I was standing at an elevation of 3,782 feet in the fog of Springer Mountain, poised to take the first of an estimated five million steps toward Mount Katahdin in Maine's Baxter State Park. The fourteen-state footpath, completed in 1937 along the spine of the Eastern mountain ranges, was conceived by Benton MacKaye, a Massachusetts conservationist and regional planner. In 1921, he published an article in an architectural journal outlining what some called a harebrained and unachievable scheme. Some friends and co-workers, I am positive, thought my hike was equally ludicrous. But I didn't care. I just wanted to get started.

As I walked north in Georgia, following the white, two-by-six-inch rectangular blazes painted on trees, I discovered that backpacking agreed with me. I naturally bent toward minimalism and had always attempted to honor the adage about beauty in simplicity. Less really is more. And that didn't mean leading an ignorant, unfulfilled life as an angry or isolated Luddite. It was about being aware that a world prepackaged with an overabundance of bells and whistles often offers nothing more than a deafening cacophony. Choices are wonderful, but just how many flavors of mustard do we really need on the grocery store shelves? Comedian George Carlin was on the mark with his wise skewerings of conspicuous consumption. Our homes, he joked, were nothing more than multi-room storage bins for unbelievable amounts of "stuff."

I felt so happy hiking. The walking was demanding but not draining. I had such an uncomplicated sense of purpose. Everything I needed was scrunched into my red-and-black external frame backpack. And with each meal, my load lightened. At night, I slept on Mother Earth's belly under stars undimmed by light pollution. By day, I befriended an assortment of characters—"Mountain Goat," "Weather Carrot," "Hippiechick,"

151

"Sleepwalker," "Six-Foot Hobbit," "Trail Chef," "Yin and Yang," "Problem Child," "Lollygagger," "Web Breaker," "Pregnant Rhino in Heat," "Judge Roy Bean," and "Bad Dog"—all pursuing their own adventures. On sunny days in Georgia, when delicate flowers known as bluets optimistically poked through rock crevices in the middle of the trail, I would lift my face skyward and ask if this splendor ever had to end. When feeling observed while writing in a journal at one of the three-sided wooden shelters along the way, I usually spotted a curious white-tailed deer watching from the underbrush.

My body toughened up as it reset its center of gravity and adjusted to carrying up to forty-five pounds of gear and food. I huffed up grueling ascents in Georgia and tried to keep my toes from turning to mush as they slammed forward in my boots on steep descents. Acquiring a "trail name" is a tradition and most hikers learn it's better to christen yourself so as not to be cursed with one you despise. Three days in, I became "The Blister Sister." Some hikers insisted I must be a nun, but I cleared up those misconceptions by pointing to a plastic bag laden with a less-than-sanitary collection of moleskin, tape, bandages, and other first-aid supplies for my afflicted feet. All I lacked was an attending podiatrist.

Besides the hefty pack, I had a heavy load on my mind too. Before I left for Georgia, my Wisconsin doctors had strongly recommended that I detour from the trail for a checkup with an oncologist. The tumors in my lungs weren't all that worried them. They were also monitoring something small but potentially suspect on my liver. They gave me the number for a clinic in Charlottesville, very close to the trail in the Blue Ridge Mountains of Virginia. I said I would think about it.

I muscled my way out of Georgia and along the North Carolina-Tennessee border, sorry I had arrived too early to see magnificent rhododendron thickets in bloom. By mid-May, I was about a month into my hike and feeling fine as I neared the Virginia border. About a quarter of the Appalachian Trail, some 525 miles, traverses the state. I promised myself I would make that doctor appointment when I neared Charlottesville.

Trail hikers tend to bunch together, creating cliques and moving along with the same clump of people. I was content to walk alone, pondering and wondering. I didn't mind the company of others when I stopped for the night, but I was equally satisfied to pitch my tent in a more isolated area. I wanted to hike my own hike, not somebody else's.

Several miles into Virginia, I met another northbound hiker who looked slightly familiar. He introduced himself as Don. I recognized his trail name, "Tiger Tunez"—a play on being a graduate of Clemson University and his last name of Looney—because that was how he signed the spiral-bound journals left in the shelters by hiking club volunteers who maintain the trail. He had introduced himself back in North Carolina where the trail crosses the Nantahala River. I was heading north out of Wesser, a little town that caters to kayakers and rafters, and he was just walking into town when we first said hello. That's when I found out he had also started his hike at Springer Mountain on April 13, a few hours ahead of me. I hadn't thought too much of that encounter because thru-hikers usually engage in such chit-chat.

When I met Don for the second time near a shelter in Virginia, he offered me crackers from his backpack. That was unusual. Hikers are usually so ravenous that, understandably, they tend to guard their victuals closely. He also told me he had been reading the observations I was recording in the trail journals. Before texting and cell phones, those dog-eared journals served as a trail grapevine along what amounted to a linear community. Word traveled north and south. Farther along in Virginia, Don confessed that he had calculated how far away I was by the time and date on my journal entries—and picked up his hiking pace so he could catch up to me in Virginia. He had fallen a bit behind when a hiker friend joined him for several days in North Carolina and Tennessee.

As the responsible adult I prided myself on being, calling the Charlottesville clinic haunted me. I kept putting it off. The truth was, I was finding the trail rhythm so magical that I wanted to keep it needle- and scan-free. Sometimes, lying in my tiny tent at night, my pack stashed under the fly and my food and toothpaste stowed in a bag hanging from a tree limb to keep it out of reach of bears and other critters, I would play a tortuous mind game. It went like this: If I did see the Virginia oncologist and he discovered more cancer, what would he and other doctors be able to do about it? It's not as if a melanoma cure had emerged in the last eighteen months. And if the Virginia oncologist found the tumors in my lungs—or the spot they were monitoring on my liver—hadn't budged or grown, then the journey to Charlottesville would be a colossal waste of time.

After the cracker-sharing episode, Don and I started hiking together, off and on. We walked at about the same pace. He told me he had planned on hiking only as far as Harpers Ferry, West Virginia, the scenic town at the confluence of the Shenandoah and Potomac Rivers. The geographic halfway point of the Appalachian Trail is in Pennsylvania, at Pine Grove Furnace State Park. But for hikers intent on reaching Maine, Harpers Ferry has a reputation as the "psychological halfway point." If northbounders make it that far, they are more likely to climb Mount Katahdin.

In Virginia, Don and I started a pattern of hitchhiking into a town every seventy-five trail miles or so to stock up on food at small country stores. At the checkout line one day, Don noticed a tabloid headline blaring the news of actor Michael Landon's liver cancer diagnosis.

"Oh, that's awful," Don said. "I always really liked him."

My stomach tensed. I just nodded.

When I realized Don and I were forming more than a casual bond—though we continued to pitch our separate tents—I was quite blunt about my own cancer.

"You've earned my trust, so I think it's only fair I tell you the gory details of my cancer surgeries and treatments," I told him as we stomped up yet another climb. "I've had the same sneaky disease that kept re-erupting in my father's body before it finally killed him.

"I never asked my father if his cancer ever made him feel like damaged goods. But I suspect it did because I know mine does, at least sometimes."

Don had witnessed the cruelties of cancer in his own family. Several years prior, doctors had reconstructed his father's digestive tract after a cancerous tumor nearly destroyed the older man's esophagus. Don had moved home temporarily to help his mother with caretaking duties.

Despite my cancer confessions, Don's steadfastness and apparent devotion didn't dwindle. This very competent hiker with the bright blue eyes and sometimes hard-to-understand drawl from the South Carolina piedmont kept showing up just about every morning when I was executing what weightlifters refer to as a "clean and jerk" to hoist my pack onto my T-shirt-clad back. We would split a packet of Pop-Tarts or boil water for oatmeal before setting off. Part of the attraction was our shared values. We both appreciated the natural world and the ability to hike together without feeling obligated to fill silences. Plus, we were both devoted baseball fans.

When I asked why he wasn't scared off yet, Don told me, "Well, I like who you are. And I've never met anybody else like you." His appreciation for individuality resonated with me. I had to admit to myself—and out loud to Don—that I had not yet been fortunate to meet anybody like this quietly persistent and patient person either.

One day after we had hiked beyond Charlottesville, I told Don about the potential trouble brewing in my liver and why I had gone silent when he mentioned the headline about Michael Landon's cancer. Still, I said I was feeling great and figured I could wait until my hike ended to see a doctor. Maybe that was a cavalier exercise in foolishness and denial, but that's what I decided. By then, I knew Don had a habit of including a short summary of each day in his succinct trail journal. It always included a plus and a minus. I asked him about his entries that day. His minus was mentioning the Landon headline to me, and his plus was hiking with me.

Not long after that conversation, we were closing in on West Virginia.

Don told me he was lengthening his hike. Instead of taking the train home in Harpers Ferry, he planned to hike to Maine with me. His work in construction as a glazier evidently allowed him three additional months off.

Beyond West Virginia, we agilely two-stepped across the millions of pointy, sharp rocks that coat the trail in Pennsylvania. During that summer's drought, we were in search of the next freshwater spring that hadn't dried to a trickle. I realized physical toughening wasn't the only change my body was undergoing. Something else—a total surprise—was also happening. Most unexpectedly, I was falling in love, or at least very strong like.

Friends can confirm that I can be sentimental, but I will never ever be mistaken for a hopeless romantic. Cinderella and those other princess stories never resonated with me. So, no, I was not—ick!—out there in the woods looking for some sort of fairy-tale love. That thought never crossed my mind. Mostly I sought time and space to knit my body and mind back together, away from demanding editors who always wanted one more story and physicians who always seemed to need one more scan, one more blood sample, or some other dreadful procedure.

I also thought maybe I could learn to be a little more forgiving with myself, the person I tended to judge most severely. I didn't feel as if I knew what wholeness was, but I was certain I had not achieved it yet. When I looked at myself, I often saw something scarred and broken, and could not imagine why anybody else would want to be around that for longer than they had to be. Humor was the shield I used to deflect the pain that sprang from those insecurities. If I kept other people laughing, maybe they would be distracted enough not to notice my messy shortcomings unfolding before them.

Don and I persevered. In New Jersey, we were rewarded with a black bear sighting and an incomparable sunset. In Connecticut, I had to break in new leather boots because the originals that had carried me from Georgia were as smooth-bottomed as the pair of Keds sneakers I'd worn as a small child. This was, er, no small "feat" for a hiker who hadn't been able to shed the name "The Blister Sister." The vendor in Wisconsin who sold me the original boots had promised to replace them if they didn't last the whole trip. He followed through by mailing that new pair to a post office in New England.

Don met my mother on the trail twice—once when she joined us with family friends for a meal and laundry session in Massachusetts, and a second time when she drove to Vermont by herself so the three of us could have a picnic on a town green. Farther along in Vermont, Hurricane Bob drenched us and everything in our backpacks for several days. The bog boards positioned over perennially wet sections of trail were sodden enough to be dangerous. When I slipped on one board and fell hard, I feared I would "turtle," that is, land on my pack and my back with my feet in the air, unable to right myself. However, I was so physically fit by then that I bounced back up like a rubber ball.

One night above the tree line in the White Mountains of New Hampshire, Don and I wedged ourselves into a space about the size of a dining room table with three other hikers who had pitched a small tent askew. It was the only flat stretch near the trail. We were so tired after rock-hopping all day that we couldn't wait for our noodles to finish cooking. We ate them almost raw. There was no space for another tent, so we pulled on all of our clothes, wormed into our sleeping bags, then spent the freezing night trying to avoid and forget the rocky edges poking us everywhere.

By the time I reached Maine, I instinctually knew how to tackle the hand-over-hand climbs and squeezes required to crawl through spills of house-size boulders. More daunting were the rains, which transformed usually fordable, bridgeless streams with rocky bottoms into raging rivers. At one crossing, the current was formidable enough to sweep away even the most surefooted hiker. Stepping in it would be folly. Instead of waiting a few days for the water level to drop, Don and I stripped off our packs and inched across the maelstrom on crisscrossed fallen logs that we hoped would be strong enough to hold our weight. The key was keeping our eyes on the opposite bank, not the roiling wetness below.

We averaged about one rest day per week. On the others, we walked twelve to twenty miles a day powered by Pop Tarts, oatmeal, peanut butter, rice, and noodles, occasionally supplemented with embarrassing episodes of gluttony at restaurants in trailside towns where proprietors were still foolish enough to offer all-you-can-eat buffets.

By the time we reached Baxter State Park in inner Maine in early October, we were lean, mean, calorie-burning hiking machines. Baxter is home to 5,270-foot Mount Katahdin, the northern terminus of the trail, and north-bounders can be barred from climbing the mountain if the weather makes it too dangerous or if rangers have shut it down for the season. After a few days of waiting for dark clouds to clear, October 8 dawned as a cold but Class A day. As I hoisted myself up boulders via metal bars bored into granite and picked my way over rime-ice-covered stones, I laughed at the way trail maintainers in Maine seemed to delight in choosing the most convoluted route. I cried at the thought of the journey being over but simultaneously relished the idea of trading my stinky sleeping bag for a mattress with sheets.

After Don and I summited Mount Katahdin together, we joined several other thru-hikers for a few days of recovery at a cabin in Maine owned by one hiker's family. Within a week, my mother came to pick us up. The three of us spent several days exploring the state's rocky coast before heading back to my mother's house in western Massachusetts. A few days later, Don took the train back to South Carolina, and I made plans to return to Wisconsin. We had no idea when we would see each other again.

I had to launch a job hunt, but my overarching worry was my health. After skipping the appointment with the Charlottesville oncologist, I knew I had to act. Reluctantly, I made an appointment at the New Hampshire oncology clinic and drove there alone from my mother's house. Whatever happened, I would have to figure out how to live with the consequences.

A young, vigilant doctor examined every inch of my exterior and performed numerous routine tests. He then ordered a series of lung X-rays and promised to call me with the results.

"Elizabeth, this will probably shock you as much as it does us, but we can't find any spots on your lungs," the doctor said on the phone a few days later. "They're clean."

My Wisconsin doctors were just as shocked when I relayed the astounding news. They didn't ask about my liver, and I didn't bring it up, content to leave well enough alone.

No doctor had a medical explanation. It could have been a delayed reaction to the chemotherapy regimen. There had been no studies, of course, about the possibility of tumors disappearing after six months spent walking, drinking spring water, inhaling mountain air, and burning every calorie that noodles, rice, oatmeal, Pop Tarts, and chocolate can provide.

I had always thought it a bunch of malarkey that Norman Cousins healed himself by laughing. Where was the science in that? Now I wasn't so sure. My questions didn't mean I was on the verge of shunning Western medicine. That would be ridiculous. Maybe I was just living proof that a body could regain equilibrium with a combination of chemotherapy and an adventure that seemed a salve for the heart and soul.

When I told my mother the astonishing news, she exhaled a "Yippee!" In the next breath, she told me how, as a stubborn baby, I had graduated from crawling to knee-walking, developing thick calluses as I barrelled across bare floors, braided rugs, and even cement. The pediatrician had told my parents not to worry. I would walk when I was ready. One day, several months before my second birthday, my mother was playing a stack of vinyl albums. She entered the living room and found me on my feet, dancing to the soundtrack of *My Fair Lady*. She burst into tears.

CHAPTER 26
EASTERN KANSAS: NEVER-ENDING KINDNESS

MILES RIDDEN: 2,403
MILES TO GO: 1,847

K ansans continued to be as warm, even-tempered, and self-effacing as the roadside sunflowers that tilted their round, petal-framed faces toward the brightest light. They approached me in grocery stores, restaurants, and post offices to ask about my trip. Not only did they grant me their undivided attention, but they acted as if they had all the time in the world to listen. And they never cringed at any worn-out references to Dorothy and Toto, even though they had likely heard enough references to Oz to last several lifetimes.

As Harold, proprietor of Bauer's Grocery in tiny Hudson, said, "We have our own pace. We're not in much of a hurry." Likewise, a nurse at a small-town hospital where I did outreach chuckled when she reminded me to "enjoy the sunsets here" because, after all, "there's nothing blocking the view." And for pity's sake, how could you not have a sweet spot in your heart for people who apologized for the weather when I mentioned tangles with menacing headwinds and crosswinds?

At the library in Walnut late on October 3, the resourceful director was so sorry I couldn't post an electronic journal entry because her sole internet link was kaput that she coordinated a Plan B. She called the library in Girard, about twenty mostly flat miles away, to reserve computer time for me the next day. In the meantime, I camped at the city park in Walnut and ate dinner at the B & J Café—cooked by the equally friendly, and also red-haired, mother of the librarian.

Girard is near the eastern edge of the Flint Hills. My back-of-the-envelope Kansas calculations had me staying at a bed and breakfast there, but Terri, the no-nonsense library director contacted by Walnut, had other thoughts on October 4. She told me her home had plenty of space because two of her three children were out on their own.

"You're staying with us tonight," she told me unequivocally. "If you don't agree, well, I'll just revoke your computer privileges," she added with a laugh.

After locking up the library, she invited me to dinner at, appropriately,

Mom's Restaurant. I accepted a ride with her but had a moment of panic when I noticed the "What part of Jesus don't you understand?" sticker affixed to her sedan's bumper.

Uh oh. Delving into a discussion about religion with people you have just met rarely turns out well. And I was not in the mood to stomach a "you're a heathen-bound-for-hell" sermon. Refreshingly, there was no such talk. Terri might have had strong Christian beliefs, but she was a librarian, not a proselytizer. Our conversation was robust and animated because she was a bright, open-minded, and inquisitive individual who kept up with politics and current events and was comfortable balancing two opposing ideas in her mind simultaneously. And she genuinely cared about people. Oh, did she ever care. I chastised myself for assuming that her religious beliefs would influence her every thought and opinion.

She asked thoughtful questions about my cancer. When a woman stopped by the table to update Terri about a mutual friend wrestling with ovarian cancer, Terri's response was, "We're going to bathe that in prayer." That approach to a difficult and sad situation sounded so soothing, especially in her calming Kansas drawl, that I realized I wouldn't have turned her down if she had made me the same offer.

That night in Terri's cozy living room, I gathered around the television with her family to watch a series of *Veggie Tales* videos produced by an outfit called Big Idea Productions. Everybody else knew the scripts by heart, but this was the first time I had witnessed vegetables acting out Bible stories. What a riot. I can't remember whether Esther was portrayed by a stalk of celery or a carrot, but the programs were entertaining—even for somebody with a less-than-comprehensive grasp of the Old and New Testaments.

While I tried to drift off in the pink-themed guest bedroom, I wondered whether my father had ever prayed during his years of illness. What would he have thought if somebody such as Terri had promised her church community would bathe him in prayer? His mother had vehemently rejected the Catholic Church several years before he and his brother were born. When she remarried, however, the family attended the Episcopal chapel affiliated with the Ohio college where her new husband taught.

In Philadelphia, my father had been quite active with our local Episcopal church. The minister's name was Taylor, which prompted my father to joke that our family spent Sunday mornings with Lord & Taylor, once a prominent department store in the region. But eventually he became disgusted with the internal politics of the church and stopped attending. When we switched to Quaker meetings in the late 1960s, my father begged off and stayed home on Sunday mornings. Our family drifted away from any sort of worship services when we moved to Massachusetts in the early

1970s. I guess my father felt comfortable with this decision because he never returned to church, even when his cancer came raging back.

I made a late-afternoon getaway from Girard the next day, October 5, because I spent time finishing my incomplete journal entry at the library. The Missouri border was just nineteen miles away, so I figured I would be camping in my seventh state that night. But near Pittsburg, a city of seventeen thousand along Highway 126, the darkening stew of a sky took on a sickening shade of green. Missouri would likely have to wait. Overpowering winds in Pittsburg convinced me to stop for an early dinner. The city no longer allowed camping in its oh-so-convenient municipal park because of the fear of inappropriate behavior by bicyclists. I figured I could worry about sleeping arrangements later.

On Pittsburg's mostly deserted main street, I sequestered a well-dressed, lone pedestrian making a beeline for the bank.

"Where is the best place to eat plenty of food?" I asked, tilting my head toward ominous clouds, feeling like a vulnerable baby sandhill crane swiveling its neck to watch for diving hawks and other airborne predators. Just as the man started to gruffly tick off a list of possibilities, a frazzled-looking woman clutching a purse and a half-eaten ice cream cone interrupted. The two of them didn't make eye contact.

"You're one of those cross-country bicyclists, aren't you?" she asked, her face just inches from mine. I nodded. "You don't want to be out in this," she said. "You'll drown. You can come to our house to spend the night. Other cyclists have pitched their tents in our huge yard. Or you're welcome to stay inside."

I was so stunned by this stranger's offer that I told her I needed to eat first. My hemming and hawing wasn't going to shake her off, though. She balanced the cone in one hand while tearing a deposit slip from the checkbook she plucked from her purse. She recited succinct directions to the address printed on the torn slip. The man, who remained silent during our exchange, gave her a disgusted look as she scurried off. He remained polite yet distant as he completed his list of restaurant recommendations and wished me luck.

A few blocks away, I found the stern man's top recommendation, an institution called Otto's Diner. Millie, an older, waste-no-steps waitress with a genuine beehive hairdo, greeted me in the nonsmoking section with a smile and a menu. As I filled up on chicken noodle soup, barbecued beef in a bun, corn, potatoes, iced tea, and cherry pie—for a whopping total of $7.21—the skies gushed. Lightning made it look as if it were high noon, and the ensuing thunder booms made diners a bit jumpy. I feared my untethered bicycle would float away.

As I polished off my pie, an older couple at the adjacent table asked where I was headed. I told them it depended on the weather. Minutes later, they invited me to their home. I politely declined, telling them that believe it or not, I already had an invitation that I would likely accept if the rain didn't ease up. *What is this, the most thoughtful and genuine community in the world?* I wrote in my journal. *Two offers within the span of an hour?* My good fortune was in overdrive, and I figured I should heed the flashing signals calling for Pittsburg to be my overnight destination—even if I had only pedaled a measly thirteen miles that day. I could have walked that distance.

Once the whooshing storm dwindled to sprinkles, I was relieved to find my bicycle upright. I pointed my front tire toward the Ninth Street address printed on the bank deposit slip. And there on the front porch was BJ, the forty-something woman with the wild curly hair.

"I knew I'd see you again, kiddo," she said, letting out her distinctive bray of laughter and introducing me to her husband, Eddie. "Let's unload your gear and put the bicycle in the garage. It's way too wet to camp in the yard."

When I saw "GO AWAY" emblazoned on their porch welcome mat, I knew I'd made the right decision. BJ confirmed my earlier suspicions, telling me that she had deliberately interrupted my conversation with the banker because she didn't like his attitude toward cross-country bicyclists and wanted to make sure I wasn't shunned.

We spent the earlier part of that damp but merry evening walking through their spacious and lush backyard garden. A centerpiece rock they'd liberated from somewhere in their travels together was shaped like Mickey Mouse, down to the distinctive ears. Later, we moved inside for a hilarious tour of the jam-packed bungalow they had called home since 1977. Each eclectic piece of furniture and artwork wedged into their cozily crowded home, including the lovely Alphonse Mucha art nouveau prints, had a backstory. We exchanged stories about politics, geography, bicycling, current events, and careers.

"It's my hometown, but we call it the Land of Value because steak dinners and everything else are a bargain," said Eddie, a round-faced man with jet-black hair who still had the mischievous grin he likely had flashed as Pittsburg's marble-shooting champion decades earlier.

BJ's job suited her effervescent personality. As a caretaker for an entourage of elderly neighbors, she ran their errands and managed their housekeeping and finances.

That evening—for the second consecutive night—I flopped down on a real mattress, my head on a feather pillow instead of a balled-up fleece jacket. I joked that this Kansas hospitality meant I wouldn't remember how to pitch my tent or sleep on the ground and would expect a team of attentive porters to fan and feed me over the Ozarks and the Appalachians.

Pedaling off the next morning, I choked up because I felt as if I were leaving two childhood friends. Part of me wanted to stay with BJ and Eddie for a week just to bask in their quirky company.

CHAPTER 27
BACK WITH A VENGEANCE

When I finished my Appalachian Trail hike in October 1991, the country was burrowed in a recession. Two-newspaper towns were shrinking to one-newspaper towns, and one-newspaper towns were downsizing to no-newspaper towns. Opportunities were so limited that I welcomed a call from Don early in 1992. He was back at work in South Carolina. I was in Wisconsin, where I had cobbled together a series of jobs that included freelance writing and housesitting.

"Are you interested in being a caretaker at a lodge that caters to Appalachian Trail hikers?" he asked in that drawl that I realized I missed.

"How do we sign up?" I responded, elated at the opportunity to reconnect. We applied. By February, the Potomac Appalachian Trail Club had hired us as caretakers at Blackburn Trail Center in northern Virginia, near Harpers Ferry, West Virginia. The Virginia-based club organizes the huge cadre of volunteers who maintain the Appalachian Trail and its connected side trails from the southern end of the Shenandoah National Park near Waynesboro, Virginia, up to Duncannon, Pennsylvania.

In early April, Don and I moved our spare belongings into the trail center's early twentieth-century log building. It's near a section of the Appalachian Trail where hikers walk the line between Virginia and West Virginia. We helped to maintain the lodge and its outbuildings, and assisted hikers, whether they were there to fill their water bottles, stay overnight in the bunk-bed-equipped hostel, take a solar shower, or relax on the expansive screened-in porch.

Time at that rustic retreat offered us an exquisite opportunity to stay connected to the hiking community while navigating our post-trail lives. In between tending to trail center duties and teaching job skills part-time to developmentally delayed teens in a nearby Virginia town, I hunted for full-time work. Physically, I was in good shape. But I was nervous because my health insurance coverage was on the verge of lapsing, and the cost of a private policy for a high-risk person like me with a pre-existing condition was astronomical. Finally, I landed a job as a reporter at a daily newspaper on the shores of Lake Michigan in Racine, Wisconsin. Don joined me later in 1993 and immediately found work as a commercial glass installer.

That first winter back in Wisconsin, I had trouble keeping food down.

At first, I blamed a stomach bug. I wasn't incapacitated, but the setback put me on edge. For weeks, I rationalized that maybe I was developing weird food allergies or reacting to the stress of daily publishing deadlines.

When my new health benefits kicked in and I was no longer at risk of being tagged with a pre-existing condition, I sought help. The thought of returning to the Madison hospital that had treated me years before scared me. So I called the New Hampshire clinic for a referral.

"Believe it or not, one of our best oncologists has just moved to Wisconsin," a woman told me. "His name is Dr. Paul LeMarbre. I think you'll like him."

Of course, she had no idea he was the same doctor who had helped design the chemotherapy regimen I had selected five years prior. Incredibly, he had just relocated to an oncology clinic in Waukesha, about forty-five minutes from my doorstep in Racine.

Everybody has explanations as to why people's paths cross at certain times. I lean toward the theory espoused by author Tony Hillerman, who earned the distinction of being an honorary Navajo for his dead-on portrayals of Indian culture in the Southwest. His police detective characters are convinced that coincidences do not exist. I suppose my reconnection with Dr. LeMarbre could be labeled as destiny, preordainment, or a harmonic convergence, but it struck me as a jolt of universal fortune, a bit of order on a chaotic planet. I scheduled an appointment in March 1994 and tried to convince myself it would be routine.

It didn't start out well. Run-of-the-mill blood tests revealed disconcerting numbers. My liver enzymes had rocketed. Dr. LeMarbre tried to reassure me that a cocktail the night before could have caused the spike. But, I hadn't sipped any alcohol for at least a week. My internal alarm buzzed.

I scheduled a CT scan for the following week. The news wasn't good. My unyielding nemesis had evidently not exhausted its sneaky bag of tricks. Extensive follow-up tests showed masses—most likely malignant melanomas—had migrated to my liver. The only relief was that it had inundated one, not both, liver lobes. Throwing up was the only hint my body had given me that something was wrong. Cancer's cold, bony fingers were once again intent on squeezing the life out of me just as I was beginning to unfurl, stand back up, and walk tall. Couldn't I borrow somebody else's body? This one required too much maintenance.

Even though the melanoma tumors in my lungs had "vanished" after my 1991 hike, that long walk unfortunately hadn't meant the rest of my organs would be spared. I had only myself to blame. I lectured myself sternly for skipping that Charlottesville oncologist and then not being more persistent about a potential liver problem during my post-hike appointment in New Hampshire. That lack of courage was now making everything more difficult for everybody. What had I been thinking?

Dr. LeMarbre was nowhere near as harsh on me as I was on myself. He seemed alarmed but not frantic. He confidently carried on as if cancer-in-the-liver conversations were part of his daily ritual. When I told him that in my cancer script the "melanoma always won," he said he understood my thinking, but that I should give his staff a chance to prove that assumption wrong. He hugged me and, very matter-of-factly and reassuringly, told me I would need surgery and that he would track down the finest doctors. His demeanor was so calming that I wasn't all that frightened.

Fear caught up with me several weeks later while I sat on an examining table facing my chief surgeon. When I squeaked out that I was under the impression only one liver lobe would be removed, he quickly corrected me. This was stage 4 cancer, the worst of the worst. My gallbladder also would have to come out, not because it was diseased, but due to its proximity to my liver. They had also discovered an unexplained mass lodged near my pancreas that was too remote to be biopsied. Somehow, cells had broken away from melanoma in my skin, my lymph system, my lungs, or elsewhere, and traveled to my abdomen. Surgery was my only option. No radiation or chemotherapy cocktail could touch this menace. If my pancreas happened to be compromised during the surgery, I would have to be on insulin treatments for the rest of my life. To top it off, if I waited to act, the cancer would likely metastasize to other organs.

"I've never done such a complicated surgery before," the surgeon told me, his gaze meeting my unblinking eyes directly. "The scan shows us only so much, so I'm not even sure what I will find when we open you up. We might not be able to do anything at all once we take a look. And, if you come through it, I don't know what kind of shape you'll be in. This is really serious." I felt like a rabbit when it glimpses a pursuing hawk's shadow and knows it can no longer outrun the razor-sharp talons poised above its neck.

I don't remember the solitary forty-five-minute drive home after that appointment. I didn't go back to the newsroom because I didn't want to talk. After I climbed the stairs to our second-story apartment with a view of Lake Michigan, I curled up with Wilbur, the cat I had rescued from a Vermont shelter. Don and I used to jokingly call him a "comfort cat" because of his innate calming abilities.

I scheduled the surgery for early July at the hospital in Waukesha. Reluctantly, I called my mother. I assured her that Don and my friends would help me through the surgery and that she could come to Wisconsin later. Hadn't she already been through enough? I explained the whole sordid situation in a letter that I mailed to my best friend from high school, an oncology nurse in Massachusetts.

On that July day, I was rolled into an operating room, and the anesthesiologist asked me to count backward from ten. I did. Then I told a joke, and he looked at me incredulously, wondering aloud how I could still be awake. When he directed me to count again, I don't think I reached five before my world went dark.

It turned out to be a five-hour operation. By the time my nurse friend opened the envelope I had mailed to her, I was already out of intensive care, where I had the audacity to throw up on the poor nurse who awakened me. Don was there to hold my hand. I hadn't asked anybody for results yet because the thought of knowing petrified me. Maybe it was true that no news was good news. At that moment, I was just happy to have survived. At least one tube was attached to each orifice, making me look and feel like a chemistry experiment gone awry. The one sprouting from my trachea limited communication with visitors and hospital staffers to nods and grunts for several days. I tried to keep the tube draining my stapled midsection covered with a bedsheet because the brownish juices it emitted periodically were not very pleasant. What a body discharged during the course of a day was obviously necessary, but the reality of it was quite disgusting.

A few days later, my surgeon slipped into my room. I was alone. It was the first time I had made eye contact with him since I had faded to anesthetized black. Instinctively, I searched his face for an unspoken answer. It's a game all cancer veterans play. Just as fortune-tellers interpret the lines on our hands, we adroitly read the sighs, smiles, frowns, and solemn glances of a doctor before he or she even utters a word. My brain, loopy with painkillers and other medications, raced through the possible permutations. Did the quick smile he flashed mean he had encouraging words, or would I need more surgery? Chemotherapy? Radiation? Or was I beyond treatment, another pitiful victim of what Stephen King has bluntly labeled "The Big C?"

He must have known the rules of the cancer game because he spoke almost immediately.

"Elizabeth," he said gently. "I feel quite positive that we removed all of the cancer. Now you just need to heal."

My mouth trembled so severely that I couldn't even shape a "thank you." Leaping from the bed with joy wasn't an option, so instead I thrust my bruised right arm upward and clenched my tethered fist.

Then, quickly returning to stoic doctor mode, he told me he was also there to extract my drainage tube. I, too, was grateful to focus on a more mundane topic.

"This is going to hurt," he said solemnly as he adeptly snapped on a

167

pair of latex gloves. "But I'll be quick about it." I braced my supine body against the mattress as he leaned over and grasped the end of the large tan plastic tube protruding from the patchwork of surgical staples and bandages covering my entire midsection. I scrunched my eyes shut as he gave it a sturdy but expert yank. For a few seconds, it felt as if a scared cat had scrambled across my innards with every claw exposed. Then it was over.

My instinct in those uncomfortable situations was to resort to humor to put other people at ease. I couldn't help it. It was a trait my father had perfected.

"Let's experiment with new ways of pain," I joked feebly when the foot-long tube dangled from his hand like a limp snake.

The surgeon smiled and then left my room. I was content to lie there for the next few hours, letting the happiness overwhelm the hurt.

The doctors and nurses told me that the more I moved, the faster my abdominal cavity would heal. I didn't need much prompting. Those magical words from my surgeon propelled me on seemingly endless forays around and around the linoleum oval of the hospital's fourth floor. Always in tow was the metal pole on wheels laden with plastic bags of various restorative juices that flowed into my recovering body.

I could never find a comfortable position in the adjustable hospital bed. One night, I bollixed up the electric bed controls so badly that I sandwiched myself between the ends of my mattress.

"I guess I shouldn't be doing sit-ups just yet," I said to the giggling nurse who freed me from the bed's evil grasp. She allowed me to rest on a vinyl-covered recliner in the hallway—the only place I could position myself so I could sleep.

I felt like I would suffocate from being cooped up in that sterile room with its hermetically sealed windows. The air, tinged with smells of chemicals and disinfectants, made me gag. I craved the caress of sunshine, the feel of real air on my crippled body, and the sound of birds singing. After a few days, I convinced the kind nurse who had liberated me from the "bed sandwich" to take me outside, even though I wasn't yet free of the pole holding my intravenous drip. She was about my age. In my hospital-issue bathrobe and slippers, I crept along the walkways near the hospital entrance. Still, I was elated to gulp down mouthfuls of air scented with equal parts perfume from the nearby flowers and exhaust from circling vehicles picking up patients.

That same nurse wanted to accompany me on my foray outside on my first day without an IV pole, but I told her I knew my way around and would be fine on my own. She relented. I told her not to be alarmed if I was gone for longer than my usual thirty minutes.

Bored with my regular shuffle around the hospital grounds, I ventured a bit farther in pursuit of green space where I could enjoy a little peace and quiet. And I was on the verge of doing so when I was abruptly interrupted by an authoritative male voice.

"Ma'am, you're going to have to slow down," said a man trailing twenty-five-or-so feet behind me as I hobbled toward a picnic table adjacent to a set of swings in a city park.

Slow down? my medicated brain puzzled. *Who* couldn't *keep up with me?* Cripes, I had fifty-plus metal staples knitting together the chevron incision in my midsection. I was hunched over like a gnome because I was afraid that straightening my spine would force the staples to pop out. Merely inhaling a full breath put a painful strain on my compromised lungs. If I were navigating any more slowly in these ridiculous hospital-issue slippers, I would be standing still.

I parked myself on a picnic table bench to catch my breath. When I looked up, I was staring directly into the green eyes of a gun-toting police officer whose leather belt was strained by a prodigious belly. *Good grief, I am* literally one step ahead of the law, I thought.

"Somebody called to report a patient walking in the neighborhood," the officer said gruffly. "We need to know who you are. Hold out your wrist so I can see your hospital bracelet."

Oh my, I thought as I squinted into the sun and thrust forward a limp and pale freckled arm bedecked with a white plastic identification strip. A hypothetical headline in the next day's newspaper flashed into my overtaxed brain: "Officer shoots rambling 33-year-old patient." I knew I had some explaining to do.

Slowly, selecting my words ever-so-carefully and hoping I sounded cogent, I told him that this must all be a tangled misunderstanding. "I just had cancer surgery," I started, and explained how liberating it had felt to venture outside.

He relaxed when a voice over his radio verified that my bracelet code confirmed me as a surgical patient at the hospital. He offered me a ride in his patrol car. I declined, saying I feared I would be too sore to extricate myself from it. He just nodded when I told him I would walk back to the hospital as soon as I regained equilibrium. He radioed his headquarters to let them know he had tracked me down. Then I heard him ask the dispatcher to call the hospital to let them know of my whereabouts. I waved as he pulled away from the park.

As I sat there, recovering, I started to put two and two together. What I hadn't relayed to the officer was that I had been restricted to a diet of crushed ice at the hospital because my body wasn't ready for liquids or solids. I'd had a severe hankering for ginger ale. I remember mentioning that ginger ale craving to a man who had slowed his car and rolled down his window to ask if I was OK. I had also told him how good it was to be free and alive. I'm sure he's the one who called the police. Looking down at myself, I realized that man had every reason to be alarmed by my presence in his neighborhood. He probably figured I had escaped from the hospital's psychiatric unit. My hair was sticking out every which way, I likely had a freedom-at-last smile plastered on my face, and logic wasn't my strongest asset that day, considering the heavy-duty painkillers I was taking.

I resolved to remain silent on the walk back to the hospital. The park where I had ended up wasn't all that far away, but I had walked at least a mile because of the circuitous route I'd navigated. I took a shorter return route. "We heard about your little adventure," one of the guards said to me, laughing, as I passed the security desk on the way to my room.

"I knew you were my favorite patient for a reason," my ally, the nurse who had first accompanied me outside, told me with a tender hug. "Good for you for getting back on your feet. We're all pulling for you."

An hour or so later, my surgeon entered my room and found me back in bed, a little tired. I watched him eye the balled-up foam slippers that I had flung near the window.

"Word has gotten around about your expedition," he announced, trying to contain a grin. "All of the security guards are talking about it. You know, we were going to keep you here a few more days, but I think your little escapade proved that you're ready to go home today."

"Well, I didn't exactly have such an exit strategy in mind when I started out this morning," I replied. "But if it's my ticket out of here, I'll take it."

CHAPTER 28
MISSOURI: AN OZARKIAN ODYSSEY, OH MY!

MILES RIDDEN: 2,689
MILES TO GO: 1,561

Missouri, my seventh state, was a mere six miles from BJ and Eddie's Pittsburg doorstep. Lolling around in their Kansas hospitality made me feel like such a slacker that I aimed for, and accomplished, an ambitious 75.5-mile day after leaving their house on October 6. I pitched my tent in a small Walnut Grove park adjacent to an elementary school. Missourians in that southern part of the Show-Me State seemed to have more of an edge, but maybe they just felt sharper to my softened, spoiled self.

They might not have been as effusive as Kansans, but they weren't unfriendly. I was touched that night by the thoughtfulness of a harried waitress trying to serve tables full of loud, demanding families with small children at the Dinner Bell. Cashew fried chicken was all the rage at these regional restaurants. It did not taste like any Chinese cuisine I had eaten before, but my growling stomach was grateful that it was warm and there was a lot of it.

After the dining room calmed down, the waitress surprised me by wishing me good luck and placing a piece of coconut cream pie before me. It was too small to sell, she explained with a smile. I had been lingering over hot tea and my journal, delaying my walk to a cold tent. Temperatures were supposed to drop into the thirties. It was no longer summer, and the dark's earlier arrival made for excruciatingly long nights.

The next day, in Marshfield, a community of about forty-three hundred near where Interstate 44 crosses Highway 38, I stopped at a convenience store to eat lunch and camel up on water. The friendly store clerk regaled me with her memories of 1976 when pelotons of cyclists participating in the Bikecentennial event rolled through her community. She was eleven years old that year when riders from around the world inaugurated the TransAmerica Bicycle Trail to celebrate this nation's two hundredth birthday. Back then, helmets were almost nonexistent, and gear was clunky and low-tech. Local businesses donated money so she and her sister could hand out free lemonade to bicyclists in their nearby don't-blink-or-you'll-miss-it hometown of Odin. She had clipped and saved a black-and-white photograph from the local newspaper showing sweaty cyclists gathered around her drink stand.

"I still laugh about that photo because of the bell-bottom pants I had on," she said. "I thought I was incredibly hip and groovy. Interacting with all of those out-of-towners was quite an education for a fifth-grader from a small town."

The second delight of that day happened when I rolled into Hartville late that same afternoon, after a sixty-nine-mile day. As I stood on the lawn in front of the county courthouse—a makeshift campground the community opens to cyclists—to scout out a level spot for my tent, I thought I was imagining a voice asking: "Would you like to stay inside tonight?" I turned to find the question came from a real person, Richard. He and his wife, Becky, were co-owners of nearby Steph's Restaurant and its adjacent hostel for bicyclists. Richard was a chatterbox extraordinaire, but I was willing to tolerate his loquaciousness to bunk where it was warm.

Frost coated the courthouse lawn the next morning. Exiting Hartville on October 8, I officially entered the intimidating Ozark Mountains, which cover at least forty thousand square miles. Many longtime residents are the descendants of hunters, trappers, and farmers who didn't need flat land. Their ancestors moved to these mountains long ago from the hill country of Appalachia. "Outsiders" intruded during the timber-cutting era of the late 1880s. Today, many calling these mountains and hollows home live hand-to-mouth. The bicycle route goes nowhere near such recreational playgrounds as Lake of the Ozarks or Branson music halls.

The uninitiated might think cyclists would be wise to load up on their Wheaties for the peaks of the Rockies. Indeed, the profile maps of climbs in Idaho, Montana, Wyoming, and Colorado look much more intimidating. But, phew, the Ozarks—where my map's ups and downs resembled an EKG readout of a heart gone berserk—issued me a sound spanking. The rhyme I hummed each climb was "inch-by-inch, it might be a cinch, but yard-by-yard, it was quite hard."

The Ozarks formed when an ancient seabed began buckling at least a million years ago. Geologists consider this rugged series of deeply eroded hills, sculpted by rivers and wind, to be some of the oldest in the world. Today the Ozarks are a rich botanical crossroads. Soils here support a mixture of pines and other softwoods, but dominant hardwoods include walnut, oak, hickory, and sassafras. An industrious entrepreneur in eastern Kansas and across Missouri could make a small fortune collecting and selling black walnuts. Homemade signs at tiny cafés, post offices, markets, and hardware stores advertised a going rate of ten dollars for a hundred pounds of hulled nuts.

Flaming yellows, oranges, and reds framed the mountain towns of Yukon, Eunice, Summersville, Alley Spring, Eminence, Owls Bend, Ellington, and Centerville in stellar autumnal glory. That beauty, however, didn't mask the deceptively difficult elevations no higher than seventeen hundred feet. The old roadways weaving these communities together were hell on quadriceps and hamstrings. No switchbacks eased the climbing. It was like riding a roller coaster—with your legs as the sole source of power. As I pedaled uphill in granny gear, the only people I passed were Amish families in horse-drawn buggies. Fortunately, I had enough wind in my lungs to sputter "hello" because I would have fallen over if I had attempted to wave. Paved shoulders had basically disappeared at the Kansas-Missouri border. For safety's sake, I wished the highway department had added an image of a bicycle to those yellow "Share the Road" signs depicting an Amish buggy.

I saw so many leathery armadillo bodies squashed on the Ozarks asphalt that I wondered if these peculiar plated animals had somehow evolved to develop the worst timing in the history of mammals. The critter carnage I had surveyed since Oregon included elk, deer, rabbits, raccoons, opossums, chipmunks, skunks, foxes, coyotes, mice, snakes, turtles, and birds. That sad tally reminded me that the open road might represent freedom to us bipedal types, but it's nothing more than a menace to animals trying to collect food for their young, migrate to their mating grounds, or protect their territorial boundaries. I didn't dismount for any armadillos, but I had gotten off my bike way back near Scott City, Kansas, to gingerly move a gorgeous but lifeless barn owl off the center line of Highway 96. Damage under its feathers suggested a truck had clipped the poor creature as it hunted in the dark for its next meal.

I had no idea where I would pitch my tent on October 9, but hunger forced me into the Quik Stop in Centerville that afternoon. My reward was learning the origin of a machine-made sign in the parking lot that read: "No Parking Unless You Are a Bob." The cheerful clerk was happy to spill the beans. Even though Centerville had a population of 194, her store somehow attracted seventeen regular customers named Bob. She had assigned nicknames to distinguish one Bob from another. For instance, Nurse Bob worked at the local hospital, Lawnmower Bob mowed municipal parks, and Pioneer Bob had left urban life behind to live in a Centerville cabin without running water. I waited around for half an hour, hoping for a Bob sighting, but unfortunately none occurred.

The idea of a bounty of Bobs kept me laughing another twelve miles to Johnson's Shut-ins State Park to do some quick calculations. Pilot Knob was definitely too far away for a late-afternoon push, but Highway N on my map was clearly marked with a restaurant symbol. Maybe there was also a church or school nearby. Just as darkness started to swallow the day and I started to get nervous that I might have pushed my luck too far, I spied a building on my left. A sign advertised it as the Blue Valley Bar. It was perched hard by the roadway, encircled by half a dozen trailer homes. Hallelujah! After sixty strenuous miles, it was time to get off the bike.

Even though it was a Monday night, country music erupted from the bar's jukebox. Over the strains of a morose George Jones, I told my traveling tale to the kind-eyed bartender. Of course, his name was Bob, but he wasn't one of the Centerville seventeen. Judging by the look on his face, I was likely one of the first cross-country cyclists to visit his bar. But he graciously directed me to the restroom and gave me permission to shoehorn my tent into the narrow, scrappy side yard.

Surveying my surroundings from a barstool, I sensed that I had entered the Cheers of the Ozarks. I could pick out Sam, Norm, Cliff, Carla, and a handful of other characters. These self-described hillbillies told jokes, shot pool, downed cans of domestic beer by the case, and sucked on endless cigarettes. Bob, wearing a Los Angeles Rams sweatshirt, served as a referee of sorts while meeting the needs of this good-natured clan. I wasn't carrying much food that day, and the tiny kitchen at the bar wasn't open on Mondays, so I figured I would make do with Slim Jims and peanuts. The woman on the barstool next to me came to my rescue. Recently retired as the bar's cook, she was back to spend a leisurely evening at her favorite haunt. When she heard about my plight, she slid off her shiny black stool. Minutes later, she reappeared with a couple of burritos she had kindly cobbled together with kitchen leftovers. I opted to delay an early exit to my tent because everybody was so friendly. I also bought more iced tea, hoping it would soothe my smoke-choked throat.

In between explaining my ride's mission, laughing, and trying to dance the two-step in my cycling cleats with a customer celebrating his birthday, I listened to poignant stories about locals' dreams, hopes, and fears. The man celebrating his birthday, who was probably close to my age, told me that six miles away he had a couch on his porch that I was welcome to use. But I politely said no, telling him I needed to be close to my bicycle and tent to prepare for an early morning departure. Another patron, Steve, who earned just above minimum wage at the local scrapyard, invited me to his trailer across the street so I could meet his wife, Laurie—a cancer survivor.

Laurie, a thirty-nine-year-old mother of three, greeted me as if I were her best friend from high school. She had worked at the local salvage yard with her husband until injuring her back. A surgeon had recently removed a disc from her back to relieve the pain, and she wasn't allowed to run or jump because she had been told that one wrong move could lead to instant paralysis. As if that wasn't enough, she had undergone a hysterectomy at age twenty-seven after being diagnosed with uterine cancer. Now her entire world consisted of a couch in a trailer, with an attentive husband, three dogs, a huge television, and cartons of cigarettes for company.

Close to midnight, Steve and Laurie insisted that I sleep on their couch. I declined, reassuring them I would be plenty toasty in my tent, and wondering how many lung cells I had already sacrificed. Before departing, I helped them dismantle their stereo and store it under the bed so their nephew—their temporary boarder while he rebuilt his messy life—wouldn't blast it when he came home drunk in the wee hours. "If you don't see any movement in the morning near my tent, come thaw me with your hair dryer," I joked before venturing into the bitter cold.

I brushed my teeth under a crown of stars. As I hunkered down into my alarmingly cold sleeping bag, I reviewed the characters I had just met in this lovely but hardscrabble region. Steve, Laurie, and their friends could have been mired in puddles of self-absorbed sorrow and depression, but instead they extended every kindness to a stranger. Despite their enormous hardships and troubles, they hadn't forgotten how to laugh—at themselves and the odd world around them. They lived about as close to the bone as one could get but were willing to share everything they had.

The temperature dipped to the high twenties that night, so I spent a healthy portion of it rolling around to keep my blood circulating. Still, I knew my sleeping bag's synthetic lining and the polypropylene hat I had pulled over my ears weren't my only sources of warmth. I was so happy to have felt kinship and to have made yet another connection on this open journey. At dawn, I was grateful to be invited back to Steve and Laurie's trailer. In their steamy bathroom, I pulled on every layer of clothing I had, including polypropylene long underwear, a fleece jacket, wind pants, a rain jacket, and lightweight gloves. My biking shoes were so stiff that I had to waddle like a penguin while crossing the road to reach my bike. The water in my bicycle bottle was an ice block, and I brushed a thick crust of frost off my tent and panniers before rolling about twelve miles to Pilot Knob for a hot breakfast.

Months later, near Christmas 2000, I sent out hundreds of Heals on Wheels thank-you cards with a photo of me and my bicycle. Of course, the Blue Valley Bar was on my list. I mailed a card to "Bob the Bartender," using a zip code from the largest neighboring community. I half-expected the envelope to be returned to me in Wisconsin within a few days, marked undeliverable.

CHAPTER 29
EXCISING INVASIVES

After my liver lobe was excised in July 1994, a series of CT scans revealed that the remaining half was boldly re-establishing itself in any available abdominal space. That spread was expected because the liver is the only internal organ that regenerates like that. What was unexpected was when my oncologist noticed "something unusual" peppering my spleen in July 1997.

A spleen biopsy is next to impossible because even a healthy one is delicate, blood-rich, and easily damaged, Dr. LeMarbre explained. He and others strongly recommended removing my spleen to keep any festering melanoma at bay. At first, I questioned the necessity of sacrificing yet another organ. But I consented. I had entrusted these doctors with my life before and had little reason to doubt their judgment.

Dr. LeMarbre was a rare and genuine combination of compassion, competence, and thoughtfulness. He and I had built a bond of trust. With him, I felt as if I was part of a solutions-driven team, not a subordinate taking orders from high above. When he entered an examination room where I waited nervously, he did not see "Melanoma Case 9564." Instead, he embraced me as an individual and as a fellow baseball fan with roots in Massachusetts. Rather than stare at the clock and calculate how much time I would suck up, he acted as if I was his only patient.

If he thought I was a lost cause medically, I never detected it. And he didn't let me drift into panic mode. During tough times, he would look me in the eye, succinctly state the facts about my health, and answer all of my questions. I had always heard, and strongly doubted, that medicine was a calling, not a career. Interacting with this soft-spoken cancer specialist left me questioning my skepticism. His calm demeanor and humanity set a standard I still use as a measuring stick for any physician. He and his nurses did not attempt to estimate what might be left of my life in months or years, and I never asked them to be such macabre odds-makers. They acted as if I would live to be 102. *Why not?* I found myself asking. *I can't die yet—not when these people are putting so much effort into keeping me alive.*

Even though a spleen is a key cog of a body's immune system, most adults can prosper without one, Dr. LeMarbre told me, confirming my own findings. Some potent bacteria are wily enough to infect the lungs, brain, and blood of a spleenless body. But a series of vaccinations and follow-up booster shots usually mitigate those threats.

In July 1997, I was admitted to the hospital on a Thursday night, a surgeon removed my spleen the next morning, and I was home by Saturday night. That schedule was as close to outpatient surgery as my doctors would allow. Post-operative laboratory tests revealed a host of unhealthy, precancerous cells in my spleen.

I was relieved to be freed of those unfit bits, but it was again up to me to regain full range of motion after a second abdominal surgery. That meant more walking, but in a different setting. The place Don and I now called home was a single-story pine-and-cedar cabin nestled among the oak and hickory trees of a six-hundred-acre nature preserve. Instead of looking out my window at expansive Lake Michigan as I had in Racine, I could sit on my porch and see a much smaller lake that glaciers had carved out eons ago. Landing there, on that mix of prairie, wetlands, and upland forests southwest of Milwaukee, was serendipitous.

From Racine, Don and I had regularly traveled an hour west to the nature preserve to work with a volunteer crew on weekends. In the spring of 1997, the private conservation organization that protected the preserve sought on-site caretakers. Once Don and I figured we could balance our full-time jobs with part-time caretaking, we applied. We moved in a few months later. The cabin was one of several buildings that the owners of a boys' camp had built decades ago.

In the early 1990s, The Nature Conservancy had purchased the property and renamed it Lulu Lake Preserve. Scientists recognized the preserve as one of Wisconsin's ecological treasures. Although the acreage had endured iterations as a farm, a boys' camp, and a corporate retreat for health care company executives, it was still a shining example of the undisturbed natural world.

In addition to Lulu Lake, biologists were enamored not only with one of the healthiest rivers in Wisconsin but also the prairies, oak savannas, fens, bogs, and an assortment of other wetlands. If a Potawatomi Indian who hunted and fished these grounds up until the early 1800s were to miraculously return today, he would still recognize the kettles, kames, moraines, outwashes, and other formations that the receding glacier left behind when it reshaped this part of the planet ten thousand or so years ago. He might lose his bearings for a few minutes when encountering the five buildings, the flattened expanse near the lake that was paved for tennis courts, and the dike that served as a railroad spur to haul travelers, ice, and other goods in the late nineteenth and early twentieth centuries. But for the most part, he would be able to find his way.

179

The land undulates, uninterrupted, from one intact ecosystem to another. That perfect fit makes it a living example of why Aldo Leopold, one of Wisconsin's premier ecologists, warned that when you start tinkering intelligently with any one part of the planet, your first act ought to be saving all of the parts. No asphalt roads, subdivisions of McMansions, or big-box stores disturb the land's flow or block the stars. Instinctively, nature knew what to do to mend these broken parts. It just needed a bit of human intervention to accelerate that journey to wholeness.

Our volunteer crew wasn't interested in taming nature. Rather, we were intent on restoring the place to a reasonable facsimile of what it was before the first white settlers arrived in the mid-1800s. Our guides were detailed plant and animal surveys from the nineteenth century and expertise from today's scientists. We cut, lopped, dragged, sawed, and sprayed with enough devout fervor to be evangelistic. So perhaps it wasn't surprising that Sundays yielded consistently fruitful turnouts. The standing joke among our core of veterans was that we did so much work on our knees, it could pass for worship. We kneeled on soil, not pews, our "altar" a makeshift desk in a garage where we consulted project maps designed by botanists and biologists. Our holy book was a field guide to plants of the Upper Midwest. We might not have been religious in the traditional sense, but that didn't mean we were faithless. Our labors were spiritually fulfilling.

Our reverence for this place ran deep. Who, after all, would dare to doubt the faith of people who believed that seed by seed, branch by branch, scarred pieces of land could be resurrected? Our tasks were deceptively simple, but what we were trying to accomplish was startlingly complex. Those layers made it intriguing.

Interacting so closely with plants, dirt, and water synced my body with different rhythms. In the depths of winter, I knew that late-night "who cooks for you" calls meant that barred owls were seeking mates. When their babies fledged in early spring, food would be plentiful. Through spring and summer, when kettles and vernal ponds hosted a cacophony of amphibian mating music, I learned how to distinguish the musical whistle of spring peepers from the jingle-bell call of chorus frogs, and to discern the distinctive banjo strum of green frogs. Those lessons made me aware that as much as we humans try to distance ourselves from the changing of the seasons, the phases of the moon, and predator-prey relationships, we cannot escape them. Our larger brains, supposedly advanced social systems, and cutting-edge technology don't absolve us of responsibility for our inheritance.

Many restoration techniques were gentle, nurturing, and quiet. But I was initially caught off guard by the assortment of loud and dangerous tools—lawnmower blades, chainsaws, weed whackers, and even fire—we employed to shape nature gone slightly awry. For instance, an elongated metal blade that whirs at the bottom of any garden-variety motorized lawn mower was most excellent for girdling trees.

As a new volunteer, I headed to a copse of aspens to execute what I laughingly referred to as "tree-killer duties." Using the sharp edge of the lawnmower blade, I cut away several layers of bark, making a single ring around each tree. Girdling involved stripping away the smooth, protective light-colored bark of opportunistic trees that invaded preserve uplands because of their ability to send out roots and shoots from an underground stem called a rhizome. While native to the region, aspens were aggressively crowding out indigenous trees and shading out native plants. Girdling eventually choked off vital nutrients flowing up their trunks. Once dead, the aspens toppled to the ground, where they decomposed and enriched the soil.

As a caretaker a few years later, when the preserve became the biggest backyard I ever had, I wandered to that same grove of aspen where I honed my tree-butchering skills. Graying trunks, small enough to be loose in my encircled arms, were each marked by a distinctive ring of missing bark. Some of the dying trees were already brittle, while others had sprouted pitiful sprays of yellow leaves.

I floated my fingers along one of the rough circular wounds, while my other hand reached for my own paler and more pliable trunk. Tracing the map that surgeons' scalpels had imprinted on my own bark, my skin, allowed me to follow the journey of my melanoma. For starters, there was the half-dollar-size indent on my freckled upper back where the first melanoma skin lesion had appeared. Just an inch or so above that was a rippling, washboard-like scar shaped like the outline of a spaceship, created when a malignant lymph node was sliced out. Adjacent to that was an expert piece of handiwork, a wan necklace-shaped scar encircling the left side of my neck where a long string of lymph nodes had been extricated. Lower down, the stark white line resembling an old-fashioned Christmas tree ornament hook, on the right side of my trunk, was the tender spot where a surgeon had separated two of my ribs to cut into my lung to confirm the oncologist's suspicions of melanoma. And that final scar, resembling a very large capital *Y* at rest on its side, splayed across the entire front of my midsection. An extension on that chevron indicated the entrance a surgeon had cut to remove my spleen.

With all of those "repairs," it was no wonder the good-natured technician at the hospital always sucked in her breath while orchestrating my CT scans. She had never seen so many surgical clips holding innards

181

together, she always told me, prompting jokes about the duct tape and baling twine keeping me intact. That was the only comforting moment during that tense, two-hour procedure that required me to be hooked up to an intravenous dye and then remain motionless, controlling my breath, so the series of pictures wouldn't be blurry.

Scientists claim that once physical pain heals, our brains cannot reinvent it. I have trouble believing that. Sometimes I can relive pain just by thinking about a particular scar. The memory makes me catch my breath and instinctively cover my torso. Maybe that's why I have to turn my head or shield my eyes so I won't wince when witnessing precious pieces of our countryside under helter-skelter assault from platoons of bulldozers, excavators, backhoes, and pile drivers. Stomach-turning "Coming Soon" signs herald new subdivisions, office complexes, and strip malls. Once you sully the lay of a landscape, it's about impossible to recover it. The optimist in me wants to live long enough to see "Coming Soon" signs that announce reclaimed wetlands, prairies, forests, and oak savannas on those same sites.

As that gaping mechanical maw gobbles its way through prairies, chews up trees by the roots, and strips away topsoil, my mind is filled with the image of a hideous and endless rape. The perpetrator never leaves, and the victim is forever pinned under its bulk, voiceless and gasping for air. An urge to excise that violent picture from my mind was what guided me to the preserve to do some doctoring of my own.

Loppers, bow saws, and my own ten fingers were the instruments I wielded to extricate what didn't belong. Those included plants such as garlic mustard, buckthorn, honeysuckle, purple loosestrife, and white clover that European settlers had brought along to their new homeland. The plants from overseas adapted beautifully, displacing their native brethren just as white settlers infiltrated land once prized by native people. Pulling, cutting, burning, and carefully applying herbicides are the only ways to euthanize these overly abundant aliens once they inundate the preserve. If the indigenous plants were to sink into oblivion because they could no longer compete with these pugnacious newcomers, then the insects, birds, and other animals that have counted on them for centuries for food and shelter also will exit—forever. I doubt that's the legacy most of us want to leave.

Fire is the scalpel of the savanna. It can quickly eradicate what doesn't belong and give a fighting chance to what does. Lightning-induced, quick-moving flames once raged across such grasslands before the early twentieth century when fearful humans doused such fires. By training with a prescribed burn crew on the preserve, I learned the value of those medicinal flames. We counted on an assortment of drip torches, flappers, rakes, and water backpacks to mimic the cleansing fires of yore sparked by lightning. Sometimes, we paddled canoes down the preserve's skinny, crooked creek, using flares to light off grasses, sedges, and dozens of other water-loving species lining its edges. Brown fluffy cattail heads would launch themselves, arcing like sizzling bottle rockets before flaming out in the lake water. The fires, which Native Americans traditionally also used to flush game for more plentiful hunting harvests, push out unwelcome alien vegetation. Native plants took note. In spring, once the sun warmed those blackened swaths of Earth, their new shoots got a head start by peeking out ahead of invasives.

Perhaps it's not all that surprising that the spelling of oncology, the word for the study of tumors, is so similar to ecology, the study of relationships between organisms and their environment. Just as I had withstood my own rounds of medicinal fire, the preserve's staunch oak trees were testaments to survival. As natives to this place, the oaks' tough bark can withstand a certain amount of heat and flame. And over the long run, fire helped to kill the pieces the trees don't need or want, thus strengthening the healthy limbs to spur new growth each spring. Like me, these trees are here for the long haul.

Periodically, my oncologist and I talked about experimenting with still-nascent melanoma vaccines. But the thought of injecting myself with the same disease I've tried so valiantly to fend off seemed counterintuitive. He agreed. Although he couldn't explain exactly why my immune system had repulsed rampant melanoma that had killed my father and so many others, he said he was reluctant to fiddle around too much with such a spunky defense. Maybe my T-cells and other white blood cells were my own internal fire burning away any unwelcome aggressors.

Sometimes I would stand, loppers and bow saw in hand, at the bottom of a hill coated with buckthorn and honeysuckle and feel overwhelmed. Where to start? If I wanted results overnight, I knew I was in the wrong place. Often, I felt as if I'd assigned myself to move the waters of the Atlantic with a teaspoon. But then there were the rewards.

One came in early April in the late 1990s near the south end of the preserve. Below two majestic bur oaks at the top of a hill was a south-facing slope above a type of wetland called a sedge meadow. In a nutshell, sedges are three-sided grasses that thrive in moist conditions. A few years earlier, my untrained eye would have labeled that slope a wilderness thicket. But my preserve lessons had taught me that it was really ecological squalor. Decades ago, grazing sheep had nibbled native grasses and flowers down to nubs, opening the way for a tangle of buckthorn, honeysuckle, white cedars, prickly ash, and thorny raspberry bushes. Our crews had spent hours clearing the overgrown snarl.

183

Each spring, we sought out just these types of bare spots to broadcast seeds of native grasses and flowers we had collected elsewhere on the preserve throughout the summer and autumn. We dried the precious and less plentiful seeds indoors in carefully marked paper bags over the winter. The more abundant seed stocks—those of little and big bluestem, goldenrod, and asters—were stored in bulging white sacks that we tied to ceiling beams in a preserve building. The idea was to keep hungry mice from gnawing at our bounty, but the room looked like it was filled with dozens of dangling, well-fed ghosts.

A flutter of light lavender caught my eye on an April visit to the newly cleared opening. I bent to take a closer look at the delicate blooming treasure: a pasqueflower. Right on cue, the rare beauty was blooming close to Easter. Walking in small circles with my head down and eyes alert, I soon counted five, six, seven, eight, nine, ten, then eleven other flowers in its vicinity. Their floppy purplish petal-like sepals and yellow centers cupped in a green leaf-life calyx coated with silky hair gave them an elegant appearance. How long, I wondered, had those seeds been buried in the hillside, shouldered out by burlier invasive species, just waiting for some sunshine so they could reappear after years of dormancy? I now had firsthand evidence that our labors were making a difference.

And that wasn't the only success. Such glories as kittentail, Jacob's ladder, shooting star, aster, goldenrod, blazing star, turtlehead, spiderwort, prairie bush clover, columbine, anemone, orchids, bloodroot, and hepatica now flourished where the competition wasn't so tough anymore. Witnessing these small but meaningful victories reminded me of my own insides.

Without the healing hands of doctors, surgeons, nurses, and anesthesiologists, I wouldn't have made it far in this eat-or-be-eaten Darwinian world where survival of the fittest counts. Left alone, the melanoma cells that manifested in my young body most likely would have continued to gorge themselves on my healthy parts, quickly reducing me to a lifeless husk to be returned to the soil. Just as we counted on fire, chemical agents, lawn mower blades, bow saws, and loppers to restore wholeness at the preserve, my physicians called on tools to excise intruders from my body.

Each spring, when we sprayed chemicals on invasive garlic mustard plants, we tried to direct them at only the "bad" species. Inevitably, however, some of the "good" plants adjacent to the garlic mustard also died from a toxic overdose. Chemotherapy, essentially chemical warfare on the body, operates on the same principle. It's powerful enough to annihilate the cancer cells, but healthy cells go down with it too. There's always the fear that everything will

CHAPTER 30
ILLINOIS: THE BIG MUDDY, FREE PIE, AND A FERRY RIDE

MILES RIDDEN: 3,015
MILES TO GO: 1,235

Seventy-four miles from the "hillbilly bar" in the Ozarks, I pedaled over the Mississippi River, the watery divide between Missouri and Illinois—my eighth state. It was October 10. Cyclists pretty much have a hello-and-goodbye relationship with the Land of Lincoln because the route crosses the state where it tapers to its skinniest point—a mere 142 miles.

Chester, the first community in Illinois, touts itself as the home of Popeye. Sure enough, its welcome sign sports a large cutout of the gravelly voiced sailor chomping on his pipe and clutching his trademark can of spinach. As if that isn't enough, an imposing Popeye statue on a pedestal in Segar Memorial Park honors Chester-native Elzie Crisler Segar, the creator of the muscular comic strip and cartoon character whose signature phrase was "I am what I am." I learned that Segar evidently based Popeye on a local scrapper, and Wimpy the hamburger fiend on his benefactor, William "Windy Bill" Schuchert, who owned the local opera house. It's a mystery as to who or what inspired sidekicks Brutus, Olive Oyl, and Swee'Pea.

The levee lands of the Mississippi River made bicycling blissful. Wheeling through farm country beyond Chester on October 11, I encountered only one car in thirty miles—and that driver was probably lost. Instead, my fellow travelers were oodles of grasshoppers and caterpillars that were on inches-at-a-time, belly-to-the-ground journeys of their own, and the flat floodplain allowed me the luxury of swerving to avoid squishing them. The windless weather was as forgiving as the landscape. I shed my thermal underwear and rode comfortably in shorts and a long-sleeved shirt. Opportunistic farmers were reaping the benefits of acres of alluvial richness, having planted what appeared to be enough soybeans to feed all of India and China. These wetlands had served as nature's sponges and filters before being plowed.

Bicycle-friendly geography wasn't all that made me pedal a little more aggressively. Part of it was anticipation. Don was driving down from Wisconsin to meet me that day. He would be my support vehicle for several days, checking on me as I pedaled into western Kentucky. Via pay phone, we set up a plan to meet early that afternoon at an intersection just west of Murphysboro above the Big Muddy River, a tributary of the Mississippi. Murphysboro was only thirty-eight miles east of Chester, so I had a short day.

I was making such good time that morning that I allowed myself to be sucked into the Bottoms Up Bar in Neunert, Illinois. I wasn't interested in alcohol, just something to calm my flip-floppy stomach. As I nibbled my way through a baked potato and a green salad, the man next to me regaled me with his favorite presidential campaign story from 2000. A local farmer with a sense of humor had rolled a pair of three-hundred-pound pumpkins into his field. He labeled one Bush and the other Gore. Then, the farmer made an editorial comment about the upcoming November vote by propping both of the giant squashes on a manure spreader.

My settled stomach and I were back on the bike by about noon. Murphysboro was only fifteen miles away. My route was clear until I reached the bridge crossing the Big Muddy. "Closed for Repair" read a giant orange sign. Oops! Off the bike, I began picking my way through the construction mess to see if I could navigate to our rendezvous site on the other side. Big, annoyingly loud machinery blocked the way. I probably could have asked one of the construction workers for permission to proceed across the bridge, but my inner shyness suddenly emerged. Bicyclists are often perceived as haughty and entitled, and I was going out of my way on this trip to show people that the me-first attitude didn't apply to everybody on two wheels. Anyway, why should I request a special privilege? So I turned around. No big deal, I could find a side street. I was not carrying a cell phone and nor was Don because signals across the country were quite spotty and roaming charges made such an investment cost-prohibitive. Unfortunately, my trail-centric map was vague, so I stopped at a house where a woman gave me a succinct detour.

Meanwhile, I was totally unaware that patient, loyal Don was already waiting on the other side of the closed bridge. He had probably been a hundred yards away—but invisible to me—when I had turned around. Also unbeknownst to me, he had asked two construction workers if they had seen a bicycle-wielding woman barging through the construction site because he assumed that was how I would handle the obstacle. Nope, they told him, no such sighting. When I didn't appear within a half hour or so of our scheduled meeting time, he traced the bicycle route all the way back to the Mississippi. Meanwhile, I completed the five-mile detour that delivered me to the other side of the bridge and, figuring that it was best to follow wilderness advice and stay put when somebody is looking for you, waited at our designated meeting spot.

I couldn't stop smiling when I saw a car with Wisconsin license plates pull up. Neither could Don. We dubbed our missed connection the version of *A Bridge Too Far* that Hollywood never made. The episode seemed uproariously funny because I was so punchy from lack of sleep. I hadn't taken a full day off since Pueblo, Colorado, so I had been riding at least a few miles every day for close to three weeks. Murphysboro was a welcome rest stop for a checklist that included a journal entry at a library, hospital outreach, a bed, a swimming pool, and a meal short on lard or grease. I didn't particularly care in what order my needs were met.

Chester, Murphysboro, and then Carbondale, which I pedaled through on October 13 after a day off, were the only stops in Illinois with more than a thousand inhabitants. The latter is a robust university city that prides itself on being the home of the Salukis, sleek hunting dogs first bred in and around ancient Egypt. My refreshed legs reveled in the gentle, rolling hills of southern Illinois after the oft-tortuous amusement ride that was the Missouri Ozarks. Oaks, hickories, maples, and sumacs were tinted with fall colors. I scoured high branches for large birds. Hawks waited for an unsuspecting rodent to make a mad dash across the asphalt. Vultures, their keen senses allowing them to smell death from afar, prepared to feast on squashed critters—the victims of bad timing. "The deader, the better" is, after all, a hungry vulture's motto.

Fair or not, long-distance bicyclists tend to judge a town's worth by its food—that is, how satisfied our stomachs are upon departure. That rudimentary ranking system prompted me to award Goreville, Illinois, an A+. The community of barely eight hundred is about twenty-six miles east of Carbondale on a rural road sandwiched between Interstates 57 and 24. When Don and I saw the Late Bloomer Café, I knew it had to be the five-star pie haven those long-ago bicycling "Cabooses" in Idaho advised me not to miss. In the late 1990s, Shirley, the owner, cook, and chief greeter, had collaborated with her husband to transform a rundown building into a cozy, cyclist-inspired respite.

Shirley's ninety-four-year-old mother, a cancer survivor, was a fixture at the corner table, where she methodically wrapped silverware in crisp paper napkins as white as her coiffed hair. After cheerful waitresses doled out heaping helpings of catfish, meatloaf, black-eyed peas, sweet potatoes, coleslaw, and iced tea, Shirley circulated the floor to make sure cross-country riders received their free slice of pie. As the sole lunchtime cyclist, I chose my favorite—cherry topped with vanilla ice cream. I was not disappointed.

"I meet all of these cyclists coming through here, and this is my way of contributing to your adventure," Shirley told me. "That makes me happy."

"Do you own a bicycle?" I asked.

"Well, I do, but I rarely take it out of the garage," she replied. "I just get too busy here. I don't have the stamina to ride across the country, but maybe someday I could do part of it."

"Hey, you could start now," I said. "My bike is leaning against your restaurant. It hardly weighs anything today because my panniers are in the car."

When I convinced her that her next round of pie-baking could wait a few minutes, we went outside so I could show her how my brakes and pedals worked.

Gamely, she got on and started riding down Goreville's main street. Don and I applauded as she circled back to the restaurant.

"That was kind of fun," she said. "Thanks for convincing me to try."

"Call me when you want to finish the Illinois section," I said, hugging her. "It's only about 140 miles long, and I'm just a one-day drive away. And I mean that."

People often argue about where the South starts and ends on maps. My taste buds tell me it's where iced tea that is almost crunchy with sugar appears on menus. On this ride, that was southern Illinois. Another tipoff is when ear-catchers such as "y'all," "reckon," "fixing to," and "yonder" creep into locals' speech. Goreville and Chicago might be in the same state and linked by Highway 57, but those are about the only characteristics the two communities have in common. In this slender southern spit of Illinois, agriculture is paramount, and the pace of life is more like molasses. The people here speak with a drawl unique to the region and are remarkably friendly, in a Kansas sort of way. One older man accompanied by his tiny dog spotted me pedaling in front of his house while fetching his mail west of Goreville. First, he hailed me to a stop and asked if I needed something to drink. Then, he announced that his house was always open, should I need food, phone, or drink. I was almost too shocked to respond.

On October 14, the day after a full moon lit up the horse camp where Don and I stayed near Robbs, Illinois, on Highway 147, I was standing in the community of Cave-In-Rock sucking on a blue raspberry frozen ice. I was just a few watery miles from my ninth state, Kentucky, waiting for the small ferry to tote us, the bike, and the car across the Ohio River. The ferry landing is at the edge of a 204-acre state park with, surprise, an actual cave in the rock. The imposing natural phenomenon was a landmark for settlers and boatmen.

The twenty-five-foot-high entrance, set in a topography of mini-badlands, has spawned boatloads of tall tales. Stories abound about how pirates such as Samuel Mason, once an officer in George Washington's

189

Revolutionary Army, and later the Harpe brothers, a pair of killers fleeing execution in Kentucky, used the cave as a base from which they preyed upon bewildered boat travelers. It's also heralded as a hideout where plunderers established a combination bar, casino, and whorehouse.

Entrepreneurial "river rats" along the Ohio River were adept at separating merchants from their valuables in the late 1700s and early 1800s. But the truth about the cave is blurry. Wild tales connected to it lack historical verification, according to the Illinois Department of Natural Resources. What is true is that this geological wonder was a well-known landmark on nineteenth-century maps. It served as a short-term shelter for pioneers and a tourist attraction for passengers on steam-powered riverboats. Hollywood producers were enamored enough of the cave's reputation that it served as a backdrop for the 1962 movie *How the West Was Won*. They chose to keep its midwestern location a secret.

Once the ferry arrived, Don drove aboard. I was the lone cyclist among a handful of cars. It was the only time on my journey that I didn't have to be atop my bicycle seat to move forward—and I still gained mileage crossing to Kentucky. Amazingly, it was a free ride.

CHAPTER 31
WHAT FUELED HIS FIRE?

For most of August 1976, my parents had our rambling house in Massachusetts entirely to themselves. My sisters and I were sent away. It was my parents' way of trying to shield us from the hideous scenario unfolding at home. They put the four of us—ages seventeen, fifteen, thirteen, and eleven—on a train to Cleveland. We spent most of the month with my mother's sister and her family and our grandparents and various other aunts and uncles in central Ohio. Being physically removed from the situation didn't make it any less painful for us. But my father was slipping away, and that was how he and my mother chose to have some of the toughest conversations of their lives.

My father was a pale, gaunt version of himself when we left. No amount of experimental chemotherapy or radiation had reined in the melanoma, and his balance and coordination were affected. Just guiding a fork to his mouth was a struggle. Pain made him so restless at night that my mother often retreated to an upstairs bedroom.

Still, my father was fueled by his usual sense, albeit somewhat diluted, of urgency. He worked diligently to complete his expansive kitchen project, which by then included painting walls and woodwork and finishing the floors. Even though he couldn't manage going to his office job, he became obsessed with sorting books and papers in his study, or tools and other miscellany in his barn workshop.

One August day, my mother was alone in the kitchen, washing dishes. Behind her, she heard the distinctive screech of the screen door opening and knew my father was standing in the front hallway. "I need to show you something in the barn," he said.

"Can't it wait until I'm finished?" she asked in an exasperated tone, not turning around.

Silence.

She faced him, and saw an expression she had never seen before.

Desperation.

"Don't you understand?" my distraught father replied. "I'm dying. Dying."

My mother had never before heard him make such a plaintive declaration. She didn't know how to reply.

She grabbed a dishtowel, and they slowly walked to the barn. My father had stacked tools and supplies in random, illogical piles. He couldn't remember what exactly he wanted to show her, and she didn't ask. It was too hard for her to speak.

My adult self so wants to calm and comfort that tender version of my father. At the same time, I want to ask that vulnerable and frightened person how a grown man could unleash such cruelty upon four little girls always so intent on pleasing him. His bullying behavior could not simply be excused as old-school parenting. He might have been born in a different generation, but as a teacher, he was a role model for classrooms of boys and was dedicated to his daughters' education. He also was acutely aware of unfairness and social injustices. For instance, when we gathered around our grandfather's television in Ohio to watch the Olympic Games, my father assured us we were not obligated to root only for American athletes.

How could a parent so rational on so many levels also be so volatile? Were his time-bomb tendencies due to his own nagging insecurities, his experiences in the Korean War, his propensity to periodically drink too much beer, or perhaps his fears that the cancer he might have thought he deserved would eventually consume him? Maybe it was a combination of all of that plus something unnamed that was broken inside.

To tease some truths from this jumble, I quizzed relatives and family friends and read dozens of condolence letters my mother had saved after he died. I didn't expect definitive answers to all of the blanks I was trying to fill in about what shaped my father's explosiveness, but I needed a narrative.

A search that began with a conversation with a military archivist at the US Navy Memorial in Washington, DC, led me to a sailor, Al Bowman. He was a Korean War veteran who had forgotten serving on the same ship with my father—and even supervised him as head yeoman—until my query prompted him to sort through the meticulous records stored in his Virginia house. Bowman uncovered photos I had never seen of my father and his fellow sailors from 1952 as their ship, the LSMR 412 (a rocket-equipped Landing Ship Medium designed to support amphibious landings), churned its way from San Diego to Korea Bay in the Yellow Sea, west of Pyongyang, the capital of North Korea. My father served his first Korean War tour on that ship. His second tour was on the USS *Catamount* (LSD-17), the Casa Grande Class Dock Loading Ship.

My father's life had gotten off to a rough start in Cleveland, Ohio. He was eighteen months old when his father died in 1933. That untimely tragedy forced his mother—the youngest in an Irish Catholic family, whose father also had died when she was a little girl—to move herself and her two sons in with her mother in Cleveland. My father's mother, a resourceful and willful independent thinker, wanted that arrangement to be temporary because she resented it when her older brothers would drink too much and roughhouse with her two boys. She continued working as a secretary. Her ticket out arrived when a friend prompted her to attend a football game at a liberal arts college in central Ohio with a professor who taught political science. Not long afterward, she married that professor, also a Cleveland native. She and her two sons joined him in a campus house in the pastoral community of Gambier.

There, my father and his older brother, both born during the Great Depression, enjoyed what many described as an idyllic childhood. Earnest, cute, kind, funny, and playful was how my father's friends described him as a little boy. He was absorbed into a tight gang of children with college-connected parents. They attended elementary school together, explored the Kokosing River, roamed the campus buildings, and were taught to swim by the coach who reigned over the college's elite swim team. My father was quite close with that coach's son, Jim. Very early on summer days and weekends, he and Jim would walk to their friend Kate's house and wait patiently on the porch steps for her to emerge. Kate, the ringleader of that young trio, would dictate what adventures were in store for the day.

My father's brother, Bill, eighteen months older, was much more studious and anointed "the academic one" early on by parents and colleagues. Bill left the local high school and graduated from Cranbrook, an upper-crust boarding school in Michigan. My father, eager to emulate his brother, tried but eventually eschewed boarding school near Cleveland. He returned to Gambier and graduated from the local high school. He wasn't a star student but was embraced and appreciated for his beautiful singing voice in theatrical and choral productions, his sense of humor, his optimism, his modesty, and his ability to put people at ease. As one mother noted, "You always liked to see Ron McGowan coming."

After graduating from high school in 1951, my father surprised everybody—probably even himself to some degree—by enlisting in the US Navy. Some claim he took that route to escape a household dominated by a high-strung and overbearing mother; others believed he did it because he wasn't ready for college. My mother was convinced he wasn't running away from his fears or anything else. It was as simple as this, she said, "Your father was a patriot. Even though his family had no history of military service, he thought it was his duty to serve his country." Unless young men qualified for some sort of deferment at that time, the army would have drafted them. Enlisting in the navy was a way to avoid the draft. The country was in the thick of the Korean War when my father boarded a train with a high school classmate that summer for basic training in San Diego.

Although my father was vigorous and eager to serve, the military, never mind the navy, likely wasn't a good fit for a sensitive freethinker who resented regimentation and was allergic to wool. Despite that, he jumped in with both feet. It was part of his pattern. In high school, he feared he was too uncoordinated to play the position of offensive end (precursor to tight end) on the varsity football team, but he diligently practiced his footwork until he earned accolades from the quarterback and coaches for his blocking skills. That single-minded intensity carried into his career.

His high school students spent very little time at desks because he was so dedicated to on-the-ground learning. In a class of his design, called Man and Environment, they studied urban renewal in downtown Philadelphia and traveled to Columbia, Maryland, for hands-on exposure to planned communities. That focused fervency, that obsession with the perfect lesson, was physically and mentally draining. The way he undervalued himself went beyond modesty and was detrimental professionally. It was as if he feared being recognized and rewarded for his hard work. Several years into his teaching career in Philadelphia, he was offered the chairmanship of the history department. Despite my mother's encouragement, he turned it down, his rationale being that teaching, not administrative duties, was his mission and love. The honor of being offered a promotion was lost on him.

After basic training in San Diego, my father was assigned to yeoman school. That meant learning how to handle an assortment of clerical and operational tasks that included generating, tracking, and organizing piles of combat reports, discharge records, letters, and other paperwork. He had learned to type in high school and was speedy on a keyboard. In addition, he was cross-trained to man a battle station on a navy ship. He returned to Ohio for a brief Christmastime visit in 1951 before returning to San Diego and then shipping out for Korea on the LSMR 412 in June 1952. On the way, the behemoth of a ship stopped in Hawaii, Midway Island, and Japan to refuel.

The smiling faces of the sailors in the black-and-white photographs that Al Bowman sent to me are achingly young and innocent. Our country, at war, referred to them as men, but they were mere eighteen- and nineteen-year-old boys. In one picture on the ship, with the sea in the background, Al Bowman, labeled as "Me" in red ink, stands bare-chested with L. L. Erskine, "Little One"; W. D. Hoy, "Dunc"; and R. S. McGowan, "McGoo." That team of yeomen served the four ships that made up Division 32. They nicknamed themselves the "Yo-Yos" and served together aboard the flagship, LSMR 412.

When my father talked to me about the war, he didn't focus on battles. Instead, he spoke about the beauty of Mount Fuji and other sights he had

195

filmed in Japan with a small movie camera when he was allowed rest and relaxation time. But when I talked years later with other sailors who served aboard LSMRs, they confirmed what my father had told my mother long ago: "It was pure hell."

The unstable ships were incredibly loud, horribly cramped, and stank fiercely of diesel fuel. Plus, sloshing waves kept the main deck wet. Seasickness was the norm because the flat-bottomed ships, designed for amphibious landings, pitched back and forth so violently. It was the equivalent, one veteran told me, "of putting a floating bathtub in a creek." Sleeping sailors had to brace themselves constantly just so they wouldn't be thrown from their bunks. Eating was a challenge because the mess hall was positioned above the propellers, which could shake food off any tray a sailor hadn't pinned to the table with his thumbs. There always seemed to be plenty of tasteless food but never any water for bathing. Most of the desalinated water was used to cool the thirsty diesel engines.

Much of the time, the ship was positioned near the city of Namp'o (formerly Chinnamp'o), close to where the Taedong River emptied into the Yellow Sea. That bay was about thirty miles west of Pyongyang. Ammunition was stacked in every conceivable open space, so sailors could easily access the tens of thousands of rockets and shells they were ordered to fire from rocket launchers and guns. The ship was basically a 220-foot-long powder keg. Some of the weaponry could shoot ammunition as far as six miles. They always fired at night, when all of that flashing ammunition turned darkness to a dusky daylight. Temperatures during that 1952–1953 winter were below freezing along the Taedong River. Loading and firing weapons required dexterity, which meant sailors had to be barehanded. Their targets were aircraft and onshore batteries, and saturation was the strategy. The LSMR 412 and its three sister ships were fired upon frequently, but no American sailors aboard them died during that tour of duty. What they never knew was how many enemy soldiers or civilians they killed. And that haunted my father.

Some soldiers emerge from war seemingly unscathed, while others come out with full-blown cases of what is now commonly known as post-traumatic stress disorder. I think my father was somewhere in the middle. That naïve, shiny-faced, red-haired Ohio boy emerged as a man with a firsthand education about the cruelties of the world and how truth can be elusive when woven into global politics. Though he kept his sense of humor, his postwar self was higher strung, quicker to anger, and hypersensitive to noise. He couldn't bear the static of a car radio on long trips, though he would tolerate our voices when my mother taught the four of us songs from her Girl Scout camp days to help pass endless hours in the backseat. A mysterious squeak emanating from some nether region of our car, however, would send him into orbit. If we couldn't fix it by padding or cushioning some errant piece of camping equipment, he had to pull over and hunt down the offending item. We had to rearrange the load until it was noiseless.

My father grew up in a household where an evening cocktail was de rigueur for his parents. My parents couldn't afford much hard liquor, so beer was my father's alcoholic beverage of choice. Alcohol brought out his aggressiveness, but he didn't necessarily need it to fuel his mean streak. He didn't drink much at home, but my mother was usually prepared to be the designated driver after parties.

No doubt the navy helped to turn my father into a world-class cusser. He often strung together his colorful sentences in front of his daughters, ignoring my mother's entreaties to stop. He didn't grasp what sponges we were. One day in Philadelphia around Christmastime, he realized she was right. My oldest sister was a toddler, playing in the living room while my parents strung popcorn and cranberries on thread, creating low-cost tree garlands. Understandably, my father became agitated when kernels broke in half or the sewing needle pierced his finger. When a neighbor stopped by to say hello, my sister innocently asked him if he wanted to help decorate the tree with the "f---ing cranberries." My father was temporarily mortified.

As funny and endearing as he could be, it seemed like a slick of anger was always roiling under the surface. He was too complex of a man for that ire to be caused by the pressures of having cancer, fighting in a war, or raising young children who needed attention from a woman he wanted to himself. Maybe his humor was a mask for the insecurities, and the anger surfaced when he feared he couldn't measure up to an ideal he had created in his own mind.

After my father was discharged from the navy, he and my mother moved to Cleveland. She taught elementary school, and he used money from the GI Bill to earn his college degree in sociology at Case Western Reserve. My father considered a career in law enforcement before settling on teaching. Even then, I think he felt he was in the academic shadow of his older brother, who was studying for his doctorate in philosophy. His parents could be condescending and dismissive of their second son, even though he excelled in college, displaying a rabid curiosity and a keen intellect. However, they also worried about his overarching quest for perfection from himself and his children. Both of them feared that the forceful discipline he exercised with us would wring all of the creativity out of us. His response was that he wanted us to know how to behave without embarrassing him in public, to think for ourselves, to be humble and empathetic, and to contribute to the world instead of take from it.

Living with such a tortured person, who always seemed to be gnawed at by something, is exhausting and exhilarating. My mother, his main sounding board, knew he counted on her for validation and praise. She can still cry about him dying so young yet also recognize that his death was liberating for those of us left behind.

"I loved your father, and I still miss him very much," my mother told me decades after he died. "As horrible as his death was, there was a sense of relief after it happened. For all of us, it meant no more walking on eggshells."

My father didn't leave much of a paper trail. One remnant I wish I had was the cache of almost-daily letters he wrote to my mother during his enlistment. Once his four-year obligation to the military ended, he demanded that she burn them all. Unfortunately, she complied. I always thought those letters might have offered me some sort of insight that I hadn't been able to garner any other way.

My mother did, however, save a dilapidated shoebox full of thick bundles of handwritten sympathy notes that friends, relatives, and co-workers sent after my father died. He wasn't around to force her to burn those. Reading them years later revealed tiny pieces of him. Nobody who wrote seemed scared of him, humiliated by him, or ashamed to know him. They rejoiced in his dedication to his students, his fairness, his radiance, his resilience, his courage, his spirit, his determination, and his clever humor. In his honor, the local parent-teacher association donated an atlas and a dictionary to the elementary school where he had done substitute teaching when we first moved to Massachusetts.

One Massachusetts neighbor who served with him on the zoning board said she admired his clear thinking and his determination to get to the root of a problem. Another, who had retired to Ashfield after serving in the US State Department, wrote how "Ron was a very special friend to me, one I was immediately in tune with, intellectually and otherwise." I discovered that my father and that friend had a mutual appreciation for puns. Evidently, one would call the other, deliver a pun, and hang up without identifying himself. It was like a secret code between two grown men.

The owner of the local hardware store marveled at my father's optimism when he came into the store to purchase a new ax handle mere weeks before his death.

"I felt he'd never be able to use it," he wrote to my mother. "Yet I guess we both had faith that a miracle might happen to save him." And a Massachusetts co-worker wrote that he "was the best thing that ever happened" to their office because "his compassionate feelings for everyone certainly wore off on us."

A mother from Philadelphia wrote about how her son started to show interest in schoolwork and began righting his abysmal academic performance after responding to my father's classroom enthusiasm and demands. That boy, who had been on the verge of flunking out of high school, was then attending Yale University.

The most poignant thoughts came from an English teacher my father taught with for at least a decade. In August 1963, the two of them had traveled with a busload of other Philadelphians participating in the March on Washington organized by Martin Luther King Jr. This fellow teacher recalled all of the times the two of them spent cussing and fussing their way through exams, laughing in the faculty lounge, and grading papers. He described my father as a "generous man who broke his heart to be fair to kids and gave his life unstintingly day after day for people and ideas he believed in and cared deeply about." He also was awed by his hopefulness.

"For he was beyond me in hope, having conquered more despair than I even knew could exist," the note continued. "Always, behind his sharpest ironies, lay the implication that there was a better way and that I and others who were specially gifted might discover it. Not that his own gifts were meager, for in humor, kindness, and understanding, he quietly outstripped us all, but it was his way and disclaim his own virtues and to set our efforts in a more favorable light. I remember his frequent praise—of fish I caught, of an apt remark in a meeting, of a comment I'd written about one of his advisees—praise so honest and unselfish I could not but believe it. By such gifts of the spirit he enriched our lives, taught me to believe and hope, as a man hopes, for the strength to outlive youth's grand illusions and the grace to do small kindnesses."

I understand fully that few are willing to speak ill of the dead, but absorbing all of those messages was a balm for me. Those insights, processed by my adult mind, allowed me to add layers to what felt like the flat, paper cutout image of my father I had stored away.

In that same shoebox, I found a heartbreakingly cheerful letter I wrote to my father shortly after my three sisters and I returned to Massachusetts in late summer 1976 from our month-long stay in Ohio. My mother's sister and her husband drove us home about a week before school started in early September. I was about to enter my sophomore year in high school. My father was in the hospital when we arrived, so I had either mailed it or hand-delivered it.

"Dear Daddy," a portion of my August 26 letter read. "The kitchen looks wonderful! We all love the painting and it was a big surprise to see it." I recounted the twelve-hour drive back from Ohio, detailing our start time, arrival time, and how long we'd stopped for lunch and dinner. I wrote about babysitting my cousin, teaching classes at the church's vacation Bible school, spending time at amusement parks, and visiting old family friends.

"There was much more that we did but I'll tell you about it when we see you. Hope you feel better," I wrote before signing off with "Love, Elizabeth" and adding, "P.S. I miss you very much and so does everybody else."

I read about fathers today who, upon being diagnosed with a terminal illness, write long, eloquent letters to their children so those adult sons and daughters have some concrete thoughts, wishes, and hopes from the parent instead of just pictures and fuzzy memories. I yearn for one of those but instead have just a few handwritten snippets. One is a grammar primer that I keep on my desk that belonged to my father. On the right side of the book, where the pages form a smooth edge, he penned this helpful tip: "Flunk Now. Avoid the June Rush."

The other remnants I have are less playful but perhaps more prescient. They are haiku scribbled in my father's barely legible handwriting on the back of a legal notepad. I have no idea when he wrote them, but the way they are squeezed between other doodles, it's as if they were composed between lesson plans or during a meeting. One reads:

Eternal sleeping
Even giants must perceive
As they grow older

Absorbing these simple yet powerful words is comforting to me because they offer some insight into his gentlest of thoughts. The haiku is only seventeen syllables. But I treasure each one.

CHAPTER 32
WESTERN KENTUCKY: LINCOLN AND THE SALT OF THE EARTH

MILES RIDDEN: 3,166.5
MILES TO GO: 1,083.5

Kentucky, my penultimate state, extended a warm and colorful welcome after Don and I exited the Ohio River ferry on the afternoon of October 14. The landscape was gentle and temperatures were in the low seventies as I pedaled the last twenty-two miles of a seventy-two-mile day. Farmers had already harvested ripe soybeans from withering foliage, but ears of corn still clung to yellowing stalks.

A mix of fiery and muted colors created a leaf-peeper haven. And unlike the conifers of the West, which really had been ablaze, these maples, oaks, sycamores, tulip poplars, ashes, beeches, and hickories just appeared to be aflame.

Unfortunately, the leaves weren't the only things "exploding." I attributed my episodes of loud and revolting gastrointestinal distress to the combination of a catch-as-catch can diet and hours on a bicycle seat. The upset was magnified each time I was exposed to the distinct stench emanating from a parade of massive chicken farms. My tender stomach roiled with each whiff of the putrid and powerful odor wafting from those cooped-up birds. The blue highways that wended through Marion, Clay, Dixon, Sebree, Beech Grove, Utica, Whitesville, Fordsville, Falls of Rough, McDaniels, and Hardin Springs were also lined with dozens of little churches. Instead of going inside one to plead for divine intervention, I pedaled to a drugstore for some Imodium capsules.

Fortunately, my stomach—and the rest of my alimentary tract—had calmed down by the time I reached Sonora on October 17. After two months of pedaling, I was on my native eastern time. I set my watch one hour ahead. The welcome sign touted the community of barely three hundred as the home of the annual Bucksnort Festival. For the ungulate-uninitiated, that's a reference to the distinct territorial grunt of male deer. I was pleased to discover Brooks General Store, which still featured a pair of old red gas pumps. The Sonora landmark was a throwback to the days when a traveler could find a sandwich, fishing bait, or a pair of nail scissors under one roof. Metal signs advertising soda, tobacco, bread, and farming equipment hung inside and outside the white clapboard building.

Rhonda, minding the store with her mother Delores, admitted to having served as Bucksnort Queen when I asked about a newspaper clipping hanging near the counter.

"The town nominated me when I was in high school," the shy but poised twenty-six-year-old explained. "I wasn't exactly pushy about competing for the title." Delores beamed and told me Rhonda not only participated in beauty pageants but was also the star of her church's plays.

Upon signing my name, travel dates, and a few observations in the store's journal dedicated to cross-country cyclists, I discovered it was just the latest in a trove of catalogued, spiral-bound notebooks. The earliest one dated to 1976, the TransAm's inaugural year.

"MeeMaw started that tradition," Delores said about her mother, Ella Mae, a native Kentuckian. "She founded this store and was so proud of being part of the cycling community."

"Clearly, you adored her," I said when Delores teared up telling me Ella Mae had died in 1999, a few weeks shy of her eighty-sixth birthday. "Selfishly, I'm so sorry I missed meeting her."

"Well, come over here and I'll tell you more," said Delores, leading me to a corner of the store that served as a shrine of sorts to Ella Mae. "Look at this," she said, her face radiant, as she thrust a framed photo my way. "On my way to MeeMaw's grave, I saw a cloud that looked like an angel floating above the cemetery. I hurried home in my car to get my camera, but that angel cloud had disappeared by the time I got back.

"So, instead I made a picture of this," she continued, pointing to a sun-pierced cloud at the center of the photo. "I didn't think much of it until I picked up the print. See, at the edge, there's a perfect profile of MeeMaw. I feel closer to her just looking at it."

Sonora had no public park, but Delores and Rhonda graciously allowed Don and me to camp in the store's backyard. After showing us the outside water spigot, Rhonda and her two little girls piled into her Nova sedan and headed off to Bible study. We kipped down between a pecan tree, a symbol of the South, and a catalpa, a tree of the North. Fortunately, it was out of earshot of nearby Interstate 65, a major route to Indianapolis. Crickets sang us to sleep.

Illinois might bear the Land of Lincoln moniker on its license plates, but Kentucky has dibs on this exquisite leader too. Just twelve miles east of Sonora, the trail passed the birthplace of the sixteenth president, now a national historic site. It was a must-stop early on October 18. Before seeking out a secure place for my bike, I sat on a bench to eat a few crackers and polish off my water. Within minutes, I was approached by an impeccably dressed, very-high-on-the-food-chain National Park Service employee who pointed to a picnic area and ordered me to move there to eat and drink. He offered nary a welcoming word before retreating to his office.

I headed to the visitor center instead. The introductory film, both poignant and informative, was narrated by actor Burgess Meredith, who played the Penguin in the *Batman* television series that had transfixed me as a child. I learned that Nancy and Thomas Lincoln paid two hundred dollars for 348 acres of land called Sinking Spring Farm in December 1808. Eking out a living on this unforgiving, unfertile red clay soil was impossible, so the Lincolns called this place home only until 1811, when they departed for Indiana. But it was here in an eighteen-by-sixteen-foot cabin with a dirt floor, one window, and a fireplace that the family, wrote author and poet Carl Sandburg, "welcomed into a world of battle and blood, of whispering dreams and wistful dust, a new child, a boy," in February 1809. He was named Abraham after his grandfather.

The National Park Service has preserved the freshwater spring as well as items such as the Lincoln family Bible and replicas of the Great Emancipator's size 14 shoes. Visitors can climb the fifty-six steps (one for each year of Lincoln's life) to meet a park ranger standing in the neoclassical memorial housing the cabin where Lincoln was supposedly born. Schoolchildren raised much of the money for the memorial, designed by John Russell Pope, the noted architect of the Thomas Jefferson Memorial in Washington, DC. The Greek temple in the woods was constructed between 1909 and 1911 of Connecticut pink granite and Tennessee marble.

The ranger leading our tour was impressively knowledgeable about Lincoln's life and immeasurable contributions to our republic. After talking with the ranger, I sussed out that there is a lack of documentation to support the cabin's authenticity. Yes, it's irrefutable that young Lincoln lived at this site with his parents, but the cabin is most likely a replica. Regardless, most visitors seemed willing to suspend disbelief because, after all, who does not want to breathe in a few of the same air molecules that maybe a young Lincoln did? The site's intimacy made it easier to grasp the essence of the person who persevered and became one of the country's most lauded presidents and eloquent writers. People can appreciate what is possible when they know that somebody so extraordinary rose from a place so ordinary.

Before leaving, I ran into yet another Park Service employee tasked with cleaning the bathrooms after about 150 students from Louisville reboarded their school buses. He asked me how far I had come, and I handed him a brochure and offered a brief trip synopsis. After tying off another trash bag, he looked at me and said, "Wow, what an undertaking. You're the kind of person I admire." I smiled, wishing that the officious employee I had met earlier, likely this man's supervisor, could have conducted himself in such a classy manner.

■ ■ ■ ■ ■ ■ ■ ■ ■

Central Kentucky is the state's bluegrass region. This vegetation might be native to parts of Utah—botanists are still debating its origins—but the species coating Kentucky was likely introduced by Europeans. Wherever it originated, the grass was named for the steel-blue hue of its spring blossoms. Native Americans referred to this pasture staple as "white man's tracks" because it sprouted wherever settlers kept cattle or plowed. Today, bluegrass is cultivated to meet Americans' compulsive need for groomed, expansive lawns.

Thick morning fog in central Kentucky made my balancing act along a spare asphalt shoulder quite dicey. I delayed my morning start until the worst of the heavy mist lifted. When impatient drivers would pull around me and then brake or swerve dramatically to avoid oncoming traffic, I would defensively veer to the right into a front yard or field, grateful there wasn't a steep drop. I would never win a contest with a hunk of metal weighing more than a ton.

During a steep climb on a narrow Highway 1295 into Kirksville, I heard a man yelling into my left ear from an open passenger window. What in the world? After more than three thousand miles of pedaling, I'd heard hundreds if not thousands of straining diesel engines. This one, too, will pass, I thought. But it didn't. I cocked my head ever so slightly and saw a decrepit black pickup truck, with three men abreast in the cab, struggling to tug an exceptionally wide load of a trailer spilling across the shoulder and over the double yellow centerlines. I could see the pores in the yeller's face. He was close enough to touch my red bicycle helmet.

What exactly was I supposed to do—tuck and roll into the underbrush? If I stopped, I would have been crushed like a beetle. I kept my steady pace. The behemoth of a trailer passed so closely that I could have hitched a ride if I had been stupid enough to grab some part of it with my left hand. Topping the hill about a hundred yards later, I spotted the yeller and his two male companions on the roadside fixing a blown tire. Not wanting to tangle with that brain trust, I stopped to admire beautiful stained-glass windows bedecking a small church on the opposite corner. Later, I was able to process the calamity I didn't want to think about earlier. If that truck tire had blown a few minutes earlier, I would have ended up in the hospital—or the morgue. That made me grateful for two young Amish boys in a buggy who waved and waited in their driveway for me to pass, before prodding their horses onto the road.

When not contending with double-wides, I appreciated the bounty of asters and goldenrod that thrived along roadsides at the edge of soybean, corn, or tobacco fields. Some days, I noticed my T-shirt was polka-dotted with the red and black of ladybugs that realized it was easier to hitch a ride on moving cotton than to fly with their own tiny wings. Along one country road, a herd of bulls kept pace with me as I sang a nonsense song at the top of my lungs. Curious, they stopped when I stopped. One of them stuck his tongue between strands of barbed wire to taste my front tire.

On October 19, the day I planned to crank out seventy-seven miles to Berea, the Methodists in Springfield made me laugh with a "When fleeing temptation, don't leave a forwarding address" message on their front yard sign. Berea is the official Gateway to the Appalachians, and Berea College is the centerpiece of that pleasant community. The college dates back to 1855, when Reverend John Fee joined forces with Kentucky politician and fellow abolitionist Cassius Clay (not the boxer, although both men were Kentucky natives) to start a school for poor whites and freed blacks. It has evolved into an inexpensive private liberal arts college where 80 percent of the fifteen hundred students are from southern Appalachia and the student-teacher ratio is an enviable eleven to one.

Students are admitted based on financial need, and each one worked ten to fifteen hours weekly in lieu of tuition while carrying a full academic load. Jobs were available in 140 areas, including the college store; crafts gallery; printing services; laundry; the college farm; the broom craft, woodcraft, and ceramics studios; and the elegant Boone Tavern Hotel and Dining Room. The latter was built in 1909 when the college president's wife sensibly refused to continue entertaining guests in her private home.

I like to think that all students bubbled with as much enthusiasm about their college experience as Rebecca, the in-state freshman from Bowling Green who circulated the relish tray the night Don and I ordered halibut in the stately dining room. After her father had died of melanoma at age thirty-three and left the family destitute, Rebecca doubted college was in her future.

"Berea is a lifesaver," she told me, admitting that she, too, lived in fear of the disease. "I never go outside without layers of sunscreen. I hope you don't either."

The student guide leading a campus tour Don and I joined the next morning was a twenty-nine-year-old political science major who had returned to the college after a post-high-school hiatus to raise a child. She repeatedly emphasized that Berea was strong on academics and did not want to be known as a hillbilly school where students with bad teeth made brooms, baskets, chairs, and crafts. Clearly, she was sensitive about the stereotypes outsiders harbor of Kentuckians. I was just heartened to know that students could honor their heritage and hand down historically valuable skills that might otherwise fade away forever.

Soon after leaving the quaint campus, I rolled onto Highway 21 and spotted the distinctive blue façade of a Walmart. I felt as if I had been thrust a hundred years forward. I wondered what Fee and Clay would think about this behemoth of a box store chock-full of imports looming around the corner from Berea's handcrafted treasures.

CHAPTER 33
NO TIME FOR GOODBYE

Writers have the luxury of reshaping sentences until words flow just so. Life doesn't permit such do-overs. But if I were allowed just one, it would be this: On that long-ago Monday in October 1976 when the empty ambulance pulled into our driveway, I wish the fifteen-year-old me had insisted that somebody drive me to the hospital so I could have said goodbye to my father, even though he was already dead. Back then, I wasn't aware I had the power to ask, so I didn't. Nobody can deny a request that isn't made. People respond to spoken questions, not silences.

What I understand now is that I needed to confirm the truth of my father's death by seeing his body. Doctors could have made arrangements if they knew I was on the way. I would not have been repulsed or scared. At the very least, I would have been able to hold his hand, kiss his cheek, or just look at him one last time. The closest I had ever been to a dead person was from a car window in Philadelphia when I glimpsed a first responder pulling a cover over a woman's body at an accident scene. The way it all ended with my father, I couldn't even remember the last time he had hugged me. That left a hole. And it made me doubly aware of how random and alarming our world can be. My father hadn't died in a war overseas or in a fiery crash. He had been in a hospital bed just two hours away. That gap remains. And I will never be able to fill it.

My father had insisted on being cremated. He didn't want a funeral or any semblance of a ceremony. Knowing his discomfort with drawing attention to himself, he probably thought he was eliminating stress and reducing expenses. Dutifully, my mother honored those wishes. My head comprehends that my mother was respecting my father's fierce pleas not to make a fuss, but my heart regrets that my mother or somebody else did not intervene. Memorial services are for those left behind—not the dead. My father's wishes discounted that, even though that wasn't likely his intent. I'm not suggesting a memorial gathering would have offered closure, whatever that trite, overused term means. I didn't even know such a word existed when I was fifteen. Now that I do, I resent how it's bandied about as some sort of antidote to grief, as if its pain magically ends on a predetermined date. It's the equivalent of asking the wounded to stuff all of their hurt and pain in a locked box so nobody is ever forced to wrestle with an uncomfortable feeling or thought again.

At the very least, a memorial service would have been unifying. People from my father's past and present would have been able to offer the support and love so many are desperate to give in traumatic times. Those insights and anecdotes can be nourishment for the hungry. My sisters and I could have heard firsthand from relatives, co-workers, and friends who he was to them and why he mattered. Though three years separated us from the life we had built in Philadelphia, friends and colleagues there wrote and called. And, lucky for us, our new New England neighbors acted instead of talking about helping. They visited, sent us thoughtful cards, made us meals, cut our firewood, helped with household chores, and often gave one of the four McGowan girls rides to places beyond walking and bicycle-riding distance.

Still, casseroles and sympathy notes didn't fill that crevasse of sorrow. I resented the look of pity in some adults' faces when they voiced condolences. I knew they were trying to be kind, but usually they didn't know what to say, and I didn't know what the correct response was. My father had always made it clear that we shouldn't make other people uncomfortable by burdening them with our problems, so it was of utmost importance that we be polite and not offend. He had also drilled into us how wrong it was to make ourselves the center of attention. The world wasn't about you and your inconsequential problems, he always reminded us. It was about those around you.

My father died during a different era. Therapists were not shuttled to every sort of tragedy involving children. The unsaid message I heard was, "Buck up, move on, and get over it." Plowing ahead was a badge of honor. My mother attended sessions of what she disparagingly called her "grief group." My sisters and I, meanwhile, got hugs and "I love you"s from our aunt, my mother's Ohio sister. She was a hospice nurse with four children of her own, and she had spent as much time as she could spare with us when my father was sick. Immediately after his death, my sisters and I resumed our regular school and work activities. We just assumed we had to figure it out and muddle along as we always had before. Something was missing, but I didn't know what it was.

School was a refuge because I could focus on the learning I loved, and I didn't have to talk about what was going on at home. I also knew that studying was my ticket out of that rural region. It wasn't as if I hated it there, I just didn't have roots there like most of my peers did. It was an isolated region and seemed like a stop along the way for me instead of a place to settle permanently. I didn't know exactly where I wanted to go or how I would get there once I graduated, I just knew I was going somewhere else. In the meantime, I didn't want to be known as that poor girl whose father had just died. So I mostly kept mum. What was there to say? Very few classmates said anything to me at school. It was easier to avoid the topic.

My mother's income was so puny that my sisters and I qualified for discounted school lunches. Each of us was issued a three-digit number that we had to recite to the lunch line cashier. I usually packed my own lunch because I didn't need to compound my fifteen-year-old awkwardness with that humiliating act. When I tried whispering the number, inevitably the din of the cafeteria drowned out my timid voice, so I had to repeat it louder. I was so self-conscious—and mortified that the older boy taking the money knew who I was—that I felt as if that horrible number were stamped on my forehead in indelible ink.

Home was a different matter. While the mood in our house was far from joyless, it was always tinged by an underlying sadness. Residual chaos and despair from my father's death floated around like atoms of oxygen that you couldn't help but suck deep into your lungs. That subject became the proverbial hulking elephant. Pretty soon it seemed as natural as a couch or a coffee table in the living room. Step gingerly enough and you could avoid bumping into it. We coped with it by retreating into our own silences. And perhaps that was fine because speaking the truth aloud might have been too much to bear.

My mother's prized, purple-flowered collection of African violets wilted, then lost their leaves in the living room.

"I just wasn't up to caring for them anymore," my mother later said. "I didn't want them to die, and I can't explain why I couldn't put the energy into keeping my houseplants alive."

Just because I didn't talk about my father much with my family didn't mean I didn't think about him. The buried sadness I carried became a bit heavier each day. I would wake up hoping to hear him yelling from the bottom of the stairs for me to hurry to stack wood, insulate the attic crawlspace, or rake leaves. To feel his presence, I would linger in his freezing-cold barn workshop. When I was sure nobody was looking, I would run my fingers over the edges of tools he had last touched just months beforehand. It was the only way I knew to connect. I silently prayed that I wasn't some sort of teenage freak when I discovered how pleased I was to find his fingerprints still pressed into the round steel can of heavy-duty soap stored under the kitchen sink. It relieved me to touch evidence of his existence. More than once, I crept into the long hall closet in the eaves next to my upstairs bedroom to seek out my father's dark blue-and-gray-striped rugby shirt. He had worn it on that last family trip to the Atlantic Ocean in July

1976. The shoulders drooped down to my elbows, but I didn't care. I closed my eyes, imagining I could still smell a mix of salt water and his Old Spice. That was the closest I could come to a hug.

Everything seemed so temporary after he was gone. Mostly, I noticed what was missing instead of what was there. Was only the pain of loss permanent? It scared me to feel farther and farther away from him as each day ticked by. After a month, I could at least comfort myself with the knowledge that just four weeks earlier my father had been alive, here with me on the planet. But what would be my touchstone after a year? Would he feel so distant that I wouldn't even remember the sound of his voice?

I also wrestled with guilt. A small part of me was worried maybe I had somehow contributed to his demise because of an incident in the summer of 1971, when I was ten. After spending that season in Oregon, we explored California before heading back east. Dai, a family friend and architect who relocated from Philadelphia to San Francisco, insisted that we stay at his apartment. One night, my older sister and I were riding with Dai in his yellow Volkswagen Beetle, sightseeing. Dai was from Wales, and his accent and everything about him seemed quite exotic to us. My father, driving the white Fairlane 500 station wagon, was behind the Beetle with the rest of our family. I wanted to relax and have fun riding in that cool car, but I kept checking out the back window because I was worried that my father wouldn't be able to keep up. The station wagon was easy to spot because it looked like a Cyclops with one burned-out headlight. That broken image made me think that my father was doomed in some inexorable way. I felt so much sorrow watching that lone light trying to penetrate the darkness that I wanted to curl up in a ball in Dai's car and cry. I didn't say anything about my feelings that night, or ever. How would I express them, and who would want to listen? A few weeks later, when we were camping in Arizona, my father noticed what he suspected was a recurrence of melanoma on his left forearm. He told only my mother, and we accelerated our trip home. When I learned he had cancer again, I was afraid I had somehow cursed him with my pity.

We kept the canister containing my father's ashes on a shelf in a low-slung, antique cupboard called a dry sink in our Massachusetts living room. When I was in high school, every time I turned the latch and opened the pair of wood doors to retrieve a dish or a tablecloth, I saw my father in that canister. He was there, yet he wasn't.

What I realized years later is that I'd been shaped just as much by his presence as I'd been by his absence. When he was alive, I knew how he wanted me to act, and when he was dead, I wondered if I was measuring up. If I had never been diagnosed with melanoma, I doubt I would have

211

been as motivated to ferret out the puzzle of my father's life. He became less of a mystery when I was able to pull back his seams and glimpse the vulnerability inside. Though I never will have a full understanding of him, I have enough of one to accept certain truths.

Maybe my tender skin has become thicker, but now I see softer, gentler images of him, mostly stripped of the hurtful, sharp edges that once cleaved me to the bone. I cherish his optimism, his empathy, his resilience, his tenacity, and the unexpected moments of innocence that even a child could recognize.

On one camping trip, he returned to our campsite, excitedly displaying what he seemed convinced was a new discovery.

"Girls," he exclaimed while holding a square of folded white tissue paper, "have you ever seen toilet paper like this? Instead of rolls, it comes in squares." My mother, older sister, and I looked at each other, not sure whether to keep the peace or tell him what it was and risk an explosion. Just before we spoke, he finished unfolding it, saw the gaping hole in the middle, and realized it was a paper-thin toilet seat cover that most people found more trouble than help.

"Oh, Daddy," we said, holding our hands over our faces in case it still wasn't safe to giggle. He just smiled sheepishly. That was our signal that we could tease him without repercussions.

He used to warn me about becoming a teacher because of the meager financial and emotional returns. Most of those comments were made in jest or frustration, but I took them to heart. I never considered that field, even though I knew he loved shaping his high school students. I do like to think that he played a role in me entering the news business and becoming a writer. As a kid, I used to hunt and peck away at a giant, heavy Underwood typewriter I had lugged home from a yard sale. The key controlling lowercase *a* was so out of whack that the letter rose high above all of the other letters on my typing projects. I just tolerated it. One day, I found that typewriter on a small bench in my bedroom. I took a closer look. A piece of paper scrolled into the carriage read: "Elizabeth: The quick brown fox jumps over the lazy dog. Love, Daddy." The lower case *a* was in alignment. I wish I had saved that note.

Knowing my father's blend of ferocity and protectiveness, it makes me cringe to think how he might have reacted had he lived long enough to see one of his daughters repeatedly diagnosed with melanoma. He would have blamed himself harshly for passing down inferior genes or letting me roast on the beach as a child. But another angle of him—the gentler side that guided me with homework or backed off enough the few times we played basketball or softball—would have been my most forceful advocate. I like to think that the way I handled my disease would have revealed to him that he knew how to raise a child with enough inner toughness to not crumple under adversity.

I don't think my father was ever as shy as I was as a child. And I know I was much more bashful at school than I ever was in my own neighborhood. In elementary school, I dreaded the first day because teachers calling roll seemed obsessed with giving every student a nickname. Usually, when they tried to abbreviate my name to one of its innumerable permutations, I just turned red and let them call me whatever they wanted to because I wouldn't speak up. Being the center of attention in those classrooms, even for that minute, was embarrassing. By the time I majored in journalism at college, I was long past that shyness. On my own schedule, I had emerged from my shell—the one well-intentioned friends, acquaintances, and teachers had always threatened to extract me from. However, those quieter childhood years had imbued me with a distinct skillset. I had become a trained observer of people's habits, patterns, personalities, contradictions, and foibles. Journalism allowed me to act on that curiosity and find my voice. Holding a notebook gave me permission to speak up and the liberty to ask questions. I could discover the story, not be the story.

I no longer cringe when people tell me how I remind them of my father. Years ago, I would have been insulted, thinking they were speaking in code about barely masked insecurity and rage. Now that I recognize I inherited more than his propensity for a deadly disease, I accept the comparison graciously. I now know they are referring to our similar smiles, senses of humor, and abilities to engage strangers and friends with genuine inquisitiveness about their lives and thoughts.

I do not idealize him for being gallant and dying what some might call a noble death. Instead, I am able to love him more fully because the perspective I have gained has made me more aware of his unique blend of attributes and flaws. What still upsets me is that he didn't get to live what we fortunate Americans refer to as a "full life." I only wish he could have had more years to put his energy into moving forward instead of battling a demon that constantly knocked him backward. Maybe, just maybe, he eventually could have achieved an inner peace and balance.

My father's ashes were still in that living room cupboard when I went away to college almost three years after he died. My mother couldn't decide where he should be buried. Eventually, she purchased a plot in the little historic cemetery on the campus of the Ohio liberal arts college where he grew up. It was adjacent to where his mother and adoptive father would eventually be buried—and 714 miles away from our house in Massachusetts. In the winter of 1980–1981, my mother hand-delivered the ashes to Ohio and picked out a gravestone. In the spring of 1981, my father's mother, who lived near the campus, arranged for a no-frills burial. There was no memorial service. His abbreviated life is marked with a small, unadorned piece of granite that simply reads: Ronald Stuart McGowan, 1932–1976.

It will forever hurt that I was never able to have even one adult conversation with my father—at least one where he answers. When I visit relatives in Ohio, I always stop at his grave. It surprises me how comforting it is to sit in front of that stone and talk to him. I never thought that would be the case.

Still, some of that long-ago anguish lingers. As a child, I used to think that having command of an adult's vocabulary would give me the ability to express that inconsolable hurt. Now I know that such language doesn't yet exist, and perhaps it never will. The ache of missing my father might shrink and fade, but it doesn't disappear. The longing to see him, to know him as an adult, never goes away. It's not as consuming or paralyzing, but it's there, like that periodic craving for a flavor you can imagine but have never tasted.

CHAPTER 34
APPALACHIA: HALLELUJAH NIGHT IN THE BIBLE BELT

MILES RIDDEN: 3,525
MILES TO GO: 725

A quintessential Kentucky scene unfolded on Highway 1209, about forty miles east of Berea. In the midst of mowed hayfield stubble, somebody had planted a crooked post strong enough to support a homemade plywood backboard. Remnants of a net still dangled from the rusty orange hoop. Not a soul was around. I wondered when a kid had last stepped up to the makeshift foul line on that country court. Had he imagined the roar of a hometown crowd as his last-second swoosh shot won his team the championship?

Basketball is just one romanticized notion of Kentucky, along with fields of bluegrass, horse farms, Daniel Boone, and Stephen Foster's song "My Old Kentucky Home." Under that shiny veneer lies a frequently ignored flip side—extreme poverty. I was immersed in the thick of it. Outside Berea, I made eye contact with an elderly man driving a creaky sedan that had probably rolled off an assembly line when Gerald Ford was president. In lieu of a government-issued license plate, a message bolted to his front bumper commanded: "Smile, God Loves You." Ironically, he looked very grumpy—and tired.

On the evening of October 20, Don and I camped next to the Stone Coal Baptist Church near Vincent, figuring I would ask for forgiveness if anybody showed up because nobody was around to grant permission. The juxtaposition between that frowning driver and my imaginary, smiling basketball player seemed a metaphor for the divide between vibrant and prosperous western Kentucky and the impoverished Appalachian region that yawned into southwestern Virginia.

Understandably, my Kentucky-bred friends are hypersensitive about outsiders' stereotypes. They go out of their way to explain that they have all of their own teeth, are not "hillbilly heroin addicts," did not marry their first cousin, and can indeed read.

I still encountered no shortage of overweight people at roadside dairy bars, parked cars perched on cinder blocks, porches laden with overstuffed furniture, and families emerging from ramshackle trailers. And the trash, oh the trash. Tires festered in ditches, carcasses of appliances and bathtubs were strewn on steep hillsides, cans, bottles, and wrappers littered the roadside, and other flotsam and jetsam swirled in creeks.

So yes, many sights in Appalachia, like jokes about the Hatfields and McCoys, are ripe for ridicule. But what's funny about grinding poverty? And why are so many Americans horrified to find out they share the country with chronically poor people with access to so little?

As I had found in the Ozarks, Kentuckians with close to nothing were the first to share the pittance they did have. I lost count of the times I was offered a cold drink, a place to pitch my tent, and small donations to my cause as I pedaled through rural towns connected by a maze of narrow, winding roads. I waved more in Kentucky than in any other state because so many people sat on their porches. The postmistress in Vincent handed me a wad of cash when I stopped in to mail a postcard on October 21. Twelve miles later, I cried at a tiny grocery store in Buckhorn on State Road 28 when a man in line behind me wrote me a check on the spot after he overheard me talking to the cashier about Heals on Wheels.

On that afternoon's ride into Hazard, I saw how the poorest of the poor scrambled to cobble together a living. Every other house or trailer had a homemade sign advertising crafts or beauty services, with one truck-leasing business doubling as a tanning salon. Many residences were tucked way back in one-lane hollows with no clear exit. No wonder I felt claustrophobic.

Pent-up nimbus clouds dropped their full load on Hazard at dinnertime, about a half hour after Don and I arrived. By then, we had come more than five hundred miles together—I on the bike and he in the car—since meeting in Illinois ten days earlier. Even if the sun had been shining, this city of fifty-four hundred in the heart of coal country would be grim. Gray Appalachia swimming in a cold rain could pitch even the most Pollyannaish optimist into a deep funk. Out of habit, I delivered a pile of brochures and cents-off sunscreen coupons to the hospital, where I engaged in a pleasant conversation with a young woman in the oncology department. It was the first time I felt I should have redirected my ride's resources. Hazard was far needier than Waukesha, Wisconsin.

It poured so hard that night in Hazard that we didn't even think about camping. Instead, we spread out my wet belongings in the cramped room of a dreary downtown inn. Don would be heading back to Wisconsin in the morning. As lightning flashed and rain lashed at our hotel windows, we feasted on a pile of fast food while watching the New York Yankees play the New York Mets in the first game of the World Series. Headlines warning of flash floods crawled across the bottom of the telecast.

On the gunmetal gray and drizzly morning of October 22, Don and I

217

said goodbye at the intersection of Highways 15 and 80 in Hazard. Early fog was so soupy that we didn't depart until ten a.m. He had a 561-mile drive to Wisconsin, and I had a 657-mile ride to the Atlantic Ocean. Intermittent rain kept me pedaling steadily through Dwarf, Emmalena, and Carrie. I didn't talk to anybody but myself until I stopped for lunch at a convenience store in the mountain town of Hindman. I knew Halloween was approaching because the town, like so many others, was festooned with goblins, skeletons, fake tombstones, witches, and bloodied corpses.

About eighteen miles later, the wet part of me was tempted to ignore the hand-lettered, cockeyed "Stop Corporate Greed" sign stuck into the soft soil of the shoulder on State Road 7. But my lonely, curious side won out, so I did a U-turn near Dema. I met three damp men huddled around a metal drum that they were feeding with heaping chunks of coal to keep warm. They cheerfully offered me a seat on a folding chair near a dilapidated vehicle that anchored one corner of a sagging tarpaulin. I felt ridiculously out of place when the wind suddenly changed, and I choked on the coarse smoke spewing from the black barrel. The men were too polite to laugh or even crack a smile. Instead, they offered me a can of soda to wash away the ashy taste on my tongue. In thick mountain accents, they explained that they were on strike from a Pittsburgh-based natural gas company and they were in the midst of a twelve-hour shift. A symphony of beeps from passing drivers indicated that the strikers weren't alone in their demands for higher wages and comprehensive health benefits. After a few minutes of small talk, I turned off my inner filter and bluntly asked the question that had gnawed at me for miles: What is it like to live in the heart of this ages-old stereotype of Appalachia?

Two of the strikers hemmed and hawed. I didn't want to pressure them because I was the one intruding. But the third, the oldest, wasn't nearly as reticent. Life in Appalachia hadn't been the same since President Lyndon Johnson had declared his war on poverty in the 1960s, he told me. Yes, what was called the Great Society had shined a spotlight on severe conditions there, but it also had brought too much unwanted attention from the outside world. That only contributed to the creation of caricatures.

"Nothing is wrong with providing health care and education to the underprivileged," he said. "Lord knows some need it." His voice quieted considerably when he spoke of the lingering pity from outsiders. "That's what we resent," he stated. "Why does this country's national anthem have to be, 'Oh, we have to help those poor people in Appalachia?'" Moving away to seek his fortune elsewhere wasn't an option. Eastern Kentucky was where he was born and where he wanted to die. The strike, he said, was about achieving dignity and justice for local workers. As for stereotypes, he said he wasn't surprised when people underestimated him. In fact, he had come to expect it. But it didn't bother him much because he felt he could hold his own in most conversations. Then his face softened. He laughed a gentle laugh while explaining that he and his neighbors defuse tense situations with visitors by referring to themselves as hillbillies—before the other person has a chance to use the epithet first.

For every convenience store I pedaled by, I counted three or four churches. Twenty-or-so miles after leaving the strikers, I was gratified to see the steeple of the Penny Road Community Church poking above the treetops on a side road near Virgie, off County Road 1469. It had been sixty-two mostly wet miles from Hazard to this tiny community of Robinson Creek, and I hadn't mapped out an overnight stop. Several cars were parked in the lot that Sunday evening. I waited for somebody to exit the small, neat church so I could ask about camping on the lush lawn. The front of the building was tastefully decorated with a simple fall harvest scene that included uncarved pumpkins and gourds mixed in with corn stalks and hay bales.

Soon, Brother Troy and his wife, Buncie, emerged. Not only did they insist that I keep my tent stowed and spend the night inside, they also invited me to the annual "Hallelujah Night for Youth." It's what you might call the anti-Halloween in a place where the holiday is viewed as a pagan event. Church children might be barred from donning costumes and trick-or-treating, but adults didn't want to deny them an evening of October fun.

The congregation couldn't have made a nonbeliever feel more welcome. Chili-covered hot dogs, chips, apples, soda, and ice cream counted as dinner before the festivities began. Kids gathered in the community room to bob for apples, mummify each other with toilet tissue, pass Lifesavers with a toothpick, and scramble for candy that burst from a busted piñata shaped like a pumpkin. Some children clearly had physical and mental challenges. But what impressed me was how the older kids looked out for the younger ones without prompting from adults. I felt as if I had a bit part in an Earl Hamner script because it was like spending an evening with John-Boy and the Walton family. One six-year-old girl even resembled the youngest Walton, Elizabeth, right down to the sprinkle of freckles across her nose. Afterward, we joined hands in a big circle and harmonized on songs heavy on hallelujahs. I didn't know the words, so I hummed along.

"Now, the church is yours," Brother Troy told me after everyone dispersed at about nine p.m. "Just please lock the door in the morning." I rolled out my sleeping bag in the staging room where parishioners were donating their labor to replace the church's drywall and roof. Early the next day, I wrote a thank-you note that I propped up on the kitchen stove and locked the door.

Fog enveloped mountain roads that were about as crooked as the Right Fork, Left Fork, Beefhide, and Greasy creeks that flowed along low points between peaks spiking to almost three thousand feet. By late morning, I had rattled, bobbed, and weaved down steep, heavily patched, one-lane State Road 195 into Ashcamp, its centerpiece a mom-and-pop grocery store.

I struck up a conversation with storekeeper Russ, who was wearing a New York Yankees cap because he admired the classy blue-and-white color combination, "not because I'm a fan of any baseball team from the Bronx." As I peppered him with questions on the store's stoop, he explained that, for the most part, people in Appalachia are descended from long lines of independent-minded folks and want to be left alone. Europeans who began settling in the crevices of Appalachia hundreds of years ago—and whose tiny, out-of-the-way family burial plots are still maintained by their descendants—once provided plenty for their families and neighbors. The terrain might have limited families to small-scale agriculture, but they each had at least a cow, some chickens, and a vegetable garden.

That ethic of self-reliance began changing during his grandparents' time when they sold their mineral rights for a song to opportunistic land agents, he explained. That gave faraway conglomerates access to Appalachian coal. Mountain people became dependent on outside dollars as coal miners.

"They broke their backs, scarred their lungs, and died doing hard labor for corporations," Russ said. "Some rely on handouts from charities or government agencies just to get by."

Inside, Russ's wife, Bula, operated the cash register. She didn't say anything but hello as I fished in my plastic bag wallet for enough change to cover the cost of a yellow delicious apple and some crackers. The look in her kind blue eyes indicated she likely had plenty of stories percolating. But why would she bother to reveal intimate details of her life to a nosy cyclist she had known for about a minute? On a whim, I handed her a brochure in exchange for my receipt. She glanced at it and asked me a few questions while she swept her long, graying hair into a makeshift bun. Once I answered them, her thoughts poured out like a waterfall.

Bula's family had lived in that mountain town for at least six generations. Her most recent heartache was trying to support four young grandchildren now that her unemployed twenty-seven-year-old daughter had filed for divorce. As business owners and churchgoers, she told me, she and her husband felt it was their responsibility to not only help their own families but also to lead outreach efforts and charity drives for destitute neighbors. For years, they had distributed donated clothes, groceries, and other supplies to people they thought were needy.

That eagerness had begun withering when disturbing incidents piled up, she said. First, a neighbor held up their store at gunpoint. Then she witnessed too many people with plenty of resources taking advantage of her generosity. She was afraid to speak up for fear of being ostracized or assaulted.

"Those rude awakenings broke my spirit," she said, her eyes tearing. "We need to get out of this business."

She took me outside and pointed to a spot on a faraway ridge framed with the coppers and crimsons of autumn. It was where Russ was building their retirement home. From that patched asphalt road, the isolated building was just a speck to the naked eye.

"These people here, they hurt my heart," she said. "I can hardly wait to leave most of them behind."

I meditated on Bula's ball of hurt as I climbed out of Ashcamp on State Road 197. Much of the roadside landscape was covered with kudzu. Decades ago, Americans became enamored with the quick-growing Asian plant because it was hailed as a miracle solution to the severe erosion caused by road-building and other engineering havoc. But it turned out to be an intensely invasive species that sprouted roughshod by outcompeting native plants. Late-fall frosts had browned the kudzu's once-green leaves, making it mercifully dormant. To me, those withered leaves symbolized how human life, too, was slowly being choked out of this shriveling region.

Ashcamp was only ten miles from Virginia, where I planned to sleep that night. I hadn't planned on covering the 517 trail miles across Kentucky in just eight days. One motivating factor for the more rushed schedule? Dogs! I'm not exaggerating when I say that at least 150 unleashed pooches chased me. They came alone or in duos or trios. And they all barked. Such unexpected ferocity was intimidating enough when I zipped along a flat stretch, never mind a steep, crooked lane on pockmarked blacktop or loose gravel. Fearing I would end up performing a grotesque gymnastics routine over the handlebars as I dodged persistent dogs, I kept my hands poised over my brakes. Uphills were equally dicey because even older, determined dogs can overtake a gear-laden bicyclist. Fortunately, most of them didn't know what to do with me once they caught up.

The way these hounds bolted down rural driveways almost had me convinced that the rotation of my wheels emitted a sound inaudible to human ears that spelled supper to them. Kentucky has a leash law, but there's evidently no penalty for ignoring it. Just how was I supposed to respond to a man who yelled, "They're not biters!" as his two large mixed-breed dogs stormed toward me near Buckhorn? *Look, buddy*, I thought as

221

I pedaled furiously, *from here it looks as if they have sharp teeth. Can you be sure they won't eat slightly roasted, freckled leg for breakfast?*

Those close canine encounters perhaps foreshadowed a wrenching event that unfolded not long after I spoke with Russ and Bula. As I grunted my way out of a hollow, incessant barking indicated I was once again being tailed. This time a trio—a German shepherd mix, a husky mix, and a mutt puppy—barreled down a trash-strewn driveway. Seconds later, a dark-blue wreck of a sedan roared around the curve behind me. The driver squealed to a halt, but yelps and revolting thuds indicated he hadn't stopped quickly enough. His balding tires had crushed two dogs. "Good Lord, I'm lucky that wasn't me," I whispered to myself while sidling up to the side of the car. The passenger rolled down his window.

"I don't know what else you could have done," I told the two stone-faced young men in the front seat. Neither made a move to open either front door. It gave me the impression that running over dogs on rural roads was as common as, say, eating lunch. Either that, or they were merely relieved that they weren't my dogs and I wasn't going to light into them. "It's a horrible incident, but I don't think it could have been avoided the way those dogs were charging," I tried again, still waiting for a response. Still, neither spoke. Even if they had, I would have had trouble hearing them over the crazy barking of the shepherd dog, the one spared by the car's tires. The driver nodded at me, but both men's faces remained eerily expressionless. Seconds later, the driver stomped on the accelerator and was gone.

The injured husky mix dragged himself to the earthen roadside, as if this was a familiar routine. The badly squashed puppy, crumpled in the middle of the lane, let out a pathetic, thin whine. I braced my bicycle over the dying creature. As I plotted how to roll him off the roadway, I heard rapid footsteps crunching on gravel.

"Snoooooopy," wailed a boy of about ten sprinting toward me from a trailer. I wanted to cover his eyes so he didn't have to watch his furry companion taking his last breaths. The boy cradled his dog's head, then looked up at me, his brown eyes wet. It was doubtful the boy's family had money to cover its own medical expenses, never mind those of a pet.

"I'm so sorry for what happened to your dog," I told the boy, still wondering if the driver would have pulled away as quickly if he had hit me instead of the dog. "Is anybody else coming to help?"

"No," he cried. "My father is inside watching the babies." Then, in a quiet but steady voice, he explained that the husky mix, injured but still alive, had broken three legs not long ago in a similar car encounter. He wiped his eyes so tears wouldn't roll down his cheeks. The blend of sadness and matter-of-factness about this pitiful ordeal reinforced my belief that he had witnessed more than his share of unpleasantness. I asked him if he had a shovel. He nodded and trudged up the driveway.

When he returned with a rusty snow shovel, the two of us gently maneuvered the still-warm puppy's body to the only vessel available—a plastic kiddie pool full of dried-up leaves. Minutes later, the boy's young mother and a boy who appeared to be his older brother chugged into the driveway. I recited the sad story, and the mother thanked me for stopping. Oddly, neither she nor the brother offered any comforting words or hugs to the heartbroken boy before driving toward the trailer. When I begged the boy to put a leash on his next puppy, he mumbled how "we tried before, but leashes just don't work." He told me he would bury Snoopy later. I waved goodbye, figuring he would complete that gloomy chore alone.

CHAPTER 35
MY GUIDE TO AGENCY

When my uncle retired from a military career that had allowed him to travel the world with his family, he opted to settle into a second career in the rural part of central Ohio where his spouse, my mother's younger sister, had grown up. They bought a small farm, complete with horses and a large fenced field where their four children could practice riding.

One summer day in the early 1970s when our family was visiting, my oldest cousin had the brilliant notion that she and I should both ride Candy, her black-and-white horse. We were both thirteen or fourteen, and neither of us was very big. The little I knew about horses I had learned from that cousin. I trusted her. She climbed into the saddle, and I got on behind her. Upon command, Candy walked, then trotted calmly around the ring. Suddenly, something set her off. The horse sped to a gallop, then began twisting and rearing. Clearly, she wanted to buck one or both of us. I was too stunned to scream. Instinctively, I grabbed the back of the saddle with one hand and the tail of my cousin's shirt with the other. That cloth and leather became my lifeline as the horse romped wildly for what was probably three or four minutes, though it seemed like an hour. Finally, perhaps exhausted, Candy stopped pitching. Slowly, I released my grip.

"I can't believe you're still back there," my cousin yelled.

"Well, what else was I supposed to do?" I barked, feeling angry and exhilarated. "Fall off and die?" It was a long drop to the ground, and the idea of being kicked or stomped by an animal wearing four metal shoes seemed brutal. Hanging on was my only option.

That pretty much captures how I navigated cancer. Nobody handed me a neatly outlined handbook and said, "Here you go, Elizabeth. Follow these steps and you're guaranteed to squeeze through the rabbit hole of melanoma unscathed." I had to write my own guidebook and edit it constantly. No single rope labeled "lifeline" was lowered magically in front of me as I untangled treatment options. Instead, dozens of mysterious ropes dangled, and I couldn't tell how securely any of them was moored just by looking. I had to tug on each one, gently at first, to find out if it could bear my weight. After handling enough of them, I became more trusting and confident.

Those test tugs were exhausting. The nitty-gritty of researching treatments, finding the right doctors, withstanding chemotherapy, or recovering from surgery was a physical and mental grind. What liberated me was consciously deciding not to be a victim of the disease. Medical authorities could only do so much to help me with sanity and stability. The rest was an "inside job." Cancer forced me to pay close attention to who I was and how I became that person. That freed me to figure out how to tinker with my personality traits. Some of that was easy, and some was really hard.

Among the simplest choices was not wasting energy engaging with people who spewed ridiculous clichés about cancer. The most odious: "God never gives us more than we can handle." And another: "What doesn't kill us makes us stronger." Maybe those aphorisms are comforting to some people, but I'm not among them. I think that too many burdens can break people in half, especially those who are isolated or unable to ask for help.

I also learned to wave off people way more depressed than I ever was about my decision not to have children. In my early twenties, I did not have a firm grasp on the genetics and inheritability of my disease—and for that matter, neither did medical professionals. My suspicion of a link was enough for me to confirm my belief that I didn't need to give birth to be a complete woman. Perhaps I lacked a maternal gene, but at no point as I crept toward age forty did I become weepy or regretful about what seemed like common sense. Why hand a potential defect and burden to the next generation? Enough was enough. My sisters and friends had children I loved to be around, and the world has plenty of children. I don't feel at all deprived, selfish, or inadequate by opting out of motherhood.

What scientists know today is that I very likely fall into a category that cancer researchers define as familial malignant melanoma. It includes families where two or more close relatives—parents, siblings, or children—have the disease. An estimated 10 percent of people with melanoma have some variation on that family history. Familial melanoma is a genetic or inherited condition, so the risk of melanoma can be passed down.

Melanoma itself is not inherited, but a susceptibility to it is. That susceptibility occurs because specific gene mutations are passed from one generation to the next. Under normal circumstances, every cell in the human body has two copies of each gene. Genes are packaged onto chromosomes. One gene is inherited from the mother, the other from the father. With familial melanoma, a mutation happens in only one copy of the gene. That means a parent with a gene mutation can pass along a copy of a normal gene or a gene with the mutation. A child whose parent has a mutation has a 50 percent chance of inheriting that mutation.

The remaining 90 percent of people diagnosed with melanoma have no family history of it. These cases are sporadic because their genes are damaged after birth. Each gene in a person's body is made up of a unique sequence of DNA, which contains the information that controls how each cell in the body grows, divides, lives, and dies. Environmental factors such as exposure to ultraviolet light can damage or mutate genes, disrupting a cell's normal function.

Only recently have two genes been linked to familial melanoma. Both of them, CDKN2A and CDK4, play vital roles in controlling when cells divide. Testing for CDKN2A is now available. Several other genes associated with an increased risk of melanoma are being studied. Scientists emphasize that they do not yet fully understand the implications of certain types of mutations and that several types of melanoma that run in families do not yet have clearly defined genetic causes.

Most oncologists agree that results of genetic tests are unlikely to change screening recommendations or clinical care for people with melanoma or those with a strong family history of the disease. In my case, testing would not have stopped my disease. It would likely just confirm what I already know and have acted on.

The most difficult part of my "inside job" was naming and then delving into behaviors I wanted to shed. Ignoring them or blaming them on somebody else was tempting. But that didn't seem fair; I needed to take responsibility.

Two themes surfaced when I zeroed in on my most glaring defects. The first involved my anger. I wanted to unearth the roots of it and figure out how to rechannel it. The second was about self-worth. I wanted to value myself more. I like to think I would have been brave enough to examine that pair of faults even if my melanoma had never surfaced. The message I absorbed from books and speakers who addressed cancer was that your mere existence meant you were worth saving. But I wasn't convinced.

The deeper I dug into my anger and how I discounted myself, the clearer it became how tightly the two were entwined. My perception of myself was what usually triggered my short fuse. On the cruelest days, I wondered if some force beyond genetics and misfortune had pegged me as incapable of achieving anything beyond enduring another surgery or chemotherapy cocktail. Maybe the truth I needed to accept was that I was unsalvageable in a world where winners lived and losers died.

Eliminating anger seemed preposterous and impossible because I didn't view it as a useless or undesirable emotion. I just wanted better control of it. On the work and personal fronts, I had benefited from transforming temporary bursts of low-grade anger into motivation to complete a project that might otherwise seem undoable. For instance, when editors told me I wouldn't be able to pursue a certain story because it was impossible, I didn't need to vent with an angry outburst. Instead, I could spin that energy into passion that spurred me into proving an editor wrong. As a reporter, I had become quite deft at calming or outmaneuvering venomous sources who tried to bait me with hurtful or provocative thoughts.

It was the same with a hike. Yes, I whined while breaking in new boots in Connecticut, the tenth state to a north-bounder trying to hike all fourteen states of the Appalachian Trail. But having a pity party wasn't going to get me to Maine because the trail didn't care about the condition of my feet, and nobody else could walk those remaining miles for me. I had watched other hikers beaten down by their attempts to adjust to new gear. They ended up quitting. Sore feet or not, I didn't want that type of ending to be my trail legacy, and I didn't want to be defeated by two pieces of leather. Instead of listening to my instinct and hitting the trail at first light, I had to swallow my frustration and spend valuable daylight rebandaging my feet.

The anger I wanted to control involved my top-blowing, irrational eruptions that reminded me of my father's volcanoes. That fury was detrimental. Strangely, though, my rage usually wasn't directed at other people. Instead, I would explode at myself, feeling inadequate and frustrated at my inability to solve a problem. Whether it was a trait I had inherited or learned didn't matter. I didn't like it, and I didn't want to make excuses for it. It scared me to have that type of turmoil lurking inside.

Maybe, I thought, I could tackle my anger the same way I had overcome my fear of heights. My self-prescribed cure for conquering my fear of high places had been simple: Face the nemesis. When I hiked the Appalachian Trail, I forced myself to climb lookout towers on mountains—the ones once used to scout for wildfires. I thought standing atop the sometimes-rickety structures would be the biggest challenge. But it wasn't. Instead, the stomach-churning part was forcing my feet to continue upward on open-air staircases made of metal grate. Looking down at the faraway ground made me freeze. So I forced myself to focus on what was at eye level. With enough practice and persistence, I succeeded. Yes, that distinctive fluttery feeling still gripped my gut periodically, and I certainly wasn't going to launch a career as a mountaineer. But I was eventually able to cross high bridges and stand at rocky overlooks without panicking.

To deal with my anger, I had to come to grips with my own internal fire tower, so to speak. Instead of climbing a physical object, however, this required peeling back my interior layers. When I did, I found surprisingly fresh scars. They were emotional wounds my father had inflicted by yelling uncontrollably, instilling fear, and hurling insults that labeled his daughters as slow or stupid. He insisted that we behave like miniature adults, performing tasks perfectly the first time. I don't know if he chose not to be aware that trial and error was a necessary part of learning and shaping confidence, or if he beat us down verbally to plug a hole in his own insecurities. Either way, his sharpness left the equivalent of deep and broad gouges on my psyche. Those marks might be invisible, but they take longer to heal than a physical wound. And the scar tissue is forever sensitive.

Blaming my father wasn't an acceptable solution though. And surgery and chemotherapy can't keep anger at bay. This time, I didn't need a scalpel or poison. I needed alertness, awareness, and the will to move beyond brokenness. I had to teach myself to calm my temper by relying on myself to intervene. When I recognized that I was on the verge of overreacting, I had to hold up a big stop sign in my brain, then grab the anger by the scruff of its neck and stare it down. Only then could I rechannel that rage toward physical activity, such as a brisk walk or a writing project. Yielding to self-pity and wallowing in it was nothing more than self-sabotage. I had to allow myself the same patience I always gave to the most reluctant, stubborn, or overly emotional sources I interviewed for newspaper articles. This requires eternal vigilance, and even to this day, I still slip and fail.

Cancer dared me to thrive. And I tried to double-dare it back. Having the tenacity to try to outsmart it helped me understand that it was all right for me to take up space in the world instead of shrinking from it. After my father died and I was still a teenager, I wondered if melanoma might strike the next generation. I used to secretly hope that if it did, it would be me because I thought I was the most inadequate sister and therefore expendable. But when I found myself in the thick of it, I was able to accept a new truth: I was strong, confident, and stubborn enough to navigate whatever nastiness was tossed at me. I would either find a way around, through, or over—or die trying.

Cancer, with its ugly, appalling unpredictability, guided me into what I define as real adulthood. My father's death might have forced me to grow up faster than many of my high school peers, but my own early encounters with melanoma propelled me to what philosophers refer to as my "agency moment." That's when I stopped being blown about by my own voids and weaknesses and began to live according to my own inner criteria. *New York Times* columnist David Brooks describes an agency moment as a time when a person gradually develops a passionate and steady capacity to drive his or her own life. For me, it wasn't a snap-of-the-fingers transformation. Rather, it was a series of aha insights that forced me to grow by gravitating toward what was challenging and rewarding instead of just fending off the intractable.

Initially, the shock of cancer fueled me to try to savor each day as if it were my last. But that was too exhausting and impossibly hard when the melanoma crept back. I needed a more measured approach. I refused to sink into a state of blind acceptance. Instead, I chose to live more deliberately and thoughtfully, keeping what mattered and paring away stagnating clutter and noise. That focus on the essentials helped me cultivate a sense of wonder and a tender reverence for life. And I gave myself permission to take detours. I might have bollixed up my career trajectory by leaving jobs to hike the Appalachian Trail, try out an internship with the National Park Service, live on a nature preserve, and ride my bike across the country, but these were healing necessities. Instead of a razzle-dazzle career, I found I was content to have a series of jobs and would bend to live with the consequences. As the old saw goes, no cemetery has a gravestone inscribed: "I wish I had worked more hours."

It was also liberating to understand that I didn't have to be a peacemaker anytime my friends or co-workers were embroiled in conflict. I could care, but I didn't need to feel guilty about choosing to conserve energy for my own struggles. Growing up in a house where I clenched my stomach constantly because my father might light into any of us at any moment made me believe that quiet, even when fragile, was preferable to confrontation. As an adult, it was a relief to realize that I didn't have to be a fixer, that I could challenge authority without being castigated, and that grown people would have to finagle their own way out of their own jams.

Another relief was becoming aware that I no longer had to apologize for being sensitive in a loud and demanding world. I didn't care if people underestimated me personally or professionally because I knew I had the grit, the gumption, the skills, and the endurance to achieve. Watching my father struggle nurtured my empathy, and wrestling with my own cancer made me better equipped to interact with and interview people in tough circumstances. What I said to people and how I said it mattered. I didn't have to tell them I cared; they could infer that from my approach and my questions. Empathy and introversion were strengths, not deficits.

As a reporter, I was accomplished at using words to demystify the world. By probing into others' lives, I was able to break down what seemed like impossibly complicated details to their barest bones and piece them back together in an understandable format that flowed. It was much more difficult to use those same tools on myself. Yet I needed to delve into my thorny patch of disquieting tangles if I didn't want to settle for some simple, saccharine fairy tale. The latter might have been more comforting, but it wouldn't have been the truth. And lies would have made me retreat, not grow.

Finding the courage to dig into hazy, painful parts of the past helped me become flexible enough to accept ambiguity, the fraught and opaque layers of human relationships, and the mistakes that adults make. That's not the same as surrender or acquiescence. For me, it meant having the maturity and perspective to forgive my father for the hurt he left behind and to understand that he was much more than the sum of his flaws. I could recognize the good and build my own legacy on that foundation. Just because I was related to him didn't mean I would have to become him. I didn't have to carry his burdens or hand them off to anybody else. And I found such solace in setting them down.

CHAPTER 36
WESTERN VIRGINIA: SNIFFING THE ATLANTIC—ALMOST

MILES RIDDEN: 3,675
MILES TO GO: 575

On winding Appalachian roads that had endured decades of abuse from gargantuan coal and timber trucks, I girded for "Get a car!" or similar taunts from passing teenagers. I didn't expect such commentary from anybody my age. When I followed a woman driving a compact car with a "May the Forest Be With You" bumper sticker into the parking lot of a small grocery store, I naïvely expected a smile or knowing nod from an ally. Instead, she rolled down her window and shouted, "Stay off the road, you idiot!"

Such venom had me on guard early on the afternoon of October 23 as I prepared to enter Virginia, my tenth and final state, on State Road 80. It's where the northern edge of the verdant Breaks Interstate Park straddles a crooked border with Kentucky. Reaching the apex of the scrappy, scrawny road, I heard one diesel engine belching behind me and saw another big rig heading toward me. I prepared to dismount. It would be safer to seek refuge in the painful puckerbush than to die defying a law of physics.

Before I could unclip my cleats, the driver of the log-laden truck heading toward me stopped—and politely waved me forward. I paused in disbelief long enough to pry my gloved left hand from my handlebars and flash him a peace sign. He nodded and smiled. I would have mailed him a commendation for courtesy if we had lingered long enough for me to jot down his address. Instead, he continued on to Kentucky, and I hurtled into Virginia.

I rolled into Council about thirty miles later. At a park that welcomed overnight cyclists, I befriended Clyde, who spent his days pitching horseshoes after a thirty-seven-year career as a coal miner. The Virginia retiree impressed me by casually nailing a ringer with almost every toss.

"I should be good at it," he said, brushing off my compliments. "This is what I do all day now. It's something to keep me busy." Barely interrupting the satisfying *clank, clank, clank* of his daily routine, he explained that the region's easily accessible coal was gone and that Appalachia now exported young people in search of safer and more lucrative opportunities. He also harrumphed about a long-promised four-lane highway connecting Virginia and West Virginia that politicians promised would miraculously boost the area's moribund economy and reduce double-digit unemployment. Clyde thought it would only speed the exodus of natives. He suggested that legislators forgo the new road and its false promise of boosting the economy, and instead divide the project's millions among residents to allow them to relocate to places where jobs were more abundant.

That night was so clear that I rolled out my sleeping bag in the park gazebo to watch the stars before I drifted off. I was awakened in the wee hours when I heard people talking several yards away. Thinking I might be a target for harassment by prowling teens, I groggily prepared my defense. Then, one person said, "Shhh, it looks like somebody is trying to sleep here. Let's go somewhere else." I was so relieved that I wanted to yell "thank you."

Wounds to the Appalachian landscape—denuded and leveled mountains, and debris-clogged streams—are the legacy of corporations' frenzy to extract the coal that fuels so many electricity-generating power plants. But just because mining, wind, and erosion have worn down these ancient mountains doesn't mean they have lost their bite. In North America, only the Rocky Mountains loom larger. The Appalachians extend roughly fifteen hundred miles from the St. Lawrence Valley in Quebec to the Gulf Coast Plain in northern Alabama. They are actually two parallel mountain chains, with the highest elevations along the easternmost spine. Depending on where you are, the two are between a hundred and three hundred miles apart.

Big A, which tops out above thirty-seven hundred feet, was my first climb out of Council on October 24. Cyclists are evidently free to choose what the "A" denotes. My calf and thigh muscles voted for arduous. Farther along, my route on Highway 80 over and around House and Barn, River, Beartown, Clinch, and Little Mountains was a lung-buster on par with the Rockies and Ozarks. Bicyclists expecting fancy switchbacks to coddle them through this territory of snaggle-toothed marvels have set their tires down in the wrong place. Whining won't get you far either. The straightforward, longtime inhabitants of these mountains have little tolerance for it— especially from somebody with enough free time to indulge in a two-wheeled venture.

Despite what the Appalachians can still dish out, I figured I had it easy compared with the crew that Alexander Spotswood assembled a few centuries ago. In 1716, the governor of the Virginia colony and a party of gentlemen, their servants, and several Indian guides set out on what researchers called an "exploratory picnic" of the Old Appalachians, also called the Blue Ridge. Those servants probably yearned for chiropractors

233

after hauling food and cases of wine, brandy, stout, champagne, rum, and cider on a two-week tour. The group claimed the lands for England before descending into the navigable Shenandoah Valley, part of the Great Valley nestled between the younger and older Appalachians.

Pothole-plagued, treacherous roads meant I could only be so freewheeling on downhills. Though I had been judicious with my brakes since Oregon, I found I had to push down harder and harder on the levers for traction. My rear brake pads had worn thin enough that I resorted to Fred Flintstone-style foot-dragging stops in a pinch. I was glad I pressed the brakes hard enough to stop in Hayters Gap, a town about thirty miles east of Council so small that no services were marked on my map.

All I wanted was a bathroom, but to my delight I also hit the jackpot in an elementary school converted to house a senior center. The seniors, hosting their weekly potluck, fed me and also loaded me up with plastic bags of apples and cookies.

Some of that loot was still dangling from my handlebars when I rolled into my old stomping grounds of Damascus twenty-three miles later, making a beeline for "The Place." For decades, this two-story clapboard house, transformed into a church-run hostel, has been welcoming cross-country travelers for very affordable overnight stays. Hikers and bicyclists converge in Damascus, at the southern edge of Virginia where North Carolina and Tennessee meet, because it is a nexus of the TransAmerica and Appalachian Trails. The last time I had rolled out my sleeping bag on one of those bed frames was during my 1991 hiking adventure from Georgia to Maine. This time around, the skies darkened by seven p.m. because it was late October. It was a pleasure to have access to electricity.

The waning daylight hours also coincided with the approaching presidential election. Don wasn't able to deliver an absentee ballot when we met in Illinois because they weren't ready yet. But the Wisconsin town clerk agreed to mail one to the post office in Christiansburg, Virginia, when I called her from Kentucky. The community of about fifteen thousand along County Road 666 is 112 bike miles beyond Damascus. Christiansburg would be a two-for-one stop because I also would pick up my final batch of brochures.

I never had a permanent address in Virginia, but nine years prior, I had established a certain intimacy with the state because one-quarter of the Appalachian Trail—more than five hundred miles—traverses it. I had absorbed its richness into my body and brain after spending weeks measuring my progress by the slant of the sun on a mountain ridge or the size of the rising moon. The part I now bicycled through had that earthy, oaky pungency of home. Waterfalls spilled near the roadways. Cows munched on grasses on open hillsides. Rocky streambeds formed watery edges in a countryside laden with lush ferns and mosses, and thickets of rhododendron and mountain laurel.

Cool evenings indicated that fall was fully present as I rolled through the Mount Rogers Recreation Area and the Grayson Highlands, between one thousand and four thousand feet in elevation. Some hardwood trees still clung to their marvelous autumnal glory, as if clutching those leafy bouquets would miraculously keep autumn from ending. Squirrels rustled among the oaks for extra acorns. They, too, must have heard the same winter report: Expect a harsh one because the brown-and-black woolly bear caterpillars were darker and thicker than usual. I swerved a herky-jerky path along my ribbon of the road to avoid these furry crawlers, cringing when I thought about the hundreds that would be eliminated by rolling herds of Michelins and Firestones.

I was never too far from Interstate 81 as I wended through Troutdale, Sugar Grove, Cedar Springs, Rural Retreat, Wytheville, Max Meadows, Draper, and Newbern in southwestern Virginia. Fortunately, this section of Virginia has a distinctly unfour-lane-like flavor. I could appreciate roadside amusements such as the "God Answers Knee Mail" sign posted outside a mom-and-pop sewing business and the "JUNK MAIL" message spray-painted on a toilet at the end of a driveway. And then there was the high-strung poultry. Near Wytheville, my morning almost began with a bang when a duck suddenly launched itself from a roadside ditch. Had I not "ducked" instinctively, that surprised creature certainly would have clocked me in the helmet, and neither of us would have emerged whole. Later that day, a chicken bolted from a yard full of free-range friends and shot across the country road in front of me, missing an ugly flattening from a semi-trailer tire by a feather's width. Did that bird regularly engage in chicken roulette just to entertain cyclists? I couldn't answer the age-old question of why the chicken crossed the road, but I knew how he did it: speedily.

After too much lunch on October 26 in the outskirts of Radford, I chugged up a steep hill. At the top, a smiling woman with a "Share the Road" bumper sticker on her Volvo waved me over to her idling car.

"Would you like a place to stay for the night?" she asked. Sarah, a nurse, explained that her husband, Thad, a doctor, had bicycled the same cross-country route with his two sons in 1998, so they now operated what amounted to a part-time cyclist hostel. He had schooled her that cyclists can be grumpy if somebody stops them midclimb, so it was best to interact after they have crested hills. Fortunately, my proceed-as-the-way-opens side quashed the inner compulsive voice yammering at me to push on to Christiansburg so I could take care of my brochure and ballot to-do list.

235

I followed the Volvo to a lovely early twentieth-century farmhouse. It was Sarah's birthday, so the three of us celebrated with sandwiches, beer, and decadent desserts at a local restaurant. Even I was finally bested by a monstrosity of a dessert that included frighteningly sweet piles of fudge brownies, whipped cream, cherries, and cookies. Thad, examining the photo on my brochure, said, "Wow, you're not the same Elizabeth who started the ride, are you?" When I looked in the bathroom mirror, I realized he was right. Not only was I leaner and more freckled, but those leg muscles he pointed out were indeed pronounced. I should have asked one of them to take a look at my injured left arm, but I was too embarrassed to mention it. I could open it about 120 degrees, and though swollen, it didn't throb unless I put direct pressure on it. I figured I would invest in physical therapy back in Wisconsin.

Leaving their house early the next morning, a Friday, wasn't an option because an impenetrable fog enveloped the New River Valley. Ironically, the New River is one of the country's oldest waterways. It flows south to north, unlike most rivers.

My late-afternoon fourteen-mile ride to Christiansburg was fog-free and simple enough. I thought I was golden when I arrived at the doorstep of what appeared to be the downtown post office just before five p.m. But I was sadly mistaken to assume the main post office would be conveniently located there. A sign on the door explained that the post office had moved to suburbia, so no dice on the brochures or the ballot that day. Undaunted, I remounted the bike, figuring I would camp near the new post office and do my pickup in the morning. The route to the new building turned into a hellish obstacle course of clogged retail strips with intermittent sidewalks. I needed a break from the beeping, so I stopped at a grocery store.

"Hey, you must be lost," I heard someone say as I dug my bicycle lock from deep in a pannier. "Where are you headed?"

When I explained my predicament, the man who introduced himself as Jim insisted on giving me a ride. "That new post office is way out there. I'm retired and have plenty of time. I'm not even shopping here, just helping myself to the free coffee."

We climbed in his car. At the post office, Jim insisted on waiting for me. The front door was locked, but a clerk answered my knock at the loading dock. Within minutes, she handed me an envelope of brochures. My ballot, mailed from the same state, proved more elusive. The friendly clerk gave me a number to call Saturday morning. Voting should not be this complicated. But I couldn't give up now. The privilege was worth the hassle. Back at the grocery store parking lot, I was grateful to find my bike whole.

From there, I dodged traffic and obstacles back to the decrepit downtown. As I repackaged my brochures near the Presbyterian church, I met Mary, the housekeeper, who allowed me to pitch my tent next to the playground. It was too early to sleep, so I ordered hot chocolate and a sandwich at a corner restaurant. The young man behind the counter refused to take my money. I started to argue, then realized my scruffy outfit and unkempt hair marked me as one of the many homeless people who gravitated there from a nearby shelter. I accepted his charity—and left my money in the tip jar instead.

My Saturday morning call to the post office from a pay phone near the church restored my faith in our postal service. My ballot had arrived. Leaving my bike locked downtown, I hoofed it partway before lucking out with a ride from a couple of good-natured Virginia Tech basketball coaches who evidently took pity on me.

At the post office counter, I used the tip of a ballpoint pen to punch out the tiny pieces of cardboard adjacent to my candidates of choice. My chads fluttered to the floor. I had left none of them hanging. On that morning of October 28—ten days before the election—I obviously had no inkling about the hanging chad debacle that would play a significant role in Florida and involve the US Supreme Court in one of this country's most protracted, drama-ridden, and memorable presidential contests.

The TransAmerica and Appalachian Trails overlap in several other southwestern Virginia communities, including Troutville, only 47.5 miles beyond Christiansburg. After voting, I arrived there late that afternoon, wearing shorts and a T-shirt. A cold front lowered temperatures to the thirties early that evening.

I found temporary warmth huddling with locals inside the Rebel Yell auction house in a converted elementary school. I laughed as winning bidders toted newly purchased lamps, furniture, dishes, artwork, radios, and knickknacks to their vehicles, thinking how hilarious my two-wheeler would look with such burdens attached. Bicycle travel is indeed a cure for consumerism.

Across the way, I found a park with a restored red Norfolk Southern X544 train caboose as the centerpiece—the perfect late-night cover for a tent-toting cyclist. My last task of the day was setting my watch back an hour to sync with eastern standard time. Abandoning daylight saving time meant it would be lighter an hour sooner in the morning but darker before six p.m.

That earlier light helped me to break away from Troutville about six thirty the next morning. Seventeen miles later, during breakfast in Buchanan, the temperature had crept from thirty-six degrees to thirty-eight degrees. My gloved fingers ached. The state's rural roads are all marked with three digits, and I had to pay close attention to the mountainous twists and turns noted on my map.

When I stopped for a sandwich at a roadside store beyond Lexington, I doubled my order after the cashier informed me that the store in Vesuvius, the eruptive-sounding community that was my destination for the night, was closed. I found Vesuvius to be the tranquil but hilly home to two-hundred-or-so residents. It's just a few miles from the Blue Ridge Parkway.

"Oh my goodness, melanoma," a Vesuvius woman out for a walk said when I asked about camping. "My husband has had surgery for that cancer, and he's still alive too. Check with the pastor at the Baptist church. He usually lets bicyclists stay under the pavilion."

Unknowingly, that woman had directed me toward more trail magic. I leaned my bike in the pavilion and knocked on the pastor's door. His family invited me inside and asked me to attend that evening's once-a-year stewardship dinner at the church. Before the meal began, I returned to the pavilion to pitch my tent—and found it littered with shreds of paper and plastic bags. An opportunistic critter had devoured my extra dinner sandwich.

The church dinner outclassed any convenience store fare. It was an evening bursting with conversation, camaraderie, and heaping helpings of fried chicken, macaroni pie, green bean casserole, cornbread, and baked apples. All I provided in exchange was a talk about my adventure.

While helping to clean the church kitchen, I talked with a parishioner, Wanda, a transplant from the south side of Milwaukee. She and her husband, Rick, and their two young daughters had moved to Vesuvius a few months earlier after a military assignment in Cuba. They were world travelers because of Rick's military career, but as Milwaukee natives, they were steeped in the Wisconsin cheese-head tradition. They insisted that I "unpitch" my tent in the pavilion and decamp to their house. There, the two girls introduced me to their treasured dog, guinea pig, and rabbit. While temperatures dipped below freezing that evening, I snuggled to sleep on their couch under a Green Bay Packers blanket.

After breakfast the next morning, Rick headed to his job at the Virginia Military Institute in Lexington.

"And you're not leaving without this," Wanda said, handing me a liverwurst-and-cheese sandwich that earned a prized spot in the zippered compartment of my left pannier.

"I guess all I'll need to make my Wisconsin-in-Virginia lunch stop complete is a place that serves Milwaukee beer," I said, thanking her.

I couldn't yet smell salt water. But I would soon. I was only 256 trail miles from the Atlantic.

CHAPTER 37
OCEANS AND FLAGS

S alt water and waves weren't part of the central Ohio landscape where my father grew up, but he became enamored with the Atlantic Ocean during his childhood summer vacations in coastal Maine and Martha's Vineyard in Massachussetts. Years later, that same water beckoned when he had his own family in Philadelphia. One of his co-workers had access to a set of three cabins on Cape Cod. That thoughtful English teacher invited colleagues to rent a cabin and share their private beach. For several summers in the late 1960s, before our family caught the camping bug, we spent a few weeks there.

Those were glorious weeks because they allowed my father to sate his appetite for the shore. We could hardly wait for the tide to recede so we could walk out on the massive, exposed ocean floor looking for shells and other treasures. My father, his pants rolled up to his knees, would join in as we dug for clams, built castles with moats, and buried willing participants up to their necks in sand. Our favorite nights were those when the large black-and-white-speckled enamel-coated kettle came out of the pantry. It meant lobster, purchased at the local seafood shack, was on the dinner menu. My sisters and I secretly professed to pitying these mottled crustaceans as they whiled away their final moments in a pan of cool water. But we hardly hesitated to wave goodbye when it came time to drop them into the boiling pot. We watched their shells turn bright red, then used nutcrackers and small mallets to liberate the sweet meat that we dipped in melted butter. Messy but delicious. After our feast, the table would be littered with an assortment of broken claws, tail parts, and carapace pieces.

Even though I usually wore a white T-shirt over my swimsuit to protect my pale freckled skin from the sun's rays on those trips, my back and legs would bake to the same red as one of our cooked lobsters. At night, I desperately wanted to be able to tumble onto the mattress upstairs and sleep like a stone, as everybody else seemed to be able to do. But I couldn't. Taking off my shirt and putting on my summer pajamas was a slow and painful process. Making contact with the sheets was excruciating, and the grains of beach sand in the bed felt like tiny needles. I found it best to position myself on my stomach and remain as still as possible. Sometimes I felt like a molting snake. My skin would peel off in big transparent pieces that I could roll up into doughy balls. I have little doubt that those summers triggered the melanoma that eventually ran amok in my cells. Tanning oils were big sellers then, with sunscreen just a blip on the public health radar screen.

Still, in my adult mind, reflecting on those Cape Cod summers conjures up pure happiness—not regret. Every day at that Cape Cod beach, my two younger sisters and I would scramble over a hodgepodge pile of rocks to mount our saddleless "steeds." To an adult, they were merely giant black rocks at the end of the jetty constructed to preserve and divide sandy beaches for vacationers. Maybe they sort of looked like lopsided animals if you squinted. But to us—three scrawny pig-tailed girls with vivid imaginations—they were Black Beauties.

"I call the horse on the end," my red-haired sister yelled as the three of us sprinted out the screen door, bolting at top speed so as not to sizzle the tender bottoms of our feet on the sun-scorched sand.

She was the same girl who used to claim the white metal swinging bar on the jungle gym in our Philadelphia backyard, thinking it always guaranteed her first dibs. As the next-to-youngest in a family with four girls, she was too naïve to realize that this was a first-come, first-served world. Nothing is guaranteed. Instead, the nimblest navigator is the one allowed to call the shots.

My sisters and I could "gallop" the beaches bareback for hours on beasts strong enough to plow through the incoming, bracing waves that splashed salt water on our hand-me-down one-piece swimsuits. Atlantic winds loosened the rubber bands in our hair as we shrieked with delight and belted out any song that came to mind. One of my favorites was "Roll on Columbia," an ode to the river in Washington State that a brave music teacher, Mrs. Kalenian, had taught to a gaggle of first-graders who needed little prodding to sing forte.

After that brief series of vacations in the late 1960s, our family began camping during our summers. We did not return to the coast of Massachusetts together until July of 1976, and it was once again at my father's insistence. By then, the melanoma was consuming him. Still, somehow, he was able to make light of his unenviable situation by cracking jokes. Upon examining some life insurance paperwork earlier that summer, he turned to my mother and quipped, "Look at this. I'm worth more dead than alive."

What he might not have been as aware of was how the cancer that had spread to his brain and the radiation and other treatments he was enduring were exaggerating his already natural predilection for becoming fixated on certain topics. That summer, the subject was flags. Recently, he had seen an advertisement in a magazine about a man in Ipswich, Massachusetts, who sewed replicas of historic flags representing particular eras in American history. My father clipped out the advertisement, and it became abundantly clear that visiting this shop was on his list of tasks to accomplish before he died. One July day, he insisted that we all pile into our sunrise-colored station wagon for a three-plus hour trip to Ipswich, a coastal town north of Boston on Plum Island Sound. Despite our vacation ritual, my mother drove.

Our first stop was the flag shop, where my father spent a few hours examining reams and reams of cloth patterns before selecting one with a distinctly northeastern flair. Half a dozen white stars representing the six New England states were arranged in a circle on a blue background. A hand-cut green pine tree was stitched into a white square in the upper-left corner, divided into four parts by a red cross. We bought the flag and headed to the beach. It was too cool for swimming, but we did wade into the water and sniff the salty sea breeze.

My father, only a few months from death, revealed once again that he had not lost his quirky and robust sense of humor. That day on the seashore, he wore a dark blue-and-gray-striped rugby shirt and rolled his pants up to midcalf. His treatments had almost completely depleted his full head of black hair, and his face was puffy and pale.

But he still had a glint in his hazel eyes when he scooped a long stringy piece of green seaweed from the sand and let the whole revolting mass swing beneath his nose. Before long, he had morphed into one of his most beloved comedic routines—the one where he tugged at one nostril to encourage the emergence of an enormous, endless, elastic booger that kept coming. Usually, when he pulled this stunt at home, the booger was imaginary. But this time he had found the perfect prop.

How could we not laugh along with this man? It wasn't a stifled chuckle that came from a sense of pity or obligation. Our family shared a genuine belly laugh.

I had forgotten about that flag until a few years ago when my mother found it folded and wrapped in a plastic drugstore bag while clearing out her attic in Massachusetts. She gave it to me, and I tucked it onto a closet shelf for several years because it was too painful for me to think about what it represented. One day, while trying to capture his essence in writing, I rummaged in my closet for the flag. I unfolded it so I could admire its artistry and the beauty in its simplicity.

Admittedly, I wanted the flag to be more than just a handsome object. I wanted its symbols to serve as a cipher that I could decode and hence discover a hidden truth about my father. But maybe it was enough that the

CHAPTER 38
EASTERN VIRGINIA: PEDALING TOWARD VICTORY

MILES RIDDEN: 3,994.5
MILES TO GO: 255.5

P edaling out of Vesuvius on October 30, I tackled my last significant ascent. It was four miles of switchbacks to the famed Blue Ridge Parkway. This scenic road stretches more than 550 miles along the backbone of the Appalachians through North Carolina and Virginia, boasting elevations as high as 6,050 feet. The TransAmerica Trail is routed on twenty-seven of those miles, which were light on cars that weekday morning well past prime leaf-peeping season. Even though voracious gypsy moth caterpillars had feasted on much of the foliage, the forest was still flush with oaks, pines, locusts, maples, and hickories.

At Rockfish Gap, the southern entrance to Shenandoah National Park, the TransAmerica and Appalachian Trails overlap one final time. By then, the temperature had more than doubled, reaching the mid-sixties. I peeled off a few layers near a marker noting that Thomas Jefferson had taken a stagecoach to a tavern here in 1818 to talk with local leaders about building his University of Virginia in "the salubrious climate of Charlottesville." I planned to spend the night in that salubrious setting myself.

I had my first sighting of our third president during a break at a Charlottesville fast-food restaurant. He stared imperiously from a framed portrait above the ketchup dispenser. Would he have considered that placement an insult or the ultimate democratic statement?

On the campus he founded, I dropped off a pile of brochures and sunscreen coupons at the university-affiliated hospital's oncology offices. That clinic was the same place my doctors had urged me to have my liver checked on my Appalachian Trail hike. I figured I should at least take a look at the clinic I had avoided nine years prior.

To ease the next morning's exit before rush hour, I ate dinner at a suburban strip mall adjacent to the TransAm route. It was dark when I left the Chinese restaurant and wheeled across the highway laden with a plastic tub of sweet and sour soup, a gift from the owners. What looked to be promising campsites behind a row of cheek-by-jowl buildings were either too exposed or bathed in the glare of security lights. I tugged on the door of a Lutheran church that, lo and behold, opened to a common area where men hunched over chessboards.

Too tired to pursue creative camping options, I secured my bike in a hidden nook outside. Back inside, I hunkered down on a flowered couch in my sleeping bag. The out-of-sight-choir practicing down the hall must have sung me to sleep. I drifted off at about nine thirty p.m., figuring I had blended in with the scenery.

I realized how wrong I was when a bright light pierced my eyes. A flashlight-wielding security guard loomed over me. I was busted and upright very quickly. He was embarrassed, and I was mortified. After I blurted the briefest version of my story, he smiled.

"Don't worry. You should be allowed to stay," he assured me. "I will call my boss and explain."

He returned in a few minutes, his sad brown eyes transmitting the verdict before he spoke. "I tried. I can't believe he said no," he sputtered. "What's wrong with people? This is a church. Where will you go now?"

"It's OK," I assured him, reminding him that I should be the one apologizing because I had started the mess by intruding without asking permission. "I have survived since mid-August. I will make it another three days."

I maneuvered my bicycle out of its secret cubbyhole. My intent was to pitch my tent on a brightly lit patch of grass about as big as a double bed near a bank across the side street. It would do until sunrise. But I didn't make it that far.

My movement activated a security light on the tiny house next door to the church. A young man in a Yale sweatshirt emerged. I could feel his stare as I tightened a bungee cord. I tried to ignore him because I wasn't in the mood for a righteous lecture from an Ivy Leaguer.

"Don't worry," I said, breaking what was becoming an uncomfortable silence. "I'm not a felon. I'm just a tired cross-country cyclist who got booted out of a church I had no business being in. I need to go."

He then did the very last thing I expected. He walked the few paces that separated us and shook my hand. "I'm Caleb," he said, smiling. "All my girlfriend, Katie, and I have is a living room couch, but we would be honored if you spent the night. We can stow your bike in our basement."

Katie greeted me, then excused herself to continue studying for an exam. Both of them were university students. Katie, from Charleston, South Carolina, was studying to be a doctor, and Caleb, from Northern Virginia, was on track to earn his law degree that December. I turned down their offer of dessert, but I must have been hungry for conversation because

Caleb and I talked until well after midnight. It reminded me of my own college days, jabbering into the wee hours about current events, philosophy, the vague but thrilling future. Caleb explained his interest in environmental and social justice law. He had a keen intellect, and his thoughtfulness and earnest joy about possibilities kept me listening.

The next morning's temperature of forty degrees signaled that I had left Virginia's mountains behind and entered the still hilly but gentler terrain of the Piedmont, French for "foothills." The soil of this region was prime for growing tobacco and, evidently, presidents. Three of the country's first five leaders made their homes in this segment of central eastern Virginia. Jefferson's Monticello and James Monroe's Ash Lawn are both on the bicycling route on the outskirts of Charlottesville. James Madison's Montpelier is in neighboring Orange County.

My two-day route through the Piedmont was a mix. One mile featured Volvos heading to tony neighborhoods, and the next, beaters pulled into driveways next to scrappy houses with upholstered furniture bedecking the front porch. A roadside constant was the patchwork of headstones denoting dozens of family cemeteries. Another was the signage explaining the bloody details of Civil War battles that had torn through these landscapes. On Halloween night, I pitched my tent under a crescent moon at the edge of a cemetery bordering a Catholic church in Buckner. To conserve my flashlight batteries, I sat near the glow of the church's security lamp while catching up on my journal. The brick steps were still warm. I had come seventy-two miles from Charlottesville. Yorktown, my final stop, was only 123 miles away.

I felt fine when I hit the road at seven a.m. on November 1 to take full advantage of limited daylight. But about sixteen miles later, I suddenly felt sick to my stomach. I wish I could have blamed it on the egg sandwich I had eaten for breakfast. But that wasn't it. I had pulled off County Road 685 at the entrance to Scotchtown—home of the state's first governor, Patrick Henry, who made the history books with his "give me liberty or give me death" proclamation—to jot down a few notes. That's when I noticed the bag that served as my waterproof wallet felt unusually light. Gone was my wad of cash. I started to cry. Why couldn't I have misplaced a pair of socks instead?

I had twenty-one miles to ruminate before reaching Ashland, the next community with services. I so wanted the money to be missing because of my own absent-mindedness in Charlottesville, not some thief. In Ashland, I immediately started my detective work at a pay phone, using valuable minutes on my calling card to track down the number of the Chinese restaurant. The woman who answered, the generous one who had given me the soup, had found the envelope of cash at my table. What a relief to know she had been expecting my call for two days. She agreed to mail it to Wisconsin so I wouldn't have to pedal extra miles by doubling back to Charlottesville. Fortunately, I had enough money in reserve to finish my ride.

Traffic on the secondary roads out of Ashland was relentless because I was not far from Richmond, the state capital, and the overloaded arteries of Interstates 95, 295, and 64. The gridlock subsided by the time I was lured into Glendale by a perfect campsite next to the Ruritan Club's playground. The slide, swings, and jungle gym looked as if they had been erected during the Eisenhower administration, but they had a down-home charm. I could walk to the country store and the port-a-potty behind it—a common and crucial rural feature.

In classic Virginia tradition, the store's shelves were jam-packed with a panoply of rat poison, spark plugs, tobacco, and an assortment of, um, well-preserved food. But what else does a bicyclist need on the final evening of her continental journey? I was sixty-one miles from Yorktown. The friendly store proprietor asked me to sign his cyclist register. His wife had undergone surgery for melanoma, so I handed him brochures and the rest of my sunscreen coupons. In the dark, I called a college friend in Washington, DC. She had offered to pick me up when I finished.

The close of any long-distance escapade is a push and pull of emotions. Endings tend to be anticlimactic because I pour so much of my heart into the anticipation as well as the follow-through. Sometimes, when tired or frustrated along the route, I wanted to reach the Atlantic, sacrifice the bike to the waves, and then soak in mineral baths for days. But other times, I imagined reaching Yorktown, washing my laundry, then repacking my panniers and investing in a new set of maps to explore whatever was around the next corner. Regardless, the short days and long nights of approaching winter were a signal it was time to head home. At least temporarily. I would miss meeting people, listening to their stories, and seeing where and how they lived. And I would miss the freeing solitude that bicycling allows, living a schedule dictated by the sun, moon, and stars.

I need not have worried about my carton of milk going sour overnight in Glendale, as early morning temperatures on November 2 hovered in the low twenties. In the morning darkness, as I folded my frost-crispy tent into its dedicated quarters and stuffed my sleeping bag into its sack for the last time, I considered how odd it would be to get up that next morning and not have to reload my panniers in such exacting fashion. The bike had been my house on wheels for so long.

I left my campsite just as first light teased the barest strands of color from the eastern sky at six thirty. Minutes later, I watched a white-tailed deer bound across a frost-coated soybean field on the verge of harvest. I stared hard, hoping to preserve that image in my permanent brain archive. That bold sign of life contrasted with the vicious killing that once plagued this acreage, now referred to as the Richmond National Battlefield. Historical markers spelled out the details of the bloody events that had unfolded there. I wondered if the developers who had named their sprawling subdivisions after those Civil War battles comprehended the legacy of that carnage. It seemed a somber site for cancer outreach, but a Wisconsin couple touring battle sites by car made an on-the-spot donation to my cause at a roadside pull-off.

Just beyond, I entered the pedaler's delight of the Tidewater. The plain descends from three hundred feet above sea level to the Atlantic Ocean. It is a mix of sediments that washed eastward as the Appalachians were forming, and silts carried inward by the mighty Atlantic. Hundreds of streams fan out from the region's four major rivers—the James, Potomac, Rappahannock, and York. Long-ago tobacco crops so depleted the region's soil that growers moved upland to the Piedmont.

The salty sea air became noticeably pungent about twenty-five miles shy of Yorktown when I crossed the Chickahominy River. That word so delighted me that I repeated it out loud to commit it to memory. The watery scenery reminded me of my August days in Oregon along the Pacific Coast. My journey across four time zones had revealed that we're not as Walmartized, Starbucksized, or homogenized as critics lament. It was reassuring and comforting that pockets of this country still retained their distinct cuisine, cultural customs, and defining speech patterns. For instance, I could use a regular fix of that soothing Virginia Piedmont/ Tidewater accent, especially the way locals pronounced "out" and "about" like the Canadians.

My ride reinforced a tenet I had learned by watching my father at his best: Maintain a sense of humor, even under duress. Without the ability to laugh, I would have ended up curling into the fetal position on the highway shoulder after abandoning my bicycle somewhere in Idaho. And that approach would likely have landed me on one of the piles of flotsam and jetsam washed up on our roadsides. I knew some of it—such as water coolers, roofing tiles, and insulation—blew off trucks with loose loads. But what about the rest of the mind-boggling detritus gumming up our countryside? How did drivers shed such an inordinate number of gloves, bungee cords, and nails? If I had collected these eyesores along the route, I could have stocked a hardware store by the time I reached Virginia. Surprisingly, I even found edibles. A produce truck must have sprung a prodigious leak because I followed a trail of vegetables along a spit of Highway 96 in Colorado. I had picked up a yellow onion as a dinner garnish.

My reverie on that November 2 afternoon was interrupted by the bumpy tread of the Colonial Parkway through the Historic Triangle of Jamestown, Williamsburg, and Yorktown. The parkway was designed to slow vehicles, so it was a bit of a tooth-jarrer, but traffic was so light that my molars didn't mind. These three cornerstone communities are a must-see for those studying early white settlement in this country. You could spend months, even years, touring Revolutionary and Civil War battlefields, learning how English settlers eked out a living in 1607 after sailing to what they christened the Jamestown Colony, and absorbing the history lesson that is Colonial Williamsburg. Historic plantations—not one of our nation's proudest legacies when you know about the misery suffered by the slaves used and abused to keep them ticking—also are part of the scenery. Cotton bales the size of double-wide trailers amazed me. I dismounted just to touch the ever-so-soft balls of the fiber clinging to roadside plants.

I arrived in the quaint community of Yorktown, named for the duke of York, with a slightly banged-up left arm and two intact tires. Remarkably, I never had a flat tire. The trail officially ended at the imposing Victory Monument. The handsome, ninety-eight-foot obelisk sculpted of Maine granite by J. Q. A. Ward is not a tribute to cross-country cyclists but a grand exit point. An elaborate fourteen-foot statue of Liberty graces the top.

The Continental Congress authorized the monument's construction on October 29, 1781, after the British surrendered to George Washington, thus ending the Revolutionary War. Bureaucratic red tape clearly existed then too because construction began in 1881 and wasn't completed until 1884.

The monument's powerful words, "One destiny, one country, one constitution," had me simultaneously catching my breath and thinking that as pure as we claim our aim is, our execution is often wobbly. My bicycle and I hogged the bottom "shelf" below Liberty for a few minutes before the first of numerous tourists approached on foot to cherish their own moment with the monolith.

Wheeling away, I remembered that friendly Idaho cyclist who had helped me bind my uncooperative rear tire with duct tape. "Shoot, you already did the hard part even before you got on the bicycle," he declared after hearing my cancer story. "Compared to all of that, this ride will be easy." No doubt my continental journey had its share of harrowing moments. Sleet storms, serpentine climbs, truck slipstreams powerful enough to suck me off the road, and that jarring spill in Oregon were all part of the adventure. When I needed motivation, I reminded myself how hard I had worked to recover from chemotherapy treatments and surgeries. That, combined with my ingrained hardheadedness, gave me the strength to persist. On some rainy or close-to-one-hundred-degree days, it was tempting to load my bike into a pickup truck. But that wasn't the purpose of my ride. It was about completing the entire journey—every stinking inch of it.

Being on the bike allowed me to experience the full force of being alive, from the drumbeat of my heart down to my microscopic capillaries. The sting of sleet on my cheeks, the scent of ash in my nostrils, the sensation of being buffeted by a persistent wind—all were my bridges to these elemental essentials. It was both liberating and mesmerizing to follow the white line of the road's shoulder, stopping when I was hungry, curious, tired, or in need of companionship. Each day seemed as new as a fluffy baby robin. I focused on breathing each conversation, each encounter, and each image into my cells. I wanted to fully absorb them so they became enduring stories I could call up like the pages of a worn classic on a library shelf.

Traveling slowly with a refreshingly simple agenda, the barest of necessities, and few tethers to the plugged-in world freed me to immerse myself in the earthly and human authenticity that I so craved. What had unfolded each day, before I once again stretched out in my sleeping bag under an endless sky, was not good or bad, because that scale did not apply. It all just was. I had to discover how to negotiate obstacles, or be patient enough for them to move from my path.

From the granite monument, I rolled to the shoreline to dip both tires— the original front tire and the replacement back tire from Montana—into the waters of the Chesapeake Bay. Tidal waters of the twenty-six-mile-long York River, called the Pamunkey by local Indians, empty here into one of our nation's most prized but ecologically compromised estuaries. I basked in a few moments of silence to ponder the last seventy-nine days. I thought about the mountains, prairies, rivers, high deserts, geysers, grasslands, and forests I had seen and smelled, the bonds I had formed with hundreds of lovely people who offered encouragement, kindness, a refuge for the night, and stories about their own dreams and fears.

Then, from a plastic bag, I extracted a worn note from Kay Ruekert, a kind soul at the Wisconsin hospital, who coordinated my donations: "Our background and circumstances may have influenced who we are, but we are responsible for who we become," she had written. "Cancer may have influenced who you are, but you can take full responsibility for what you have become—an inspiration for all."

As waves of salt water licked at my tires and doused my feet, I forced myself to read her message out loud, as if my father were standing next to me, also savoring this gorgeous and peaceful setting. I had accomplished what I set out to do.

There, by the ocean he so loved, I could finally hear his strong baritone speaking the cathartic words that children of any age crave from a parent: "I am so proud of you."

Onward.

ABOUT THE AUTHOR

E lizabeth McGowan was born in Waterbury, Connecticut in 1961, where her father, Ronald McGowan, taught at a private school. His gift for teaching took the family to Philadelphia a couple of years later. She grew up in Philadelphia and Ashfield, Massachusetts—a tiny town—where she and her three sisters spent much of their childhoods tiptoeing around their explosive father.

At such a young age, McGowan could never have imagined how her future would unfold—trying to beat back the same cancer that killed her father when she was just fifteen. In her early twenties, she was diagnosed with melanoma—a deadly form of skin cancer—in the same place on the back of her neck where her father's disease was originally diagnosed.

McGowan graduated from the University of Missouri-Columbia School of Journalism. She started her career at daily newspapers in Wisconsin and Vermont, where she worked while enduring several bouts of melanoma.

In the 1990s, she won numerous explanatory writing and reporting awards from the Wisconsin Newspaper Association, the Milwaukee Press Club, the American Heart Association, and the Wisconsin Association of School Boards while a general assignment and feature writer, first for *The Janesville Gazette* and then for *The Racine Journal Times*.

In 2007, McGowan won second place in the Cleveland Press Club's Ohio Excellence in Journalism Awards contest in the public service/ investigative category for two stories published by Crain Communications about the five-year anniversary of September 11; one story focused on the compromised health of cleanup workers, and the other on the environmental complications associated with razing the Deutsche Bank building near the Twin Towers site in New York.

In 2013, she won the Pulitzer Prize for National Reporting for "The Dilbit Disaster: Inside the Biggest Oil Spill You've Never Heard Of." She was the lead reporter for a three-person team at the digital news startup, InsideClimate News. The e-book version of the series won the Rachel Carson Book Award from the Society of Environmental Journalists that same year. The "Dilbit Disaster" series won the James Aronson Award for social justice reporting in 2013 along with an honorable mention for the John B. Oakes Award for Distinguished Environmental Reporting; it was also a finalist for the Scripps Howard Foundation Award.

She was inspired to embark on a cross-country bicycle adventure in 2000 after her oncologist at Waukesha Memorial Hospital in Wisconsin declared her to be five years cancer-free. *Outpedaling 'The Big C': My Healing Cycle Across America*, a gripping story about grit, fear, recovery, and discovery, is her first book.

Today, McGowan is a freelance energy and environment reporter in Washington, DC. Links to her articles can be found at www.energynews. us/author/emcgowan and www.renewalnews.org.

During her award-winning journalism career, she also has narrated a two-part documentary for PBS, given numerous radio interviews about her investigative pieces, and participated on panels at venues as varied as the World Conference of Science Journalists, Columbia University School of Journalism, the National Press Club, the Poynter Institute for Journalism, *The Baltimore Sun*, the Maryland Humanities Council, the Society of Environmental Journalists, and the Tom Tom Festival in Charlottesville, Virginia.

McGowan has lived in Washington, DC, with her husband, Don, since 2001. She continues to pursue hiking and bicycling adventures, and is vigilant about wearing sunscreen and regular melanoma checkups.